Safeguarding the Atom:
A Critical Appraisal

sipri

Stockholm International Peace Research Institute

SIPRI is an independent institute for research into problems of peace and conflict, especially those of arms control and disarmament. It was established in 1966 to commemorate Sweden's 150 years of unbroken peace.

The institute is financed by the Swedish Parliament. The staff, the Governing Board and the Scientific Council are international.

The Board is not responsible for the views expressed in the publications of the Institute.

sipri

Stockholm International Peace Research Institute
Pipers Väg 28, S-171 73 Solna, Sweden
Cable: Peaceresearch Stockholm
Telephone: 08-55 97 00

Safeguarding the Atom:
A Critical Appraisal

David Fischer and Paul Szasz
Edited by Jozef Goldblat

sipri

Stockholm International Peace Research Institute

Taylor & Francis
London and Philadelphia
1985

UK   Taylor & Francis Ltd, 4 John St, London WC1N 2ET

USA   Taylor & Francis Inc., 232 Cherry St, Philadelphia, PA 19106-1906

British Library Cataloguing in Publication Data

Fischer, David
    Safeguarding the Atom: A Critical Appraisal
    1. Nuclear Arms Control
    I. Title.   II. Fzasz, Paul   III. Goldblat, Jozef
    IV. Stockholm International Peace Research Institute
    327.'74   JX1974.7
    ISBN 0-85066-306-7

Cover design by Malvern Lumsden
Typeset by Georgia Origination, Liverpool
Printed in Great Britain by Taylor & Francis (Printers) Ltd, Basingstoke, Hants.

Foreword

Since the entry into force of the Non-Proliferation Treaty, the nuclear weapon powers have exercised virtually no restraint in their nuclear weapon policies: they have pressed ahead unremittingly with new technologies in warheads and delivery systems. Among the non-nuclear weapon states the story is a different one: things have gone better than many people feared. In the late 1950s and early 1960s there were a number of informed predictions that, by the mid-1980s, the nuclear weapon states would number between 15 and 25. This has not happened. The non-proliferation regime has—so far—held remarkably well.

This book is a study of one element in that regime—the safeguards system of the International Atomic Energy Agency. SIPRI published a monograph on safeguards 10 years ago. It was then among the very few publications which dealt with this subject comprehensively (SIPRI, *Safeguards Against Nuclear Proliferation* (MIT Press, Cambridge, MA, and Almqvist & Wiksell, Stockholm, 1975). In the past 10 years there have been many developments in the system. The present book is an updated review.

This book is not simply descriptive. It contains a critical appraisal and proposals for ways of improving existing procedures, and adapting them to the political and technological changes of recent years. It is written for the informed layman as well as for the specialist: the safeguards system has many points of interest for arms control in general and, in particular, for the verification of compliance.

The main author is David Fischer, a former high official of the IAEA. Paul Szasz, formerly a legal and safeguards officer of the IAEA and now a Director in the UN Office of Legal Affairs, describes the political and legal aspects of sanctions for non-compliance with the safeguards obligations. The conclusions and recommendations have been prepared by SIPRI, which bears sole responsibility for them.

The book was edited by Jozef Goldblat, senior researcher at SIPRI, who is in charge of the arms control and disarmament programme. We are grateful to Billie Bielckus for her expert editing work.

Frank Blackaby

January 1985

Director

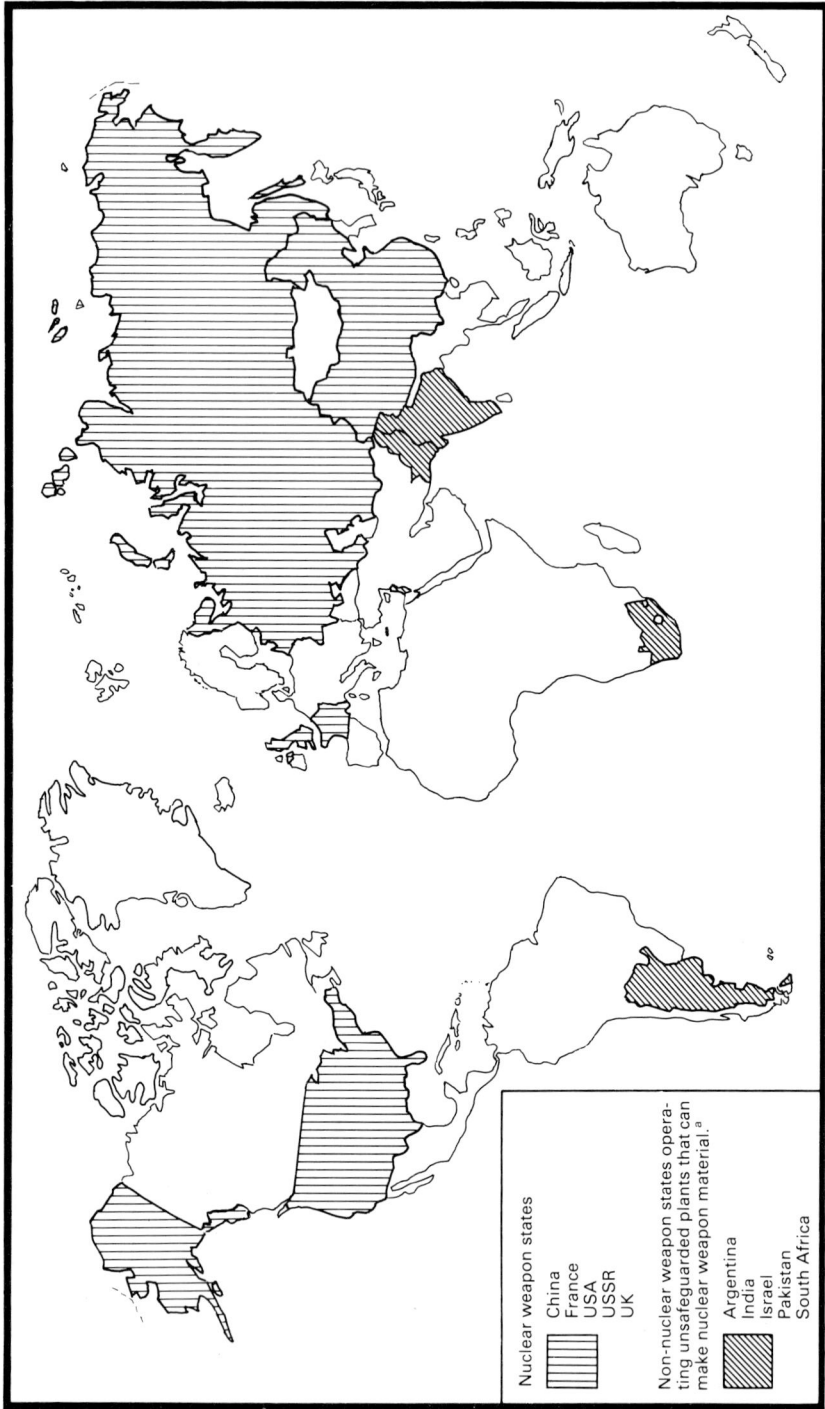

Nuclear weapon states

China
France
USA
USSR
UK

Non-nuclear weapon states operating unsafeguarded plants that can
make nuclear weapon material.[a]

Argentina
India
Israel
Pakistan
South Africa

[a]The status of Brazil is uncertain.

Contents

Preface

The objective of nuclear safeguards is to deter the diversion of nuclear material from peaceful activities to military purposes by the risk of early detection. But the deterrent role of safeguards is secondary to that of building confidence between nations by demonstrating that states which have undertaken not to acquire nuclear weapons abide by their undertakings.

Safeguards were in fact introduced before the 1968 Treaty on the Non-Proliferation of Nuclear Weapons (NPT), but now their future is to a great extent linked to that of the NPT. Indeed, they play a key role in verifying the effectiveness of restraints on the spread of nuclear weapons.

The detailed review of international safeguards which is made in this book reveals a series of shortcomings, both avoidable and unavoidable. Avoidable shortcomings can be remedied in part by action of the International Atomic Energy Agency (IAEA), but chiefly by action of the states themselves. The most serious limitation lies in the fact that not all non-nuclear weapon states have accepted comprehensive control of their nuclear activities. Five or six states that have not done so operate unsafeguarded plants that can make material directly useable in nuclear weapons; some of these states are highly influential in the world community. This is a disturbing situation because where safeguards stop the risks of proliferation begin.

On the whole, however, IAEA safeguards have proved essential not only to guard against nuclear weapon proliferation, but also to advance the peaceful uses of nuclear energy. They constitute, moreover, the first practical experiment in systematic international verification of arms control obligations, including on-site inspection of important installations on the territory of sovereign states. This provides a most valuable precedent for more far-reaching measures of arms limitation.

In 1995 the parties to the NPT must decide whether the Treaty should continue in force indefinitely or should be extended only for a fixed period of time. It is crucial, therefore, that the non-proliferation regime, which is the *raison d'être* of safeguards, should be substantially strengthened before that date. Whether this actually happens will depend on the continued restraint of those states which have significant nuclear activities and which have chosen not to join the NPT and not to accept full-scope safeguards. Equally critical is the attitude of the nuclear weapon powers party to the NPT, who are expected to provide tangible proofs that they are taking seriously the pledges they have made to bring the nuclear arms race under control and to reverse it. If this does not happen, there is a danger that the non-proliferation regime—together with the laboriously constructed edifice of safeguards—may disintegrate, with all the dangers to world security that such a development would bring.

Jozef Goldblat
January 1985   Editor

Glossary

The terms explained or defined in this glossary are italicized.

ARIE

Actual routine inspection effort—an estimate by the IAEA of the number of *man-days* that the IAEA's inspectors will spend at a particular nuclear plant or store during one year. This estimate is usually much lower than the maximum number of man-days permitted by the safeguards system under which the plant is being safeguarded. The term may also be used to refer to the inspection effort of the national or regional safeguarding authority (in the case of Japan and EURATOM respectively).

Bulk handling facility (BHF)

A plant or store that handles nuclear material in bulk (e.g., in the form of liquid, gas, powder, pellets, 'pebbles', wire or sheets) as distinct from a plant in which the material is in separate (discrete) and identifiable components. Typical BHFs are reprocessing and enrichment plants, plants for fabricating fuel elements, plants for converting uranium oxide into the gas uranium hexafluoride (UF_6) to be fed into an enrichment plant or for converting uranium oxide into uranium metal.

CANDU

Canadian deuterium uranium reactor—the most common *heavy water reactor*, fuelled with natural uranium and cooled and moderated by *heavy water*. The large Canadian research reactors (known as the NRX-type) are also HWRs but of a somewhat different design.

Chain reaction

The continuing process of nuclear fission in which the neutrons released by one fission cause at least one other fission. In a nuclear weapon an extremely rapid, multiplying chain reaction causes the explosive release of energy. In a reactor the pace of the chain reaction is controlled to produce heat for power or neutrons for research purposes.

Containment and surveillance (C/S)

Containment is the use of the physical features of a plant or store to restrict access to it (e.g., by sealing it off) and

xiii

Containment and surveillance (C/S) (Contd)	thus prevent the clandestine movement of nuclear material into or out of it. Surveillance means chiefly the use of instruments to detect any unreported movement of or tampering with safeguarded items.
Conversion time	See also *detection goals*. The time needed to convert the nuclear material at hand (e.g., spent fuel) into the metallic components of a nuclear explosive device.
Core (reactor core)	The central portion of a reactor containing the fuel elements and, usually, the moderator.
Detection goals	The goals which the IAEA sets for its safeguards at individual plants or types of plant, e.g., the smallest amount of material the diversion of which the IAEA should be able to detect (the *significant quantity*) or, putting it another way, the largest amount a diverter might be able to get away with, undetected; the longest time that should elapse between a diversion at the plant and its detection (detection time); how probable should it be that the IAEA will detect the diversion (detection probability). In setting these goals the IAEA takes into account the amount of material needed to manufacture a nuclear explosive (*threshold amount*), the time that would be needed to do so (*conversion time)* and the diversion strategies that the IAEA will seek to counter.
EEC	The European Economic Community or Common Market, which now comprises Belgium, Denmark, France, FR Germany, Greece, Ireland, Italy, Luxembourg, the Netherlands and the United Kingdom. The membership of Portugal and Spain is the subject of negotiation.
Enriched uranium	Natural uranium contains 0.7 per cent of the fissile isotope uranium-235, the remainder is the fertile (i.e., convertible into plutonium) isotope uranium-238. By various means (e.g., by passing it in gaseous form through the membranes of a *gaseous diffusion plant* or rotating it in a gas *ultracentrifuge*) one increases the proportion of uranium-235 to uranium-238. When the percentage of uranium-235 reaches 20 per cent, the material is termed 'highly enriched uranium' although the charge of a nuclear explosive is much more highly enriched (90 per cent). Highly enriched uranium was in the bomb dropped on Hiroshima, that dropped on Nagasaki used plutonium-239.
EURATOM	The European Atomic Energy Community established in 1957 by the Treaty of Rome as the nuclear branch of the EEC.

EURODIF	European Gaseous Diffusion Uranium Enrichment Consortium—*a gaseous diffusion* undertaking launched by France with capital also provided by Belgium, Italy and Spain (and, originally, Iran) to help meet their needs for enriched fuel.
FA	Facility attachment—the detailed plan for safeguarding a particular plant. The FA may include an estimate of annual routine inspection (*ARIE*), define the *material balance areas (MBAs)*, and indicate the strategic points to which the IAEA's inspector may have access during routine inspections and at which safeguards instruments may be installed.
FAO	The Food and Agriculture Organization of the United Nations, which has its headquarters in Rome.
(Fast) breeder reactor (FBR)	A nuclear reactor that produces more fissile material than it consumes. It normally does this by converting a 'blanket' of fertile uranium-238 into fissile *plutonium*; in the process it 'burns up' less of its plutonium fuel than the plutonium that it 'breeds' in the blanket.
Fertile material	Material composed of atoms which easily absorb (capture) neutrons and turn into *fissile material*. Uranium-238 is fertile material.
Fissile material	Material composed of atoms which readily *fission* (such as ^{235}U and ^{239}Pu) when struck by a thermal (slow) neutron.
Fission reaction	The process in which a neutron strikes the nucleus of an atom and splits it into fragments—several neutrons are emitted at high speed, and heat and radiation are released.
Gaseous diffusion	As used in the nuclear energy context this refers to a method of enriching uranium based on the fact that atoms or molecules of different mass (weight) will pass (diffuse) through a porous barrier or membrane at different rates. The method is thus used to separate uranium-235 from uranium-238. As a rule gaseous diffusion plants are large and require much electricity. The *NWS* used and still use such plants to produce weapon-grade uranium-235 as well as low-enriched uranium for *LWR*s.
Gigawatt	One thousand megawatts (*MW*)—here used only to denote electric generating capacity.
G-77	The 'Group of Seventy-Seven'—a term used to denote the developing countries acting as a bloc. The group originally consisted of 77 developing countries; it now contains many more.

Heavy water (deuterium oxide or D_2O)	Water composed of molecules of a heavy isotope of hydrogen (deuterium, which has two neutrons in its nucleus; 'ordinary' hydrogen has only one) and oxygen.
Heavy water reactor (HWR)	See also *CANDU*. A reactor that uses *heavy water* as a moderator. Other moderators are ordinary (light) water and graphite. The moderator slows down the neutrons emitted by uranium-235, plutonium or by the nuclei of other fissioning atoms. This permits the fertile uranium-238 to 'capture' the neutrons and thus turn into plutonium-239. Heavy water (and also graphite) is a more effective moderator than light water and makes it possible to produce a self-sustaining chain reaction with natural uranium; with light water as a moderator it is necessary to use enriched uranium to produce a chain reaction.
HTGR	High temperature gas-cooled reactor—an advanced reactor type which uses enriched uranium for fuel, graphite as a moderator and helium as a coolant. The fuel can be in the form of 'pebbles' and in that case the reactor should be safeguarded as a *bulk handling facility*.
Hot cell	A shielded room with remote handling equipment for analysing and experimenting with highly radioactive materials. A hot cell can be used to *reprocess* small amounts of spent fuel but it is not a reprocessing plant.
IAEA	The International Atomic Energy Agency (headquarters in Vienna). Its Statute, which came into force in July 1957, endows the Agency with the twin purposes of promoting the peaceful uses of atomic energy and ensuring that nuclear activities with which the IAEA is associated are not used to further any military purpose.
INFCE	An 'International Fuel Cycle Evaluation' made by over 40 countries from 1978 to 1980, chiefly at IAEA headquarters, on the proposal of President Carter.
INFCIRC	Information Circular—one of a series of unclassified, general purpose *IAEA* circulars used to bring to general notice the contents of an important document or an important decision or communication. Safeguards documents circulated in this form include the safeguards systems, safeguards agreements, and the contents of the *Trigger List* and *London (Suppliers') Guidelines*. When the IAEA circulates documents (such as the last two) at the request of the state or states concerned it takes no responsibility for the contents of the document.
ISMA	International Satellite Monitoring Agency—a French proposal.

INFA	International Nuclear Fuel Agency—a US proposal designed to ensure fuel supplies to countries that renounce nuclear weapons and all sensitive nuclear facilities.
IPS	International Plutonium Storage—a scheme for storing surplus separated plutonium under the control of the IAEA so as to prevent governments from stockpiling it. The IAEA's Statute authorizes the IAEA to 'require deposit' with it of 'any excess' of separated plutonium as a safeguards measure (see Article XII.A.5 of the Statute, reproduced in Appendix I).
Light water reactor (LWR)	Today the most common type of power and research reactor, moderated and cooled by ordinary 'light' water. See also *heavy water reactor*.
London (Suppliers') Guidelines	A set of guidelines (reproduced in Appendix VIII) that most of the main suppliers of nuclear plants and materials agreed to in London in 1975–77.
Man-day	'A day during which a single inspector has access to a facility at any time for a total of no more than eight hours' is the succint definition given by the model NPT safeguards agreement.
Material balance area (MBA)	An area inside or outside a nuclear plant which is constructed or laid out in such a manner that it is possible to measure, count or otherwise determine every transfer of nuclear material into or out of it as well as all nuclear material in it (i.e., its 'physical inventory' of nuclear material). A typical MBA is a store of fresh fuel, or the bay in which spent fuel is stored or the core of a reactor.
MFCC	Multinational Fuel Cycle Centre—also referred to as a Regional Fuel Cycle Centre. A scheme put forward in the mid-1970s for pooling the resources of several countries in a joint fuel cycle plant (a reprocessing plant), the main aim being to deter the construction of many smaller 'proliferation prone' national plants.
MUF	Material unaccounted for. Defined by the model NPT safeguards agreement as 'the difference between book inventory and physical inventory'. When the operator of a nuclear plant takes stock (makes a physical inventory) of the material in his plant, the amount of material that he finds may differ from the amount he has calculated to be there; any difference is termed MUF. The calculation of what material should be there is made by taking the amount found at the previous physical inventory, adding

MUF (Contd)	all inputs and estimated production and deducting shipments, 'burn-up', measured discards, estimated losses, etc.
MW (or MW(e))	Megawatt, or one million (electric) watts. This is the unit usually used to indicate the electrical power that a power plant generates when it is operated at full capacity.
MW(th)	Megawatt thermal or one million (thermal) watts. The unit used to indicate the total power that a research reactor generates when it is operated at full power.
NNPA	The United States Nuclear Non-Proliferation Act of 1978. This Act substantially amended (in the direction of much stricter controls on nuclear exports) the Atomic Energy Act of 1954 which had been the basis for the United States' 'Atoms for Peace' programme from 1954 until 1978.
NNWS	Non-nuclear weapon state(s). Various meanings have been given to this term. The most common (and that used in this book) is to denote a state that has not made and tested (exploded) a nuclear weapon. However, the NPT clearly indicates that making and exploding any nuclear device for any purpose, whether military or peaceful, means that the state that does it should be regarded as a *NWS* (nuclear weapon state) but only if it did so before 1 January 1967. Where does this leave India which in 1974 exploded a nuclear device but ostensibly for peaceful purposes? In this book India is regarded as a NNWS (and it so regards itself).
NPT	The Treaty on the Non-Proliferation of Nuclear Weapons or 'Non-Proliferation Treaty'. The NPT was the product of negotiations in the Eighteen-Nation Disarmament Committee (ENDC) in Geneva from 1965 to 1968 and especially of the US–Soviet agreement in 1967 on what it should contain. On 12 June 1968 the General Assembly of the United Nations commended the draft treaty that the ENDC had submitted to it and expressed the hope "for the widest adherence to the Treaty". The Treaty was opened for signature on 1 July 1968 and came into force on 5 March 1970 when the necessary ratifications had been deposited with the three depository governments (the USSR, the UK and the USA).
NWS	Nuclear weapon state(s). Under Article IX.3 of the NPT, the term means a state "which has manufactured and exploded a nuclear weapon or other nuclear explosive device prior to 1 January 1967", i.e., China, France, the USSR, the UK and the USA.

OECD	The Organization for Economic Cooperation and Development. Its membership includes all countries in Western Europe and the USA, Canada, Japan, Australia and New Zealand, i.e., almost all the free market industrialized countries. The OECD is the successor to the OEEC (the Organization for European Economic Cooperation) established after World War II to administer the Marshall Plan.
Plutonium	An element which is artificially manufactured (it hardly exists in nature). Although there are other ways of manufacturing plutonium, almost all is produced in nuclear reactors. When the nucleus of an atom of uranium-238 captures an extra neutron (usually emitted by the fissioning of another nucleus in a nuclear chain reaction) it is eventually transformed into plutonium-239. Plutonium-240 is produced when plutonium-239 captures a neutron instead of fissioning under the impact of the neutron. Plutonium-239 is the preferred isotope for making nuclear explosives or weapons; plutonium-240 complicates the construction of an explosive because of its high rate of spontaneous fission. Generally speaking, the longer nuclear fuel is irradiated (i.e., the higher the 'burn-up') the more plutonium-240 will be produced.
(Plutonium) recycle	Use of *plutonium* as part of the fuel for a nuclear reactor. The plutonium may replace or partly replace uranium-235 and thus 'enrich' the fuel. The commercial alternative to recycling is to use the plutonium in an *FBR* or to store it for later use.
Reprocessing	Chemical treatment of spent fuel so as to separate the plutonium and remaining uranium from the unwanted waste products.
SAGSI	The *IAEA*'s Standing Advisory Group on Safeguards Implementation.
SIR	The *IAEA*'s annual, classified 'Safeguards Implementation Report'.
Significant quantity (SQ)	The approximate amount of nuclear material (not only fissile material; see also *threshold amount*) which the *IAEA* considers a state would need to manufacture its (first) nuclear explosive. In defining such quantities the *IAEA* takes into account matters such as the degree of enrichment of the material and any process that may be needed to convert it into a nuclear explosive. For material that can be directly used as an explosive, the SQ is the same as the *threshold amount*.
Spent fuel	Fuel removed from a reactor after use. It is usually

Spent fuel (Contd)

removed when it contains too little fissile and fertile material and too high a proportion of fission by-products to sustain an economical operation of the reactor.

Threshold amount

The approximate amount of *fissile material* needed to make a nuclear explosive device. *SAGSI's* recommendations about the quantities the IAEA should assume for this purpose are based on a United Nations 1967 report on the *Effects of the Possible Use of Nuclear Weapons* (UN document A/6858 of 6 October 1967). They make allowance for *fissile material* that is likely to be lost in manufacturing the nuclear device. It is understood that *SAGSI's* recommendations assume that it will be the first nuclear explosive device made by the country concerned; the amounts needed might be smaller in countries that have had much experience in making such devices and where very sophisticated techniques can be used.

Trigger List

A list of the materials (besides source and fissile material), plant components and equipment the export of which to an *NNWS* requires the application of safeguards on the plant in which it is used or on the material which it uses, processes, etc. The list is only relevant to exports to non-NPT NNWS since in NPT NNWS virtually all nuclear material is required to be safeguarded. The original Trigger List was agreed in 1974. It has since been expanded. It forms part of the 1977 *London (Suppliers') Guidelines*.

Ultracentrifuge

In the nuclear context this means a rotating vessel used to enrich uranium. The heavier isotopes of uranium hexafluoride gas concentrate at the walls of the rotating centrifuge and are drawn off.

UNPICPUNE

The United Nations Conference for the Promotion of International Cooperation in the Peaceful Uses of Nuclear Energy, now expected to be held in 1986.

Unesco

The United Nations Educational, Scientific and Cultural Organization. It has its headquarters in Paris.

URENCO

Uranium Enrichment Company—created in 1970 by the signing of the Treaty of Almelo by FR Germany, the UK and the Netherlands.

Yellowcake

Uranium concentrate (U_3O_8). Converted into the gas uranium hexafluoride (UF_6) in preparation for enriching and into purified uranium oxide (UO_2) for use in a natural uranium reactor.

Part I

International Safeguards

David Fischer

Chapter 1. Overview

Superscript numbers refer to the notes and references at the end of each chapter

'International nuclear safeguards' have chiefly come to mean an arrangement under which the International Atomic Energy Agency (IAEA) verifies a pledge by a state that it will not use its nuclear activities to make a nuclear weapon or any other kind of nuclear explosive.

Safeguards were needed because of the spread of the peaceful uses of nuclear energy and of the fact that nations can use or misuse peaceful nuclear plants to make nuclear weapons. Safeguards began modestly in the early 1950s when the USA, reversing its earlier policy, started to export research reactors and their fuel to 'friendly' countries and required them to accept US controls and inspection to verify 'peaceful use'. They became international in the full sense in 1959 when the IAEA began to apply its own safeguards to supplies of plant and material. Later the IAEA took over this task from the USA and other suppliers.

In 1968 the nations most directly concerned agreed on a Treaty on the Non-Proliferation of Nuclear Weapons (NPT) (reproduced here as Appendix IX) with the aim "... to avert the danger of ... [nuclear] war"[1] that would follow from the further spread of nuclear weapons. In the same year the United Nations General Assembly, by an overwhelming majority, commended the Treaty and expressed hopes for the widest adherence to it.[2] Many saw the NPT as a major step towards the distant goal of a universal, internationally verified, non-proliferation regime and as "a vitally important and indispensable step on the road to real disarmament", as the UK representative put it.[3]

The NPT assigns to the safeguards of the IAEA the cardinal role of verifying that the non-nuclear weapon states (NNWS) party to the NPT are fulfilling their obligation not to divert their peaceful nuclear activities to nuclear weapons or other nuclear explosive devices.

The NPT therefore requires each NNWS party to conclude an agreement with the IAEA, within a prescribed time-limit, so that the IAEA may apply its safeguards to all the state's peaceful nuclear activities. After the NPT entered into force in March 1970 the IAEA drew up a detailed 'model' agreement (IAEA Document INFCIRC/153, reproduced in Appendix V) to be used as a basis for the negotiations with the states concerned.

By 1 January 1985 there were 124 parties to the NPT (including three nuclear weapon states—the USSR, the United Kingdom and the USA). Of the 121 NNWS concerned 78 had also concluded the required safeguards agreements

3

with the IAEA. Forty-three states were thus in default of their obligation to conclude such an agreement (and some were as much as 10 years in default!). The position is, however, better than might appear from these figures since every NNWS party to the NPT which had a 'safeguardable' nuclear plant or nuclear material had concluded the standard agreement with the IAEA.[4]

IAEA safeguards had been in operation for nearly 10 years before the NPT came into force. In fact the experience gained in applying IAEA safeguards helped in the negotiation of the NPT and in the decision to give the IAEA responsibility for verifying compliance. These pre-NPT safeguards were embodied in a system approved in 1965 and extended in 1966 and 1968 (IAEA Document INFCIRC/66/Rev. 2, reproduced in Appendix IV). This is the system that the IAEA still applies to some or all of the nuclear plants in the 10 NNWS that have significant nuclear plants and that have not adhered to the NPT.

The NPT is the driving motor of the international non-proliferation regime, and the IAEA's NPT safeguards verify that the NPT is functioning properly. But the non-proliferation regime is much more extensive than the Treaty and its safeguards. It includes the various policies, institutions, treaties, agreements and sets of rules aimed at preventing or slowing down the spread of nuclear weapons. The regime's verification measures also include, although perhaps less directly, the safeguards the IAEA is applying in NNWS not parties to the NPT, the safeguards of the Common Market countries applied by their nuclear arm (EURATOM) jointly with the IAEA, the safeguards and other measures foreseen in the Treaty for the Prohibition of Nuclear Arms in Latin America (the Treaty of Tlatelolco) and the various checks applied by individual states, including satellite observation, that is, 'national technical means' of verification.[5] It was the latter that first revealed to the world the existence of the Dimona reactor in Israel and South Africa's apparent preparations for a nuclear test in the Kalahari desert.

The export policies of the main supplier states also play an important role in buttressing (or heedlessly weakening) the NPT regime. It is a truism that no export controls, however rigorous, can in the long run prevent a state from obtaining the means of making nuclear explosives, if it is determined to do so and has (as perhaps 30 countries have today) the capacity to build the necessary nuclear plant. On the other hand the lax policies followed by Canada, France and FR Germany in the 1950s and early 1960s helped India, Israel, Pakistan and South Africa acquire the technology for making weapon-usable material; the USSR assisted China to do the same and the US policy paid too much attention to promotion and too little to adequate safeguards. As recent experience has shown, overly restrictive policies carry their own risks but it is interesting to note that, except for China, no country has acquired the technology to make nuclear weapon material as a result of nuclear trade with the USSR. The USSR requires the return of all spent fuel used in Soviet-supplied reactors and does not export any of the so-called sensitive technologies (essentially the technologies for reprocessing spent fuel so as to recover the plutonium, for enriching uranium and for producing heavy water).

The foreign policies of the more powerful countries as conducted in their relations with other governments are also an important element in the NPT regime. Thus US diplomacy helped to speed the conclusion of a safeguards agreement between the IAEA and EURATOM while Soviet support helped the IAEA to negotiate a fully effective agreement with India for safeguards on two power reactors using Soviet heavy water. But in other cases states have attached more importance to selling their nuclear plants or to bilateral political relations than to effective safeguards.

Almost all the IAEA's experience in applying safeguards to the fuel cycles of sophisticated nuclear industries has been gained during the past 10 years. IAEA safeguards have taken some hard knocks in this process—especially after the Israeli bombing of the Iraqi nuclear research centre in 1981—and some other painful lessons have been learned by governments and the public about the inherent limitations of any international system of verification. But the achievements have also been considerable. For the first time in history, nations have freely accepted systematic inspection by foreigners to verify that they are carrying out the undertakings they have assumed in international agreements. IAEA inspectors now (or will soon) regularly visit and check peaceful operation of nuclear plants in every nation operating a nuclear reactor except one—the People's Republic of China.[6] About 98 per cent of the nuclear plants outside the five nuclear weapon states are under IAEA safeguards.

The NNWS that make greatest use of nuclear technology are the eight Common Market NNWS (especially FR Germany) and Japan. By far the larger part of the IAEA's verification takes place in these NPT countries, a matter of some sensitivity in both FR Germany and Japan. Another large and growing share of the effort is devoted to the NPT NNWS of Eastern Europe, and yet another large share to Canada, Sweden, Switzerland (all NPT parties) and Spain (not a party to the NPT). To many people the risk of proliferation in most of these countries may seem low or non-existent, but the IAEA as an international organization cannot make subjective judgements of this kind, and the extent of its safeguards effort must be determined in the first place by the size and complexity of the nuclear industry of the country concerned.

In the countries of the European Economic Community (EEC) the EURATOM system underpins IAEA safeguards and is becoming increasingly multinational as more nations join the Community. A 'state system' of safeguards plays a similar role in Japan although obviously no national system can achieve the same degree of political credibility as a multinational one operated by 10 (possibly soon 12) states, 2 of which are nuclear weapon states.

The main strength of IAEA safeguards is that in every case they are applied after the voluntary decision of the government concerned. In the NPT case the decision, which is taken chiefly on the basis of national security considerations, is that by formally renouncing nuclear weapons the state will best serve its own national interest and that IAEA safeguards will show the world that it is abiding by its renunciation.[7] IAEA safeguards are thus first and foremost a means of promoting greater confidence between nations; the extent to which they actually deter states from breaking their word is secondary to their role of building confidence. As the international web of treaty obligations and the coverage of safeguards become more extensive, it becomes safer and thus easier to renounce nuclear weapons and to maintain that renunciation. In this sense the system nurtures itself, provided of course that states believe that IAEA safeguards will in fact detect and make known any forbidden nuclear activities in other states. As the technical barriers to proliferation continue to be eroded, the political commitment to non-proliferation and its international verification become more important.

Since governments accept the NPT and its safeguards by their own free decision (although sometimes as a condition for continued nuclear supply) there is a strong presumption that they will normally abide by their peaceful, no-explosive-use, pledges and that breaches of safeguards agreements are unlikely. (The same logic applies to non-NPT safeguards agreements which are also entirely voluntary.) The IAEA has in fact, year after year, reached the conclusion that all nuclear material under its safeguards remained in peaceful nuclear activities or was otherwise adequately accounted for (with two temporary exceptions when it was unable fully to verify peaceful use at two similar plants in two non-NPT countries, India and Pakistan). But the IAEA cannot entirely discount the possibility of a breach of its undertakings by any state in which it applies safeguards. If it did there would be no need for safeguards.

It is, of course, possible that a state might think that by joining the NPT it can more easily get hold of the plant needed to make nuclear weapon material and that, having got it, it would 'break-out' of the NPT at short notice with nuclear weapons in its hands. This also seems unlikely. Those states that wished to have the plant to make nuclear weapon material without safeguards have refused to join the NPT (Argentina, India, Israel, Pakistan and South Africa). Moreover, so far at least, non-NPT countries have been able to import or otherwise obtain nuclear plants including 'sensitive' (weapon-material producing) plants at least as easily as the parties to the NPT.

The main inherent weakness of safeguards is the extent to which they depend upon stable international relations, North–South as well as East–West, and upon the willingness of governments to co-operate with the IAEA in helping it to apply safeguards to the national nuclear fuel cycle. During the Cold War of the 1950s the superpowers and their allies were unable to agree, either on a concerted effort to stop proliferation or on a comprehensive safeguards system. In those parts of the Third World where recent war or internal strife breed distrust, safeguards are only reluctantly or partly accepted, significant gaps remain, and even where safeguards coverage is complete their application may become difficult and uncertain and their credibility may be called into doubt. There are several examples: the coverage of safeguards leaves out critical plants in Argentina, India, Israel, Pakistan and South Africa. It may become incomplete in Brazil and Chile, which have also not joined the NPT or brought the Treaty of Tlatelolco into force. The

IAEA has encountered difficulties—subsequently resolved—in applying safe-guards at one plant in Pakistan, and in arranging inspections on Iran, Iraq and Libya (all parties to the NPT).[8] Partly as a result of such difficulties the credibility of its safeguards in Iraq was flatly rejected by Israel and seriously questioned by part of the Western press after the Israeli attack. The matter did not end there. To ensure that Israel's rights as a member of the IAEA were not eroded by the organization's annual General Conference, the USA temporarily withdrew from the IAEA from September 1982 to March 1983 and threatened to pull out entirely at the September 1984 General Conference. The attack on the Iraqi centre and the threat of US withdrawal are likely to trouble the IAEA for many years.

The NPT regime and IAEA safeguards are therefore fragile commodities. They would be severely damaged if ever IAEA-safeguarded fuel were found to have been diverted. They would suffer grave damage, too, if any country were to withdraw its Treaty obligations or denounce a safeguards agreement with the IAEA and proceed to use previously safeguarded plant or material to make a nuclear explosive. Given this inherent fragility, IAEA safeguards have on the whole fared well so far and one may hope that the longer they remain intact, the more accepted and entrenched they will become.

IAEA safeguards have by now become an indispensable component of most other parts of the non-proliferation regime. A non-proliferation treaty lacking IAEA verification would be almost inconceivable today. Multinational and national export policies, such as those of the London Suppliers' Group and the formalized policies of Australia, Canada, Sweden and the USA, explicitly rely on IAEA safeguards to verify that their supplies are not diverted (and in the latter four cases require IAEA safeguards on the entire nuclear industry of the importing NNWS). It would be nearly impossible today to revive the bilateral safeguards of the early 1950s, or to renegotiate the NPT so as to re-assign the verification task to another entity or entities.

The international community thus has an important stake in the continued effectiveness of IAEA safeguards. They have helped to create confidence that, at least for the present, the spread of nuclear weapons has stopped in the indus-trialized world and in much of the Third World. They have promoted inter-national nuclear trade and co-operation; in fact there would be little nuclear commerce without them. They have provided the world's first experiment in systematic on-site inspection by an international body, which may thus serve as an example for other more far-reaching arms controls.

Applying safeguards is only one of the IAEA's activities. Most of the others are concerned with promoting the peaceful uses of nuclear energy. (In the majority of Third World countries this means promoting nuclear science applications in agri-culture, medicine, and so on, rather than in electric power production.) Since 1970, however, the balance in the IAEA's work has shifted steadily away from promotion to regulation (safety rules as well as safeguards) and the cost of IAEA safeguards is now roughly the same as that of all other technical programmes put together or about one-third of the IAEA's regular budget.

It is, nevertheless, sometimes argued that to charge an institution with both the promotion and regulation of nuclear energy must lead to a conflict of interest, and that there should be a sharper separation in the IAEA between the two types of activity—perhaps responsibility for safeguards should be assigned to a separate international organization and the IAEA absorbed into an international agency with a wider mandate to promote all forms of energy. Part I of this book examines this as well as the other main issues raised in the overview.

Two final observations can be made. First, it has been pointed out that the rate of *overt* proliferation declined from three states in the decade 1945–54, to two in 1955–64, to one (if the Indian explosion is to be so regarded) in 1965–74 and to none in the decade 1975–84. Why has the rest of the world not followed (at least, so far) the same path as the five nuclear weapon states (NWS)? Perhaps one or two of the threshold states (most likely, Israel) have some pre-assembled 'bombs in the basement', but all that one can be reasonably sure of in the other cases (India, Pakistan, South Africa and Argentina) is that they have, or soon will have, stocks of unsafeguarded plutonium or enriched uranium. This is a far cry from the bristling nuclear arsenals of the superpowers or even from that of the least formidable of the NWS. Moreover, the gap between the five NWS and the rest of the world is steadily increasing as the NWS pour vast resources into their nuclear arsenals.

The fact that most NNWS have tolerated this situation is a rather remarkable phenomenon, but it cannot last indefinitely. The number of NWS cannot remain forever at five. It must either go down or go up, more probably the latter.

Second, it is said with much reason that the main weakness of the non-proliferation regime today is the lack of progress in arms control, in other words, the failure of the NWS to honour the commitments they made in Article VI and in the Preamble of the NPT, a failure they will hopefully redress well before 1995 when the NPT comes up for renewal.

But no major country is likely to quit the Treaty just because the NWS have largely ignored their pledges. The political and economic loss (and in cases like FR Germany and Japan, the political penalty) would be far too great.

The Treaty's weakness in this regard is rather the large number of parties, chiefly in the Third World, that would stand to lose so little by leaving it (or would so believe). More than half the NPT parties have no nuclear programme at all, and no nuclear plants that could be damaged by a cut-off of nuclear supplies. Many of them probably regard any nuclear threat as remote or, at worst, as coming from countries not restrained by the Treaty. In other words, if the NPT were ever to begin unravelling it would not do so because the centre no longer holds (as was the case in the league of Nations, with the USA deciding not to join and Germany and Japan pulling out) but rather because the fringes begin to fray, perhaps as a result of a test by one of the threshold countries. It may be best to be prepared for this unlikely but not unthinkable contingency which, though very damaging, need not be fatal to the non-proliferation regime.

But this question lies outside the scope of this book, intended as a critical appraisal of international safeguards rather than the regime on which they depend.

Notes and references

[1] Preamble to the NPT Treaty, see Appendix IX.
[2] UNGA Resolution 2373 (XXII) 95 votes for, 4 against (Albania, Cuba, Tanzania, Zambia) and 21 abstentions.
[3] UN publication OPI/372 1969, p. 22.
[4] One, Viet Nam, had negotiated the agreement and was about to conclude it (see IAEA Annual Report for 1983).
[5] The chief role of satellite observation (one of the main 'national technical means') is to keep track of the nuclear arsenals of the other superpower. Its non-proliferation role is incidental but potentially useful.
[6] The IAEA is applying safeguards on all nuclear plants and material in Taiwan (generally considered as part of Chna), apparently with the tacit consent of the government of the People's Republic of China.
[7] Similar considerations probably apply in states that are parties to the Treaty of Tlatelolco but not to the NPT, the only state in this category today being Colombia. In the case of the non-NPT agreements (namely, those with Argentina, Brazil, Chile, Cuba, India, Pakistan, the People's Democratic Republic of Korea, Spain, and South Africa) the state accepts the obligation not to use the *safeguarded* items for any military purpose or to make nuclear explosives of any kind. The state does not, however, formally renounce nuclear weapons or other nuclear explosives and is legally free to use unsafeguarded plants to make nuclear weapon material. Argentina, India, Israel, Pakistan and South Africa have such unsafeguarded plants.
[8] The IAEA encountered difficulties of a different kind in superimposing its safeguards on those of EURATOM. This has led on occasion to similar though much less intractable difficulties in regard to Japan which keeps a close eye on the IAEA's relations with EURATOM and seeks to avoid being treated less favourably.

Chapter 2. The three main elements

International nuclear safeguards may be seen as a collective political activity carried out by a large group of states (comprising today most of the international community) operating through an international organization, designed to verify that states are abiding by the obligations they have accepted in safeguards agreements with the organization.

To gauge the strengths and weaknesses of these safeguards one must look at them as a whole and assess the political as well as the technical efficacy of the system.

The IAEA Statute establishes safeguards as one of the two main functions of the organization.[1] Indeed, it is doubtful whether there would be an IAEA were there no need for international safeguards. Its other functions could have been left to existing UN agencies, many of which had already moved into various uses of nuclear energy.

I. The Board of Governors

The Statute assigns responsibility for safeguards to the IAEA's Board of Governors. This purely political committee, consisting today of representatives of the 35 member states, creates, adapts, oversees and plays a key role in arranging to finance the entire legal and technical apparatus of safeguards. Specifically, the Board:

1. Draws up, promulgates and (very occasionally) modifies the safeguards systems of the IAEA. On the basis of these systems the Secretariat of the IAEA negotiates safeguards agreements with states.

2. Approves each individual agreement on behalf of the IAEA.

3. Oversees the implementation of safeguards on the basis of reports to it by the Director General, who also consults the Board on all major issues of safeguards policy and on the chief problems that arise.

4. Approves the IAEA's annual budget including the allocation for safeguards. The budget must also be approved by the annual 'General Conference' of all member states,[2] but the Conference cannot change the budget unless the Board, too, agrees. In practice the General Conference has always accepted the Board's proposals.

11

5. Determines (on the basis of proposals by the Director General) the general structure and organization of the Department of Safeguards as well as the appointment of the head of that Department, the Directors of its seven divisions and of all inspectors.

6. Determines whether a state is failing to comply with its safeguards agreement. (This determination would be made on the basis of a report by the Director General. So far there has been no such report.) In the event of a determination of non-compliance, the Board would submit a report direct to the General Assembly and Security Council of the United Nations as well as to all member states of the IAEA. It may also curtail assistance and call for the return of nuclear supplies.

On the Board's recommendation, the General Conference has in recent years approved a special scale for safeguards' costs which has virtually frozen the contributions of developing countries.

Most UN bodies have, like the IAEA, a bicameral system of government, an executive board of limited membership and a general conference or assembly of all member states. However, the way the IAEA's Statute concentrates authority, particularly in the domain of safeguards, in its executive Board of Governors, rather than in the General Conference (or in the hands of the Director General) is unusual and deliberate. When the Statute of the IAEA was negotiated (1954–56) it was so framed as to ensure that the Board would be the more 'safeguards-minded' of the two bodies.[3]

The Board may thus be said to constitute the IAEA's *collective* interface with its member states on whose behalf the IAEA is applying safeguards. The Board is also the first element in determining the effectiveness of safeguards.

II. IAEA–state relations

The second element, which is also a crucial though more diffuse interface, is that between the IAEA and *individual* states, in the negotiation of safeguards agreements, in the designation and acceptance of inspectors and in the day-to-day application of safeguards in the nuclear plants of the states concerned.

III. The IAEA Secretariat

The third element is the IAEA Secretariat itself as an international unit for verifying the workings of a complex, high-technology industry and its associated research and development. Numerous factors determine the Secretariat's ability to do its job effectively: the extent to which safeguards cover the nuclear fuel cycles of all NNWS, the extent of safeguards coverage in states where such coverage is not complete, the resources available to the IAEA, the efficacy of its organization, direction and administration and, above all, the quality of the direction and support it gets from the Board and the co-operation it gets from the states in which it applies safeguards. It should go without saying that the integrity, technical competence and the political skill and courage of the Secretariat are vital for the success of safeguards.

Before looking at how IAEA safeguards work in practice, one should be aware of the inherent limits to the IAEA's freedom of action.

Notes and references

[1] Szasz, P., *The Law and Practices of the International Atomic Energy Agency* (IAEA, Vienna, 1970). This is the indispensable source book on the early history of the IAEA. Szasz points out that although the Statute deals extensively with safeguards its treatment of the matter is "by no means complete or free of ambiguities". The Statute's provisions dealing with safeguards are reproduced in Appendix I.

[2] The General Conference and the Board of Governors are the governing bodies of the IAEA. All member states may participate in the General Conference. Its annual meeting usually lasts one week and is largely taken up with a 'general debate' during which delegates, *inter alia*, express their government's views about the future work of the IAEA and extol their nation's achievements in nuclear energy. The General Conference also debates the budget, takes decisions on membership and on certain political issues.

[3] For instance, by requiring that states "... most advanced in the technology of atomic energy including the production of source materials ... " (see the *IAEA Statute*, IAEA, Vienna, 1980, Article VI.A.I) should have virtually permanent seats on an initially fairly small board (23 members compared with 35 in 1985). Most though not all of the states in this category support effective safeguards and are politically powerful group or bloc leaders (in 1984–85 the USA, USSR, UK, France, FR Germany, Japan, Australia, Belgium, Canada, Egypt, all in the 'pro-safeguards' camp; Brazil and India, usually not supporters of safeguards; and the People's Republic of China, attitude not yet clear).

Chapter 3. The political framework and constraints

I. What can safeguards do?

At first sight the aim of international safeguards should be to help to *stop* the spread of nuclear weapons and, in the broadest sense, it is this purpose that they are bound to serve. Under the NPT, "Each NNWS Party to the Treaty undertakes to accept safeguards . . . for the verification of its obligations assumed under this Treaty with a view to *preventing* diversion of nuclear energy from peaceful uses to nuclear weapons or other nuclear explosive devices" (see Appendix IX).

However, to assume that the IAEA can literally 'prevent' diversion would be to ignore the political realities of the modern world and the means at the IAEA's disposal.

Unlike the sovereign states with which it deals, the IAEA can use no force; it can neither compel a state to do anything nor physically prevent it from doing anything. If the IAEA found that a state was diverting, the sanctions it could invoke would be largely formal: it would ask the state to desist, report the diversion to the Security Council and the General Assembly of the UN, and it could also curtail or seek to curtail nuclear supplies and suspend the state from membership of the IAEA.[1]

The IAEA's job under the NPT, as the above quotation also makes clear, is the limited but important one of verifying that the state concerned is observing its undertaking not to use its nuclear programme to make nuclear explosives of any kind, and to sound the alarm if it detects a breach of the state's undertaking. It will also sound the alarm if it is unable to carry out its verification task effectively, for instance, because the state does not permit effective inspection. Of course, the risk that it may be detected fairly promptly if it attempts a clandestine diversion is expected to serve as a powerful deterrent to most states. The deterrent purpose of safeguards is made clear in the description of its technical objective (in para 28 of INFCIRC/153, see Appendix V), namely, ". . . the timely detection of diversion of significant quantities of nuclear material from peaceful nuclear activities to the manufacture of nuclear weapons or of other nuclear explosive devices or for purposes unknown, *and the deterrence of such diversion by early detection*".[2]

The point has already been made in chapter 1 that safeguards are accepted voluntarily. A state which wishes to keep open the option of making nuclear weapons (or to be perceived as keeping it open) is hardly likely to place its entire nuclear industry under safeguards. The five NNWS—Argentina, India, Israel,

Pakistan and South Africa—that have plainly chosen to make unsafeguarded weapon-usable material illustrate this point. Each has declined to ratify the NPT.

Another factor that may lessen any incentive to clandestine diversion, particularly in NPT NNWS, is that the NPT explicitly affirms the right of a party to withdraw from the Treaty (giving three months' notice) if "it decides that extraordinary events, related to the subject matter of this Treaty, have jeopardized the supreme interests of its country".[3] (The NPT requires the state to inform the UN Security Council of the reasons why it has found it necessary to withdraw.) In other words, if a country considers that a situation has arisen which makes it imperative for it to open or re-open the nuclear weapon option, it can legally revoke its renunciation of such weapons rather than seek to acquire them illegally by diversion. Withdrawal might of course be interpreted by other states as notice of the country's intention to 'go nuclear' and could have very serious consequences. Although one or two states have at times referred to the possibility of withdrawal, no country has withdrawn either from the NPT or the Partial Test Ban Treaty of 1963, which contains a similar provision and which bans nuclear testing in all environments except underground.

With these three factors militating against diversion (the voluntary, confidence-building object of safeguards, their secondary deterrent effect and the possibility of withdrawal from the NPT) it is hardly surprising that year after year the IAEA has formally achieved its objectives and with two exceptions, mentioned below, has been able to conclude that all nuclear material in the NNWS, non-NPT as well as NPT, to which the IAEA was applying safeguards, was satisfactorily accounted for.[4]

This annual confirmation has, however, been given with several express technical reservations by the IAEA. The chief reservation is that in numerous cases the IAEA has been unable to achieve the quantitative safeguards goals that it has set for itself. For instance, the IAEA may not have been able to verify non-diversion *within the number of days or weeks it has prescribed for verification at a particular type of plant* (but could nevertheless, somewhat later, confirm that the material was still present or properly accounted for). Such technical reservations have not invalidated the general conclusion of compliance. Moreover, the IAEA's record in achieving its quantitative goals is gradually improving as more manpower and better instruments become available.

II. The case of KANUPP

Potentially more serious in its implications was one of the two exceptions in which the IAEA was for a considerable time unable to confirm compliance. The KANUPP nuclear power plant in Pakistan is a natural uranium-fuelled heavy-water-moderated reactor known as a 'CANDU'-type and manufactured in Canada. For technical reasons this type of reactor has some advantages in countries with a relatively unsophisticated industrial infrastructure. However, it also lends itself more easily to diversion and is more difficult to safeguard effectively than the so-called light water reactor which is now the standard model in almost all industrial and many developing countries and accounts for nearly 90 per cent of the world's nuclear power plants. Canada has supplied CANDUs or heavy water research reactors[5] to three *non*-NPT NNWS (Argentine, India and Pakistan) and to two parties to the NPT (the Republic of Korea and Taiwan). The Cirus heavy water research reactor which Canada supplied to India and a similar type of reactor, the Dimona reactor which France supplied to (non-NPT) Israel, are the chief sources of unsafeguarded plutonium in Israel and India and of the nuclear explosive used in the Indian test of 1974.

When Pakistan, not being under NPT safeguards, began to manufacture its own unsafeguarded natural-uranium nuclear fuel elements and thus provide an unsafeguarded source of fuel for the KANUPP reactor, it became necessary to install additional safeguards equipment at the reactor. Pakistan objected on the grounds that this was not explicitly foreseen in the initial safeguards agreement. During some two years of negotiation and frequent reports on the matter to the IAEA Board of Governors, Pakistan agreed, step by step, to accept additional equipment and other safeguards measures that were adequate for the IAEA's purposes. About the same time a similar case arose in India, but India agreed without undue delay to adequate additional measures.

The IAEA was careful not to imply that Pakistan had diverted any nuclear material during the safeguards 'interregnum' (although the possibility that Pakistan did divert some material cannot, of course, be entirely excluded). The case illustrates, however, the extent to which the effectiveness of safeguards depends on the willing co-operation of the state. It shows, too, the difficulties that the IAEA experiences when technical or other developments require an upgrading of the original safeguards agreement. It also illustrates another point, which will be examined later, namely, that if a country did decide to divert, it would be likely to take measures to ensure that the IAEA would be unable to prove the diversion, the easiest being to prevent inspectors (or surveillance instruments) from doing their job properly by obstructing access. Being unable to prove diversion the IAEA would be in a position to state only that it was no longer able to verify the absence of diversion. In practice this is likely to be the furthest that the IAEA can go in most cases. The model NPT safeguards agreement expressly foresees this as the most likely contingency.[6]

Above all, the KANUPP case highlights the problems that can arise if the IAEA has the right to safeguard some but not all of the nuclear material and plants in a state—especially if some of the unsafeguarded plants are crucial points in the state's fuel cycle and, together with the safeguarded plants, enable it to make weapon-usable material.

III. Stockpiling safeguarded weapon material

Other limitations need to be noted. International safeguards cannot and do not seek to prevent any state, including NPT NNWS, from producing *safeguarded* plutonium or *safeguarded* highly enriched uranium that could be used for weapons as well as for peaceful purposes. If the state were to use such material to make a nuclear explosive, it would of course be violating the safeguards agreement (and the NPT, if it were a party to the Treaty). Nevertheless, it is quite legal for a state to develop its nuclear industry to the point at which it is able to stockpile, *under safeguards*, significant amounts of weapon-usable material. Several NPT NNWS are today at that point and more will reach it as time goes on. The main exporting countries have tried to limit the spread of such capacity by imposing export controls.[7]

IV. Inflated expectations

Related to this limitation is the fact that international safeguards cannot, except very indirectly, give any indication about the nuclear intentions of states. Safeguards can only deal with measurable and observable facts—past and present—and not with future intentions. They have been likened to a radar set that scans the sky and discloses what is there but not what might be over the time horizon. It is conceivable, therefore, that a state might ratify the NPT and place all its activities under safeguards so as to make it easier to acquire weapon-material capacity, with the secret intention of denouncing or violating the Treaty and its safeguards agreement at a later date. This is, in fact, one of the charges that the Israeli government made to justify its attack on the Iraqi nuclear centre.

Whatever may or may not have been Iraq's long-term intentions, the IAEA and France have put forward convincing arguments to show that any violation of the IAEA's safeguards agreement with Iraq, which is a party to the NPT, would have been promptly detected.[8] Nevertheless, the Israeli attack and Israel's subsequent allegations about the inadequacy of IAEA safeguards damaged the credibility of IAEA safeguards in many Western countries. Iraq had made matters worse by refusing for some time to admit IAEA inspectors because of the danger of Iranian attack (but it was persuaded to change its mind and an inspection was in fact carried out shortly before the Israeli attack).

Some of the media criticism directed against the IAEA reflected inflated—and therefore disappointed—belief in the power and authority of the IAEA. It came as a shock to many to learn that IAEA inspectors may, as a rule, visit only nuclear plants notified to the IAEA, that the IAEA usually has to give advance notice of the arrival of inspectors and that it must get the government's agreement to the list of inspectors that it sends to any country.

Yet these are the realities of a world of sovereign states. Any international or regional or bilateral system of verification will inevitably be subject to most of these or similar constraints. No country would, for instance, allow international inspectors (always foreigners in the case of IAEA inspections) to roam freely around its territory in search of unreported plant or material. Every country has, and usually uses, the right to require that the inspectors be always accompanied by its own official(s)—which implies some advance notice in most cases. Every country will reserve its right to exclude inspectors who are personally unacceptable. Of course, any country that built undeclared facilities or stores would run the risk of detection by 'national technical means' of verification (chiefly satellite observation by the superpowers), as in the case of the Dimona reactor and the suspected South African nuclear test preparations.[9] France has made proposals for an international satellite monitoring agency (ISMA) and if this bears fruit, as unfortunately does not seem likely in the near future, it could provide a valuable reinforcement to the verification of safeguards agreements, although its main task would lie elsewhere and it might not be able to detect small nuclear plants (e.g., pilot centrifuge enrichment plants).

The existing constraints on the IAEA's choice of inspectors and their freedom of action can nevertheless, in some cases, seriously affect the efficacy of its safeguards operation, as is shown in later chapters of this book.

Finally, and from a broader perspective, the confirmation that the IAEA has given each year about compliance with agreements is only meaningful, from a non-proliferation point of view, to the extent that the nuclear fuel cycles of all the world's NNWS are subject to safeguards and to the non-proliferation regime. Its coverage has greatly increased both in extent and in efficacy since 1970 but, as noted above, there are still serious gaps, notably in Argentina, India, Israel, Pakistan and South Africa.

V. IAEA safeguards in nuclear weapon states

The differences between pre-NPT and NPT IAEA safeguards are examined later. In the meantime, it should be stressed that there is a great difference between the purpose and scope of the safeguards that the IAEA applies in nuclear weapon and in NPT non-nuclear weapon states, although both are based on the model NPT safeguards agreement and use the same safeguarding techniques and approaches.[10] In the case of a NNWS party to the NPT the object is to verify that there is no diversion of any nuclear material in the state to nuclear weapons or other nuclear explosives. This obviously makes little sense in a nuclear weapon state (NWS). Moreover, each of the NWS reserves the right to withdraw any facility or material from safeguards and use it in the military domain.

It could be asked what purpose do safeguards serve in a NWS? The answer is that they demonstrate that the NWS is willing to accept the 'burden' of safeguards under what has been irreverently called the 'equality of misery' principle—namely that the fuel cycles of *all* states must be equally 'liable' to safeguards and exposed to the same risks of industrial espionage, and that all states must accept the same responsibilities for reporting to the IAEA and incurring some additional costs. Otherwise, it was averred, nuclear industry in the NNWS would be handicapped in competing with its counterparts in the NWS. They also provide some limited training and experience for the IAEA in advanced nuclear R&D centres. Finally and perhaps most important, they demonstrate the willingness of the NWS to accept the principle of international on-site verification, thus establishing, it may be hoped, a precedent for more far-reaching arms control measures.

VI. Prospects for improvement

Most of the constraints on IAEA safeguards described in this chapter reflect the very limited authority that states are prepared to give today to any international organization. In short they reflect the existing international structure, and they are unlikely to change for a very long time. The IAEA and other bodies applying safeguards have to work within them as best they can. Nevertheless, there are several steps that could be taken to ensure that, within these limitations, IAEA safeguards operate as effectively as possible and that the risks of further proliferation are minimized. Some of these steps can be taken by the IAEA itself, others by governments acting jointly in agreed supply policies, and some by individual states in their political and diplomatic relations with each other. But before identifying shortcomings and suggesting possible remedies let us first see how the IAEA system works in practice.

Notes and references

[1] The range of sanctions that the IAEA could and other states might apply is discussed in Part II.

[2] INFCIRC/153, para. 28 (see Appendix V).

[3] NPT Article X (see Appendix IX). The article lays down the procedure to be followed for such withdrawal.

[4] As Hans Blix, the Director General of IAEA has put it, "States do not invite inspection to deter themselves from diversion . . ." (Hans Blix, Statement to ESARDA, Venice, 14 May 1984). The standard annual conclusion of the IAEA so far, is that ". . . it is reasonable to conclude that the nuclear material under Agency safeguards . . . remained in peaceful uses or was otherwise adequately accounted for". (e.g., IAEA Annual Report for 1982, para. 54.)

[5] The trade name CANDU (Canadian deuterium uranium reactor) is usually given only to power reactors of this design.

[6] INFCIRC/153, para. 19 (see Appendix V).

[7] As an international body the IAEA cannot act as the agent of the exporting state and cannot usually 'enforce' any of its export controls other than the condition that the exported item and its products will be placed and remain under IAEA safeguards and will not be used for proscribed purposes. The IAEA cannot, for instance, enforce an exporter's requirement that the fuel it supplies should not be reprocessed without the exporter's prior consent.

8   The IAEA planned to inspect the reactor every fortnight as soon as it became critical. Under France's agreement with Iraq, French technical staff would have worked in its centre for 10 years and France and Iraq would have jointly laid down and carried out the reactor research programme.

9   South Africa denied that the installations detected by a Soviet satellite in a remote part of the Kalahari desert were intended for a nuclear test. However, the British, French, US and West German governments were reasonably sure that a test was planned and put strong pressure on Pretoria to desist. There have been some suggestions that the preparations were an elaborate bluff.

10 The USA and the UK accept IAEA safeguards on all their civilian nuclear plants, i.e., on all those that they regard as not having to do with national security. Their safeguards agreements with the IAEA have been in force for several years. Each country has given the IAEA a list of all 'eligible' plants or parts of plants, from which the IAEA may select any for the full application of safeguards procedures, including routine inspection. An agreement with France, which has offered a more restricted list than the USA or UK, is also in force. The agreement with the USSR is awaiting formal approval. The IAEA can only afford to select a very limited number of the 'eligible' plants for the full application of safeguards. The inspection effort of the IAEA in France, the UK and the USA in 1983, amounted only to about 6 per cent of the IAEA's total inspection effort (see Tempus, P. [Deputy Director General for Safeguards], 'Progress in safeguards: 1983 implementation', *IAEA Bulletin*, September 1984).

Chapter 4. The technical basis

I. How the safeguards system evolved

In 1958 Japan asked the IAEA to arrange for the supply of fuel (Canadian uranium) for a small research reactor, thus triggering the first application of IAEA safeguards. It became necessary to negotiate a detailed agreement with Japan on the basis of the broadly worded provisions of the IAEA statute (these are reproduced in Appendix I). It was clear that for future agreements it would be better to have a set of rules, approved by the Board, so that if states came to the IAEA for assistance they would know in advance what their safeguards obligations and rights would be, so that the Secretariat would know what it should propose or require in future negotiations and so that safeguards agreements should be as uniform as possible in their key provisions.

With difficulty and against much opposition from India, supported by the USSR and other countries, the Board was able in January 1961 to approve a system of safeguards to cover reactors up to a capacity of 100 MW(th).[1] In the same year the Board brought into force a document containing procedures for designating inspectors, arrangements for inspections and inspectors' rights of access. This document, GC(V)INF/39, reproduced in Appendix VII, still governs IAEA inspections in states not parties to the NPT or the Tlatelolco Treaty.

In 1963 the Board set about reviewing the 1961 safeguards document (INFCIRC/26). In the more congenial atmosphere of detente the Board made good progress and in 1965 it approved a new set of rules known as 'The Agency's Safeguards System (1965)' or more usually, today, as 'INFCIRC/66'. This document, together with its later extensions (INFCIRC/66/Rev. 2, reproduced in Appendix IV) still serves as the framework for all IAEA safeguards agreements with states not parties to the NPT or the Tlatelolco Treaty.

Soon after the NPT entered into force on 5 March 1970 the Board set up a committee to advise it on the contents of the safeguards agreement that each NPT NNWS would have to conclude with the IAEA under Article III.1 of the Treaty. Another NPT article gives these NNWS a limited time to conclude these agreements. Under this and other spurs the committee completed its work in March 1971 and in April the model agreement (INFCIRC/153, reproduced in Appendix V) it had drafted was approved by the Board.[2] The Secretariat has since used INFCIRC/153 as the basis for negotiating all agreements with NPT NNWS and with parties to the Treaty of Tlatelolco, and to a considerable extent too for those with NWS, whether parties to the NPT or not. Later chapters show in greater detail how INFCIRC/66 and the model NPT safeguards agreement INFCIRC/153 are structured and what system defects have come to light in applying them. But it may be helpful now to explain briefly how the general approach changed between 1963–68 (INFCIRC/66/Rev. 2) and 1970 (INFCIRC/153).

The core of INFCIRC/66/Rev. 2 consists of five sets of safeguards procedures. The first three sets, contained in the original 1965 document, cover (a) all types of plant (General Procedures), (b) reactors and (c) nuclear material in R&D facilities, sealed stores and 'other locations'. The fourth and fifth, added in 1966 and 1968, cover (d) reprocessing plants and (e) conversion and fuel fabrication plants. When INFCIRC/66/Rev. 2 was drawn up there was no coherent, technically and quantitatively oriented concept on which to base it. The document makes no attempt to spell out the technical aims of the procedures that it prescribes or the methods to be used to achieve such aims (although implicitly it envisages meticulous accounting of materials and verification of this accounting by the inspectors).

INFCIRC/66/Rev. 2 relies heavily on the presence of inspectors at the plant to detect any breach of a safeguards agreement and sets very high limits on the annual number of inspections. For instance, it permits continuous inspection of large power reactors, or, at least, an unlimited number of inspection visits (described as "the right of access at all times"). For the same plant the model NPT safeguards agreement (INFCIRC/153) prescribes a maximum of 50 man-days of inspection. In practice the IAEA now usually considers that 12–14 man-days a year is enough inspection of a large light water reactor.

Since INFCIRC/66/Rev. 2 is designed to deal with a wide variety of supply arrangements and other circumstances under which safeguards will be applied, it is cast in general terms, as a set of guidelines. It gives no guidance, however, on many points that have to be covered in a safeguards agreement (e.g., who bears what costs, procedures in the event of a breach of agreement, procedures for settling of disputes). The NPT document (INFCIRC/153), on the other hand, is a complete, detailed model safeguards agreement.

When the NPT began to emerge from the Geneva negotiations (1965–68) it became likely that the entire nuclear industry of countries such as FR Germany would eventually move under IAEA safeguards. This spurred research into ways of making those safeguards less 'burdensome' and 'intrusive' and thus diminish the risk that they would raise the cost of operating nuclear plants or that IAEA inspectors would spy out industrial secrets.

The new concept that emerged appears in the Preamble of the NPT itself and it is also evident in Article III of the Treaty. Thus, in NPT NNWS safeguards would follow the "flow" of *nuclear material* (and not, as in most INFCIRC/66/Rev. 2 agreements, apply to *nuclear plants*).[3] Where possible "instruments and other techniques" were to do the work of human inspectors. Under normal circumstances inspectors would only be allowed to go to previously agreed "strategic points" in the plant.

These principles and their consequences inspire much of the technical approach of INFCIRC/153.

Japan's still relatively small nuclear industry was already under INFCIRC/66/Rev. 2 safeguards but Japan had the scientific and industrial resources to build an unsafeguarded fuel cycle. It was most desirable, therefore, that the Japanese Diet be persuaded to ratify the NPT. In return for such ratification Japan was able to ensure that it would receive safeguards treatment not less favourable than that accorded to FR Germany and other EURATOM NNWS. A second Japanese aim was to set up an "oversight" committee of the Board on which those countries that would bear the full weight of safeguards would be amply represented and able to prevent undue superpower/Secretariat control of the safeguards operation. Out of this idea emerged eventually the IAEA's Standing Advisory Group on Safeguards Implementation (SAGSI); not a committee of the Board but a group of nationally chosen experts advising the Director General and, through him, the Board itself.

Despite their differences of approach, both INFCIRC/66 and INFCIRC/153 (and in fact all regional and national systems) make use today of three essential methods of verification. They are *material accountancy*, *containment* and *surveillance*. Before applying these methods, however, it is necessary to define and quantify the aims of the system. What, in terms of quantity, is it trying to detect, how quickly and with what degree of assurance?

II. The technical aims

As has been shown, the technical objective of NPT safeguards is defined as "... the *timely detection* of diversion of *significant quantities* of nuclear material from peaceful nuclear activities to the manufacture of nuclear weapons or of other nuclear explosive devices or for purposes unknown, and deterrence of such diversion by the *risk of early detection*".[4]

In setting goals for safeguards, "timely" detection and "significant" quantity must be defined.

On the advice of SAGSI,[5] the IAEA has set the 'significant quantity' at roughly the amount of material that a state would need to make its first nuclear explosive device, taking into account the waste and losses that the state would probably incur, namely (*a*) 8 kg of plutonium, or (*b*) 25 kg of uranium-235 contained in uranium enriched to 20 per cent or more, or (*c*) 8 kg of uranium-233.[6]

Defining "timely" detection is a more uncertain process. The IAEA relates it to the estimated time that would be needed to convert diverted material into the components of a nuclear explosive device. This time will obviously vary according to the nature of the material, being very short for separated plutonium or highly enriched uranium and much longer for natural uranium or spent fuel which cannot be directly used as an explosive. Also on SAGSI's advice the IAEA has set conversion and detection times at: (*a*) 7–10 days for plutonium or highly enriched uranium in metallic form; (*b*) 1–3 months for plutonium in irradiated fuel; and (*c*) about one year for natural or low-enriched uranium.[7]

The third term in the safeguards objective, 'the risk of early detection', lies in the eye of the potential diverter and cannot be quantified. However, what can be quantified to some extent is the probability that the IAEA will detect the diversion of a significant quantity of nuclear material. The IAEA aims at achieving, through material accountancy, a 90–95 per cent likelihood of detecting such a diversion and a less than 5 per cent likelihood of sounding a false alarm.[8]

A state that contemplated diversion would have to consider not only the risk of being detected but also the consequences of such detection. The question of possible sanctions is examined in detail in Part II. As indicated there the sanctions that the IAEA itself could impose consist chiefly of bringing a diversion to the world's attention. What would happen after that is very uncertain and would depend on many factors which lie beyond the scope of this book.

III. *The methods*

Returning now to the three essential methods of verification, the model NPT safeguards agreement (INFCIRC/153) describes the use of the first, *material accountancy*, "as a safeguards measure of fundamental importance". Its aim is to determine ". . . in respect of each material balance area (MBA) . . . the amount of material unaccounted for (MUF) over a specific period . . .".[9]

An MBA may be an entire nuclear plant or a part of it. For an area to qualify as an MBA it must be possible to determine (measure, count, identify) all material that moves into or out of the area as well as the amount and composition (inventory) of the material in it. An example of an MBA is the fresh fuel store of a reactor.[10] To determine how much material is unaccounted for the operator records (and reports to the IAEA) how much material is in the MBA at the beginning of the specified period, all material brought into the MBA or produced in it, all material taken out, lost or scrapped. From these records the operator calculates how much material should be in the MBA. (The calculated amount is known as the "book inventory".) At the end of the specified period the operator takes stock (the "ending physical inventory") of the material that is actually present in the MBA. The difference (if any) between this amount and the book inventory is the amount of material unaccounted for. The amount established by the physical inventory is the starting point ("beginning physical inventory") for calculating the book inventory of the next specified period.

Containment and *surveillance* are described in the model NPT safeguards agreement as important measures to complement material accountancy.[11]

Containment consists of making use of physical barriers in the plant, such as the pressure vessel of a reactor, the walls and doors of a storage area or the sheath of a container, so as to restrict access to the nuclear material inside it and thus prevent or hamper the clandestine movement of the material. For this purpose it is usually necessary to seal off the area or container.[12]

Surveillance means chiefly the use of instruments such as automatic cameras, video recorders or other electronic aids so as to detect any unreported movement or any tampering with safeguarded items.

IV. Verification procedures

To put into practice and to verify the results of material accountancy, containment and surveillance all existing safeguards make use today of four procedures, namely *design review*, maintenance of plant operating *records*, *reports* on plant operation and *on-site inspections*.

Design review

The IAEA examines (but may not seek to change) the overall design of the nuclear plant so as to develop a detailed plan for safeguarding it, for example, for defining MBAs and strategic points needed for material accountancy and to decide where to apply seals or install surveillance instruments. After verifying that the plant is, in fact, as designed, and that there are, for instance, no unreported channels for removing nuclear material, the IAEA negotiates a detailed *facility attachment*. The negotiation may be with the operator or the national authority or both. The facility attachment is thus an agreed detailed plan for safeguarding the plant and it sets out the obligations of the operator and the rights and obligations of the IAEA. Any change in the facility attachment must be agreed to by both parties. The facility attachments for the nuclear plants in the state concerned then become part of the *subsidiary arrangements* to that state's safeguards agreement. The main part of these subsidiary arrangements deals with more general matters applying to all plants in the country (how records shall be kept, in what form reports are to be drawn up and transmitted and inspections arranged, safety measures, and so on), that are not already dealt with in the safeguards agreement itself.[13] The subsidiary arrangements and their facility attachments are a crucial supplement to the safeguards agreement. Like the agreement itself, the subsidiary arrangements have to be negotiated with the state—the IAEA cannot 'impose' them on the state. However, the IAEA tries to keep subsidiary arrangements as uniform as possible.

Maintenance of records

The operator of the plant must keep accurate accounts of all nuclear material in use at the plant as well as of all material that the plant receives, produces, uses up, or sends out.

Reports

On the basis of these records the *national authority concerned* (not the operator) sends the IAEA regular (usually monthly) reports showing the quantity of nuclear material in each MBA of a safeguarded plant as well as any changes (receipts, shipments, production losses) since the previous report. The IAEA uses these reports to keep its own set of accounts of nuclear material in the plants.

The national authority must also send the IAEA a report whenever the operator takes a physical inventory of the nuclear material.

Inspections

On-site inspection is the crucial procedure to confirm the veracity of the data yielded by the other three procedures. The IAEA carries out inspections for a variety of purposes, for example:

1. To check design information.

2. To check (count, measure and possibly seal) material before it is shipped abroad or when it arrives in a country.

3. When the plant has started operation, to check that the reports sent to the IAEA are consistent with the plant's operating records. The inspector is also usually present at each physical inventory-taking and checks the location, identity, quantity and composition of nuclear material at the plant. Finally, the inspector will look into any causes of MUF and of differences between the reports sent to the IAEA by the shippers and receivers of nuclear material. In both NPT safeguards agreements and INFCIRC/66 safeguards agreements the inspections described in this paragraph are classified as "routine inspections". During these inspections the IAEA's inspectors may (under NPT safeguards agreements) have access only to "strategic points" specified in the facility attachment. However, the NPT safeguards agreement makes it plain that there must be enough, properly located, strategic points to provide, normally, "the information necessary and sufficient to implement safeguards" and to verify such information.

4. If, however, the national authorities report that there has been or may have been a loss of nuclear material or a breakdown of containment or if the IAEA considers that the information reaching it is inadequate, it may, after consulting the national authorities, carry out "special inspections". In these inspections the IAEA may, with the agreement of the national authorities, send its inspectors to places not specified in the facility attachment and may obtain additional information.

5. The model NPT safeguards agreement also describes in broad terms the tasks that the inspector may carry out during these inspections. It also specifies certain important limitations on the inspector's freedom of action. For instance, he may check the consistency of records and reports, oversee the inventory taking, and, *provided that the facility attachment so permits*, install surveillance equipment and other equipment for independent measurements and apply IAEA

seals and similar devices. In most cases the inspector is not allowed to take action himself but must "observe" the actions of the operator, for instance, so as to be able to satisfy himself that the samples of nuclear material that the operator takes (and of which he gives a duplicate to the inspector) are representative and that the measurements the operator makes are both representative and accurate. The inspector may also make arrangements with the national authorities for additional sample taking or measurements.

This summary of the relevant part of the model NPT safeguards agreement gives a rough idea of what an inspector actually does when he visits a nuclear plant. But it may be helpful to give a concrete example.

The most common type of reactor, the light water reactor, is usually divided into the three areas through which the fuel moves step by step: (*a*) the fresh fuel store; (*b*) the reactor itself; and (*c*) the spent fuel store.

The first task of the inspector is to examine the operating records and check that they tally with the reports sent to the IAEA since the last inspection. The records and their corresponding reports will show how much and what kind of nuclear material there should be in each area. The inspector will verify this by counting the number of fresh fuel and spent fuel assemblies and checking their identity numbers. He may then check a representative selection of fuel assemblies to ensure that they are not dummies—in other words that the fresh fuel is indeed low-enriched uranium and of the enrichment specified for the reactor. To test whether the spent fuel is indeed 'spent', in other words that the spent fuel assemblies have been irradiated and are not dummies, a commercially-available 'Night Vision Device' can be used to verify that fuel assemblies in the spent fuel pond are emitting the characteristic Cherenkov glow (a bluish light emitted by irradiated fuel immersed in water, but not by fresh fuel or dummies). The device amplifies the glow so that it may be readily detected in darkness, even when the image is too faint to be seen by the naked eye. An improved version of the Night Vision Device (using ultraviolet filtering techniques) is under development which can be used under normal ambient lighting conditions, that is, in daytime.

During most inspections the reactor will be in operation and its core will be inaccessible. However, if a seal has been applied to the core, the inspector will check that it is intact. He will also run through the tape or film from the surveillance cameras which will have taken a picture every 15 to 20 minutes of the outside of the reactor core and of the spent fuel bay. This will show whether there has been any unreported opening of the reactor core and any unreported removal of fuel elements from the core or the bay. Usually two tamper-indicating surveillance cameras are operated in tandem in case one should fail and also to make it difficult to fool a camera, for instance, by putting a picture of the reactor core on a screen in front of it and carrying out clandestine activities behind the screen.

The core of the standard light water reactor is normally opened at 12–18-month intervals, one-third of the spent fuel is removed and fresh fuel is inserted. This offers the opportunity for taking an inventory of all the nuclear material present in the reactor and its storage areas. The inspector will normally verify the operator's inventory by counting the assemblies and by making independent measurements and analyses.

As we shall see later this is a somewhat idealized scenario. Moreover, verification is much easier at reactors (although this applies to some types of reactor more than others) where the material is in the form of separate and identical assemblies, often carrying an identification number, than in a plant where the nuclear material flows through in a continuous or intermittent stream (as in a reprocessing, enrichment or fuel fabrication plant).

Frequency of inspections

The model NPT safeguards agreement lays down elaborate rules for calculating the maximum frequency of inspection in terms of inspection man-days per year[14] at various types and capacities of plant. This can vary from one inspection a year for small reactors and fuel stores up to continuous inspection in the case of plants processing or handling large quantities of sensitive nuclear material (e.g., separated plutonium or highly enriched uranium).

The agreement also provides five rather complex guidelines to help determine the IAEA's *actual* routine inspection effort (e.g., number of inspection man-days per year) at any plant.[15] The guidelines relate to (*a*) the form of nuclear material; (*b*) the state's own system for accounting and controlling nuclear material, and other organizational questions; (*c*) the nature of the state's fuel cycle and characteristics of its nuclear plants; (*d*) the extent to which the fuel cycle is autonomous or dependent on external supplies; and (*e*) technical progress in safeguards. The only case where an explicit attempt has been made to apply the second guideline is in the IAEA's safeguards agreements with EURATOM and Japan. There has been no attempt to apply the fourth guideline. Implicitly, the first and to some extent the third and fifth guidelines are taken into account when the IAEA draws up inspection plans for different types of plant (e.g., fabrication plants making highly or low-enriched fuel, or CANDU or light water reactors).

Arrangements for inspections

The model NPT safeguards agreement also contains detailed rules for getting the agreement of the state concerned to the designation of the officials whom the IAEA wishes to assign to inspect its plants, for giving advance notice of inspections, and for the way in which inspectors must carry out their work at the plant. The advance notice required for each inspection varies from at least one day to at least one week before the visit to the plant. If, as in most cases, the inspector comes from abroad the IAEA must inform the state of the time and place of his arrival. It should be stressed that advance notice or joint planning of inspections is generally useful and sometimes essential for both the inspector and the operator. Inspection timetables must take account of those of the operator, for example, when the latter plans to open the reactor or take a physical inventory.

The agreement does, however, permit the IAEA to carry out, without advance notification, "a portion of the routine inspection . . . in accordance with the principle of random sampling". In practice, and largely for the reasons just explained, the IAEA hardly ever makes unannounced inspections. The first such inspection in an NPT country (Sweden) was, for instance, only made in 1983.[16]

The procedures for designating inspectors are equally detailed. The state concerned is supposed to inform the IAEA within 30 days whether it accepts the inspectors proposed by the Director General. It may withdraw this acceptance at any time. If the state rejects a proposed designation or withdraws its approval of an inspector whom it had previously accepted the IAEA has to put forward alternative name(s). However, if the state repeatedly refuses the IAEA's designations and if its refusals would impede inspections the Board would consider the matter ". . . with a view to appropriate action".

The most explicit among several rules governing the conduct of inspectors is that the inspector may neither operate a plant nor direct the staff of the plant to carry out any operation; he must simply request the desired operation. The state also has the right to "have inspectors accompanied" by its own representative provided that this does not delay the inspector or impede his work. The exercise of this right might plainly diminish the element of surprise in an unannounced inspection. However, the presence of a national official can often be helpful in cutting through red tape, getting things done and sometimes translating requests.

V. Confidence and secrecy

In applying safeguards the IAEA staff is bound to obtain a large amount of information about the nuclear plants and programmes of the states concerned, for instance, when IAEA staff review plant design, check records of plant operations or inspect certain types of plant. Although most of this information is in the public domain, some of it may concern new processes and novel designs, or plant performance, or size of stocks of material. It may thus be of commercial value. Therefore, the technically advanced NNWS such as Belgium, FR Germany, Italy and Japan feared that the NPT would place their nuclear industry at a disadvantage in relation to that of the nuclear weapon states since all NNWS plants would be under safeguards while the NWS were under no such obligation even with regard to their purely civilian plants (in fact, as mentioned above, the USA and the UK as well as France and the USSR[17] have placed some or all of their civilian plants under IAEA safeguards of a kind).

Because of these concerns the model agreement lays down strict rules regarding the publication of information obtained in implementing safeguards agreements. At most, "summarized information" on safeguarded nuclear material[18] ". . . may be published upon declaration of the Board if the States [note plural] directly concerned agree".

VI. Non-NPT guidelines

It should be noted that in most of the matters referred to above, the non-NPT safeguards guidelines (INFCIRC/66) place fewer restrictions on the IAEA and the inspectors than the model NPT agreement (but also place fewer obligations on the state). The non-NPT safeguards guidelines (and the non-NPT safeguards agreements) place no limitation on the inspector's freedom of access within the plant, fewer restrictions on the range of his activities within the plant and are much more liberal in setting the maxima for inspection effort.[19] However, the requirements in regard to the procedures for designating inspectors[20] and for giving advance notice of inspections as well as for preserving the confidentiality of information are much the same in both systems. These matters are examined in greater detail in chapter 11.

Notes and references

[1] This safeguards system is set forth in IAEA document INFCIRC/26. See also Szasz, P., *The Law and Practices of the International Atomic Energy Agency* (IAEA, Vienna, 1970), pp. 550–53. Ben Sanders provides extensive coverage of the early history of safeguards in SIPRI, *Safeguards Against Nuclear Proliferation* (MIT Press, Cambridge, MA and Almqvist & Wiksell, Stockholm, 1975).

[2] SIPRI (note 1), pp. 6–7.

[3] Though this distinction (between applying safeguards to plants or to nuclear material only) became an article of faith when the model NPT safeguards agreement was drawn up and in negotiations with EURATOM, it does not usually make much practical difference. To safeguard nuclear material the IAEA must safeguard the plant in which it is being processed, used or stored and it must have information about and access to the plant. However, in those cases where the distinction can be of importance—e.g., where the IAEA may not be able to apply safeguards because the state maintains that the plant has been emptied or does not yet contain nuclear material—the distinction's effect is to diminish the credibility of safeguards and of the assurance that safeguards coverage is complete.

[4] INFCIRC/153, para. 28 (see Appendix V).

[5] See chapter 9.

[6] *IAEA Safeguards, Aims, Limitations and Achievements*, IAEA/SG/INF.4, 1983, p. 26.

[7] Note 6, p. 29.

[8] Note 6, p. 31.

[9] INFCIRC/153, paras 2a and 30 (see Appendix V).

[10] The tendency is to regard the entire reactors as MBAs.

[11] INFCIRC/153, para. 29 (see Appendix V).

[12] *IAEA Safeguards—An Introduction*, IAEA/SG/INF.3, 1983, p. 24. See also an article by a former head of the IAEA Safeguards Department, Grümm, H., 'Nuclear safeguards—a basic task of the International Atomic Energy Agency (IAEA)', *New Scientist*, 27 October 1983.

[13] See SIPRI (note 1), pp. 25–26.

14 One "man-day" is defined as "a day during which a single inspector has access to a facility at any time for a total of not more than eight hours". One man-year of inspection is 300 man-days (INFCIRC/153, para. 109).

15 INFCIRC/153, para. 81 (see Appendix V).

16 Unlike the public and the press, senior IAEA inspectors tend to be doubtful of the safeguards value of 'surprise' visits and the author believes that the 1983 'unannounced' inspection was carried out more 'for the record' than because it was considered operationally useful. However, unannounced inspections may be useful where the layout of the plant can be changed fairly quickly so as to make weapon-usable material. 'Unannounced' inspections are thus a part of the agreed regime for gas-centrifuge enrichment plants.

17 As noted, at the time of writing the IAEA–Soviet safeguards agreement is awaiting formal approval.

18 In practice the IAEA has been able to go somewhat further than this injunction would imply. The IAEA's annual reports contain a list of all nuclear plants in which safeguards are being applied and an indication of the progress made in concluding a facility attachment for each plant. With this and one or two other exceptions the Board has insisted on a strict application of the confidentiality rules.

19 The non-NPT safeguards guidelines (INFCIRC/66) also set limits only to the *number of inspections* that the IAEA may make during one year at a plant of a given type and size and they do not limit the length of each inspection or the *number of inspectors* that may take part in it. The model NPT safeguards agreement (INFCIRC/153) sets limits to the number of inspection *man-days* that can be spent at a plant. This is a much more inflexible constraint.

20 The procedures for designating inspectors, giving advance notice of inspections and the injunctions about the conduct of inspectors are not contained in the non-NPT safeguards agreement guidelines but in a separate document, the *Inspectors Document* (the Annex to IAEA document GC(V)/INF/39) (see Appendix VII).

Chapter 5. The risk of secret nuclear plants

I. Confidence in the IAEA's coverage

In each NPT NNWS the IAEA's safeguards are expected to cover virtually all nuclear material (other than ore and concentrates) within the country's frontiers.[1] In the non-NPT case they should cover all plant and material referred to directly in the relevant safeguards agreement.

Yet how can the IAEA (and the world at large) be confident that its coverage is in fact complete? No country would permit IAEA inspectors unlimited territorial access, and under all safeguards agreements the extent of IAEA safeguards coverage depends almost entirely on information given by the country or countries concerned.[2] In the NPT case the information is given solely *by the country in which the safeguards are applied*, firstly in the form of an 'initial report' that is required to identify all nuclear material in the country.[3] In certain non-NPT cases information may also be given initially by a country supplying hardware or technology, but in time the IAEA will depend almost entirely on the recipient state.[4] In either case how can the IAEA be sure that the country has told the full tale?

II. Completeness of the 'initial report'

It might be thought that the IAEA would have greater assurance about the completeness of the NPT 'initial report' if it had been safeguarding a country's entire nuclear programme under INFCIRC/66 since the country imported its first reactor (or if the IAEA had taken over all its bilateral safeguards agreements at an early stage) than if it had entered the scene only much later. Finland, Japan and most developing NPT NNWS are in the first category; Canada, Sweden, the East European allies of the USSR, and EURATOM are in the second.

In practice, however, there is little difference between the two categories. On obvious political grounds one may assume that the East European, Canadian and Swedish 'initial reports' were complete. The multinational character of EURATOM probably rules out any real possibility of a deliberately false report; moreover the USA must still have a pretty complete picture of the nuclear material in the EURATOM NNWS.

But it still remains a fact that in 1977, when the IAEA–EURATOM agreement came into force, the IAEA had no option but to trust EURATOM's initial report (and the initial reports of Canada, Sweden and of the East European countries concerned) to the extent of assuming that they were adequate enough to enable the IAEA to begin discharging its right and *obligation*[5] to apply safeguards on *all* nuclear material in the countries concerned.[6] Thereafter the IAEA would independently verify the amount of nuclear material in each country but its starting point would have to be the amount initially declared. This point is stressed since it is, perhaps rightly, an article of faith for the IAEA that it cannot rely upon any verification except its own—yet in several cases it has had to begin its operation by what amounts to an act of faith in the government's (or EURATOM's) initial report. This could present special verification problems if any country *known to have been producing unsafeguarded weapon-usable material* were to adhere to the NPT (e.g., Argentina, India, Israel, Pakistan, South Africa).

III. *The possibility of subsequent secret construction*

Even if one assumes that the initial reports of the 1970s were comprehensive, this would not by itself prevent the countries concerned from subsequently building secret plants or secretly producing material. Indeed, IAEA safeguards do not and cannot exclude the possible existence of a secret plant and one of their main objects in NPT NNWS is to verify that there is no diversion of material to such a plant. But by themselves IAEA safeguards would have a much harder task in detecting an *independent* undeclared cycle *that made no use of safeguarded material.*

IV. *How can the IAEA's information be supplemented?*

Some means of supplementing the information given by states do nevertheless exist, even in the NPT case.

It seems likely that the 'national technical means of verification' of the super-powers would discover a secret reactor or sizeable enrichment or reprocessing plants.[7] As is shown below the problem is how the IAEA could make use of information gathered in this way unless it were officially communicated to the organization.

The Treaty of Tlatelolco makes provisions for 'special inspections' *at the request of a state.* Special inspections of this kind are not explicitly foreseen in the IAEA Statute and are not contemplated under either of the two IAEA safeguards systems but they would give additional assurance in countries parties to the Tlatelolco Treaty that no unsafeguarded plant was being built or operated. Such inspections could play an even more important role in other regional nuclear weapon-free zones where regional tensions and mutual distrust are much sharper than in Latin America.

It is possible that the clauses in the model NPT agreement that relate to 'special inspections' *at the request of the IAEA* might provide the legal basis on which the IAEA could propose to inspect an unreported plant of which it had got wind, whether or not these clauses were intended for that purpose. Paragraph 73(b) of the model NPT safeguards agreement foresees that the IAEA may make "special inspections" if it "considers that the information made available by the State . . . is not adequate for the Agency to fulfil its responsibilities under the Agreement" to apply safeguards to all nuclear material in the country.

The authority given to the IAEA in paragraph 73(b) is supplemented by paragraph 77 of the model agreement. Under that paragraph the IAEA "may obtain access in agreement with the state . . . *to locations in addition to* the access specified . . . for *ad hoc* and *routine* inspections". Paragraph 77 places *no geographical limit* on such additional access, no requirement, for instance, that it should be confined to other previously inaccessible parts of the same plant[8] (although this may well have been the intention of the drafters).

Paragraph 77 also provides that if a dispute arises about the need for additional access, the matter will be submitted to the Board of Governors or to arbitration, but if the Board considers that such access is 'essential and urgent' to verify the absence of diversion it may require the state to permit access without delay.

One may speculate that if the state's conscience were clear it would promptly agree to an IAEA request for additional access, while a refusal to do so would arouse suspicions that the state had something to hide (although there might well be other reasons for such a refusal). If the state did refuse it would be open to the Board to conclude that the IAEA was no longer able to verify the absence of diversion. As noted, this is probably the furthest the IAEA would be able to go in identifying a likely diversion. The state would not be likely to permit the IAEA to catch it red-handed in the act of diverting, nor to test a nuclear explosive while it was still a party to the NPT.

As far as is known the IAEA has not given consideration to the possibility of using this path to gain access to any undeclared facility. It has tended rather to assume that it can do little about undeclared plant or material unless such plant or material is discovered by chance during an inspection of a declared facility or declared material or unless its own accounting—for instance, an inexplicably large MUF—pointed clearly in the direction of some undeclared activity.

V. The non-NPT case

At the early stages of implementing a non-NPT safeguards agreement the IAEA can usually be reasonably sure that it *is* safeguarding all the items it is supposed to safeguard. The IAEA will automatically receive (or be able to obtain) corroboratory information from the supplying state about the hardware it has supplied.

Such assurance may become much more doubtful when safeguards are to be applied to plants built by the importing state on the basis of supplied technology. In fact this problem can arise quite early if only technology and no hardware has been supplied, as the following case will show.

The Franco-Pakistani reprocessing plant agreement

The question at issue in this case was whether Pakistan was reporting and placing under IAEA safeguards all items that it was required to report under the 1977 Franco-Pakistani-IAEA safeguards agreement covering the transfer of a reprocessing plant and reprocessing technology from France to Pakistan. One clause of that agreement stipulates that any reprocessing plant that Pakistan builds within a specified period and that uses the 'solvent extraction' technique must be placed under safeguards. Since solvent extraction is the only technique in use today, this means, in effect, that Pakistan is obliged to place under safeguards any reprocessing plant that it constructs during the prescribed period.

There were, however, two snags. The prescribed period began when the IAEA was informed (as it was by both France and Pakistan) of the first significant transfer of technology under the agreement (France sent Pakistan the blueprints for the plant). The agreement also required both countries to inform the IAEA of the length of the prescribed period. Neither did. Since France decided not to go ahead with the export of the plant the agreement, though not officially abrogated by either party, went into some kind of legal limbo.

The second snag was that, as is normally the case under such agreements, the IAEA could place the plant under safeguards only when notified of its transfer by the importer or the exporter or by both.

The IAEA learned *unofficially* that the length of the prescribed period was the same as that in a similar but much more extensive agreement concluded between Brazil and FR Germany, namely, 20 years. It also learned, again *unofficially* but from different sources, that Pakistan was in fact building one or two reprocessing plants using the solvent extraction technique. In fact the media were full of such reports. But no official notification came from either Pakistan or France. The IAEA sent a number of official enquiries to Pakistan asking it to confirm that it had duly reported all that it was obliged to report under the agreement, but received only bland replies. The IAEA took the matter up again informally after it discovered that the Pakistani budget for the year in question made provision for the construction of a reprocessing plant, but again the IAEA's queries were side-stepped. France was unwilling to make any official reports for fear of reopening the question of its own supply obligations or casting doubt on continued legal validity of the agreement. In the absence of an official notification from either government and in view of the ambiguous status of the notification clause, there was little more that the IAEA could do.

The incident illustrates several points:

1. It underlines the unsatisfactory nature of safeguards that apply only to a part of the nuclear activities of the country concerned. The type of clause which caused difficulties in this case is, of course, unnecessary in NPT safeguards agreements which unequivocally require the country concerned to place all nuclear material "in all [peaceful] nuclear activities" under IAEA safeguards (the qualification "peaceful" was intended—but has never been used—to permit NPT NNWS to withdraw nuclear materials for use in permissible nuclear military activities, for example, to propel naval vessels.

2. It casts some doubt on the efficacy of similar clauses in the Brazilian–West German agreement containing the 20-year time-clock and, indeed, on provisions in several other agreements regarding the use by the importing country of technology received from the exporter. These clauses stipulate that if such technology is used by the importer to build new plants they must be placed under IAEA safeguards. But it is usually up to the importer to inform the IAEA of any such replicated plants.

3. It illustrates the degree to which the IAEA depends upon the willing co-operation of the state or states concerned and the difficulties it has in taking effective action if such co-operation is withheld.

4. Ironically it also shows that safeguards, at least, might have been better served if France, ignoring US pressure, had gone ahead with the originally planned export of the plant itself which would then assuredly have come under safeguards—the "replication" or "use of supplied" technology issue would, then, not have arisen.

5. Finally, the incident shows how difficult it is for the IAEA to make effective use of information which is given to it 'unofficially' but not formally transmitted.

It should be noted that the unreported and unsafeguarded reprocessing plant is likely to be that which Pakistan would use to reprocess fuel from the KANUPP reactor. This reactor was the subject of a protracted difference between the IAEA and Pakistan in the course of which the IAEA felt obliged to report that it was no longer able to verify fully the provisions of the relevant safeguards agreement—in other words, to verify the absence of diversion. The existence of an unsafeguarded reprocessing plant obviously heightened the IAEA's concern about KANUPP. It should also be noted, however, that if Pakistan does reprocess fuel from the KANUPP reactor, the agreement relating to that reactor requires that the reprocessing plant be placed under IAEA safeguards, *while* it is handling KANUPP fuel.

Notes and references

1 "Within its territory, under its jurisdiction or . . . under its control anywhere . . ." is the language used by the NPT. The NPT does not require safeguards on material being used for a military non-explosive purpose but no NPT NNWS has yet availed itself of this option—see chapter 12.

2 It may be argued that if the main purpose of ratifying the NPT and accepting comprehensive safeguards is to build confidence, a state would stand to lose far more than it could gain by deliberately withholding vital information, and thus violating its safeguards agreement and, implicitly, the NPT, by a form of "anticipatory" diversion (see Blix, quoted in note 4 to chapter 3). But a state may believe that it would run a much lower risk of detection, if it hid away an undeclared stock of plutonium or enriched uranium than if it attempted, later, to divert such material from declared and safeguarded plants.

3 In non-NPT cases, safeguards can spread through much of the fuel cycle by coming into contact with safeguarded items. For instance, unsafeguarded fresh fuel going into a safeguarded reactor remains under safeguards when it emerges as spent fuel. If unsafeguarded spent fuel is put into a safeguarded reprocessing plant, it and its products (e.g., the extracted plutonium) remain under safeguards through all subsequent generations.

4 The USA, UK, USSR and France do, however, inform the IAEA of exports of nuclear material to all NNWS (IAEA document INFCIRC/207 and INFCIRC/207/Add. 1). NPT NNWS also inform the IAEA of all their exports of nuclear materials (but not of nuclear plant, except to non-NPT NNWS).

5 INFCIRC/153, para. 2 (see Appendix V).

6 The IAEA did, of course, verify that the material in the plants, stores, etc., identified by EURATOM, tallied with EURATOM's initial report. The IAEA could not, however, verify that EURATOM had notified to it every plant, store, etc., in the five nations concerned (i.e., Belgium, FR Germany, Italy, Luxembourg and the Netherlands, which were initially covered by the IAEA–EURATOM agreement. Before joining the Common Market, Denmark and Greece were covered by separate NPT safeguards agreements with the IAEA. There was no nuclear material or plant in Ireland). In fact, EURATOM apparently overlooked some items; notifications of previously unlisted items are still occasionally being sent by EURATOM to the IAEA! (personal communication to the author).

7 Although there has so far been no published indication that they detected Argentina's pilot (gaseous diffusion) enrichment plant.

8 The argument that the IAEA has at least a residual right to unlimited access in cases of doubt is strengthened by Article A.6 of the Statute. Under this article IAEA inspectors "shall have access at all times to all places and data and to any person who by reason of his occupation deals with materials, equipment or facilities which are required by this Statute to be safeguarded..." EURATOM has a similar right under Article 81 of the Rome Treaty. The formula was first used in some US bilateral safeguards agreements.

Chapter 6. Limits to the present approach

I. Cheating the accounting system

Les us now look at some of the main problems the IAEA runs into in applying its three safeguards 'measures'—material accountancy, containment and surveillance—and its four safeguards procedures—design review, records, reports and inspections—and examine some suggested solutions.

It is appropriate to ask first how valid the entire approach is. The approach is well summed up in paragraph 30 of the model NPT safeguards agreement. This states that "... the technical conclusion of the Agency's verification activities shall be a statement, in respect of each *material balance area*, of the amount of *material unaccounted* for over a specific period ..."[1]

The approach is premised on the assumption that a state planning to obtain nuclear explosives—that is, weapon-usable material—by a diversion will do so by trying to deceive the IAEA's accounting system so that, for instance, the diverted material does not show up as MUF, or by attributing MUF to causes other than diversion (e.g., measurement uncertainties). This deception could take the form, for instance, of: (*a*) falsifying records or reports;[2] (*b*) substituting dummy fuel elements, possibly containing fission products, for fuel elements that had been diverted; (*c*) simultaneously diverting small quantities of fuel (much less than a significant quantity) from a large number of plants; (*d*) draining off a small part of the liquid or gaseous flow of nuclear material and attributing the loss to uncertainty in the accuracy of the measuring instruments; or (*e*) clandestinely introducing unsafeguarded material into the appropriate plant and irradiating it or enriching it and withdrawing it before detection. A variant of this would be to 'borrow' fuel elements from other plants, not being inspected at the time, and insert them in place of diverted fuel.

All these diversion scenarios as well as the strategies the IAEA draws up to foil them *assume that the IAEA safeguards system will be in full operation while the diverter attempts to deceive it.*

Diversion of safeguarded material *under the eye of the IAEA's safeguards* is indeed one of the ways in which the NPT NNWS might attempt to obtain nuclear weapon-usable material. But it is not the only way nor is it necessarily the most likely one. The following are some alternative diversion scenarios.

A secret fuel cycle? (scenario A)

Assume that a highly industrialized NPT NNWS such as FR Germany or Japan decides to obtain some unsafeguarded weapon-usable material.[3]

Both FR Germany and Japan have some workable, though costly, domestic sources of uranium. Both have mastered the technology of uranium enrichment by gas centrifuges which are manufactured in plants that are not under safeguards since the plants contain no uranium or so little as to fall under the exemption clause.[4] It is, thus, at least arguable that if either country were prepared to violate its NPT obligations (extremely unlikely) and decided to obtain unsafeguarded highly enriched uranium it would be more likely to build a small undeclared centrifuge enrichment plant and process its own undeclared uranium through it than to attempt to divert enriched uranium from a safeguarded plant under the eyes of the IAEA inspectorate (and of EURATOM, in the case of FR Germany).[5]

It may be countered that it is not the IAEA's business nor within its powers to look for undeclared plants. In chapter 5 questions have been raised about this assumption.

Non-co-operation (scenario B)

A moderately industrialized NPT country with a fuel cycle that includes a reprocessing or enrichment plant (there is no NPT NNWS in this category today) decides to acquire unsafeguarded weapon-usable material. It might of course follow a similar route as in scenario A and clandestinely build an unsafeguarded enrichment plant or an unsafeguarded plutonium fuel cycle (reactor, heavy water, reprocessing, etc.). But for some inexplicable reason it decides rather to divert safeguarded material.

If plutonium is sought it might do so by diverting spent fuel to an undeclared (i.e., clandestine) reprocessing plant or by diverting plutonium direct from its safeguarded reprocessing plant. If highly enriched uranium is the object, the country would presumably divert direct from its safeguarded enrichment plant.

In either case, it would run a risk of detection and probably a high risk *if it permitted the IAEA to operate its safeguards fully and effectively*.

Again it is at least arguable that rather than run the risk of actually being detected in a diversion and 'convicted' by the IAEA before the bar of world opinion, the country would attempt to blur the issue by taking steps to ensure that IAEA safeguards cannot function properly—especially by impeding inspections. There are many simple administrative expedients at a state's disposal. It can delay its reply to proposals for the designation of inspectors, it can reject such proposals, it can attempt to set limits on the number of inspectors, delay the granting of visas, refuse to admit inspectors on security or other grounds. In other words, it can deploy all the impediments that an artful and recalcitrant bureaucracy can think up. They might be coupled with lengthy delays in submitting reports, sloppy keeping of records and reports, failure by 'oversight' to notify the IAEA of an inventory taking, refusal to install necessary surveillance instruments.

The IAEA has in fact already experienced almost all these impediments at one time or another though in each case, so far, they could be attributed to normal bureaucratic delays, inexperienced national accounting and control systems and genuine, though not necessarily valid, national concerns.[6] As subsequent events bore out they did not cloak a diversion.

A combination of such stratagems would probably make it impossible for the IAEA to reach an unassailable conclusion that the diversion of a significant quantity of nuclear material had taken place. As mentioned in chapter 3 the IAEA would, at most (and probably after considerable delay), have to conclude that it was unable to verify the absence of diversion. Before doing so it would have to "afford the State every reasonable opportunity to furnish the Board with any necessary reassurance"[7]—a further opportunity for delaying tactics in the absence of a clearly demonstrated diversion. While the Board's inability to verify the absence of diversion would trigger the "sanctions" foreseen in the IAEA's Statute—that is, to sound the international alarm and, possibly, curtail assistance—the remaining element of uncertainty about what the state had actually done might mitigate the consequences of such an alarm. Unless of course the state proceeded to a test explosion.

The law's delay (scenario C)

Another form of delay and obstruction (not necessarily masking any intention to divert) would be to provoke a legal dispute and to resist the application of effective safeguards on legal grounds. This type of problem has already arisen in cases where the IAEA has attempted (in the end successfully) to update obsolete facility attachments so as to permit the IAEA to install new surveillance equipment, and it is likely to occur more frequently in future as better equipment becomes available. In such cases the IAEA has been accused of attempting 'unilaterally' to change previously agreed arrangements. In the end the government has usually given in but, as we have noted in one case (Pakistan), only after considerable delay.

This kind of problem can arise under both NPT and non-NPT safeguards agreements and not only because of advances in safeguards equipment. A finding by the IAEA that its routine inspection effort (which is specified in NPT safeguards agreements only) needs to be increased, is also likely to be strongly resisted.

A type of legal problem that may arise under non-NPT safeguards agreements but is less likely (although not impossible) in the NPT context is a dispute as to whether a particular plant must, in terms of the agreement, be submitted to IAEA safeguards. It should be noted that such a problem has already arisen in regard to a pilot reprocessing plant in Pakistan.

II. Broadening the approach

The first two scenarios describe sequences of events that could occur in NPT NNWS. For many reasons they are improbable.

Why should a state ratify the NPT and accept full-scope safeguards if it wishes to keep the nuclear weapon option open? If it chooses not to ratify, the solution is simple—build an unsafeguarded fuel cycle to the extent necessary to produce weapon-usable material, as four non-NPT countries (India, Israel, Pakistan and South Africa) have already done and a fifth (Argentina) appears to be doing.

Nevertheless, scenarios A and B are no more improbable than certain others that IAEA safeguards strategies already seek to foil. A reasonable conclusion, therefore, is that in its consideration of diversion scenarios and of measures it can take to defeat them the IAEA should not confine itself to diversion under a fully operating safeguards regime. It should take a further look at the question of access to unreported plant and material, at the measures to be taken in the event of deliberate attempts to frustrate the effective operation of safeguards and at possible measures to avoid disputes arising when the IAEA considers it necessary to update facility attachments.

It may also be desirable to draw up a series of *automatic* internal IAEA procedures. This might list 'trigger' events that should automatically be reported to the Board and recommendations about the action the Director General and the Board should take.

It should be stressed that the IAEA has not so far detected any discrepancy or faced any situation under an NPT safeguards agreement which pointed to attempted diversion and that there has only been one non-NPT case (KANUPP) in which the IAEA was unsure for some time that its safeguards would have detected the diversion of a significant quantity of nuclear material.

The examples given in this chapter, and especially some of the NPT examples, also suggest a few more fundamental questions. If a country like FR Germany, Japan, Sweden or Switzerland decided that its security had deteriorated so much that it must have nuclear weapons, is there really any probability that it would try to get them by attempting, at some risk, to cheat the IAEA's accounting system? For instance (one of the quickest and the most discussed way) by taking advantage of the measurement uncertainty at a large reprocessing or enrichment plant and surreptitiously 'embezzling' enough plutonium for a few nuclear explosions each year? Is it not much more probable that such a country would use its legal right to withdraw from the NPT, having perhaps prepared all the non-nuclear components of a nuclear arsenal and the means of its delivery and having built up, quite legally, large stores of *safeguarded* fissile material?

The consequences of such a withdrawal might be grave but not less grave and much less humiliating than being caught 'in flagrante delicto'.

This raises the question of whether one should clarify the *political* as well as the technical aim of IAEA safeguards in so far as they are intended to serve as a deterrent. The political aim might perhaps be to confront a would-be NWS with such a risk of detection that it would prefer to withdraw from the NPT.

It is, of course, more difficult (perhaps impossible) to quantify the elements involved; certainly more difficult than to quantify the elements of material accountancy (a 'significant quantity', 'timeliness of detection' and 'risk of detection').

But it does suggest that besides refining the techniques of material accountancy (*which are essential*) the IAEA should give more attention to political realities in defining its safeguards approaches. In particular it must avoid the risk of giving ammunition to its critics by setting quantified aims that are so exacting that the IAEA cannot in practice achieve them (some of its 'timeliness goals' already fall into this category), yet being perfectly able to force any would-be NWS to come out into the open rather than to cheat.

It may be countered that the principal aim of safeguards is to build confidence and not to deter, and that stringent material accountancy is essential for the confidence-building process. To this one may answer that setting aims that cannot be achieved (and that one is subsequently required to admit have not been achieved) is not a very effective way of building confidence.

Notes and references

1 See Appendix V.
2 This would probably mean that the state would have to falsify its own national accounting, or keep two sets of accounts.
3 The assumption is of course highly improbable today—quite apart from the absence of motivation, the political consequences of a detected breach of NPT and other commitments would be quite out of proportion to whatever marginal military advantage might be gained. Nevertheless, as noted in chapter 1, the IAEA deploys more of its safeguards effort in FR Germany and Japan than in any other country because the size of the IAEA's safeguards activities is geared to the size and sophistication of the fuel cycle of the country concerned, on the valid grounds that the IAEA can never rule out the possibility of diversion.
4 Whether or not such plants should be brought under safeguards by amending the model NPT safeguards agreement is another question, which is examined later in this book.
5 Of course the country concerned might run some risk that US or Soviet satellites would detect the clandestine plant.
6 INFCIRC/153, para. 19 (see Appendix V) and most non-NPT agreements give the Board the right, if it decides that an action by the state is "essential and urgent to ensure verification . . ." that no diversion is taking place, ". . . to call upon the state to take the required action without delay . . ." The Director General has never so far proposed that the Board should exercise this right and experience suggests that the Board would be reluctant to do so unless the obstructionism took a particularly blatant form—e.g., continued refusal to admit any inspectors.
7 INFCIRC/153, para. 19 (see Appendix V).

Chapter 7. Problems with safeguards methods

I. *Material accountancy*

The IAEA runs into several problems in achieving the goal of detecting the diversion of a significant *quantity* of nuclear material. These problems differ widely according to the type and size of plant and the nature of the process to which the IAEA is applying safeguards. Let us first see how effectively material accountancy operates in various types of reactor.

The light water reactor (LWR)

It is relatively easy to achieve the 'quantity' goal and, in fact, to do much better than that at the most common type of reactor, the light water reactor. The United States introduced this type of reactor (originally for warships) in the 1950s and the USSR introduced it soon afterwards. In recent years it has become the sole commercial nuclear power reactor choice of all East and West European countries (except Romania), of Japan, South Africa, and of all developing countries except Argentina, India and Pakistan. The LWR accounted for 84 per cent of the total capacity of nuclear power reactors built or under construction at the end of 1983 (323 out of 385 gigawatts (GW)) and more than 90 per cent of those imported from or on order from other countries (67 out of 72 GW). It is also by far the most widely used type of research reactor. Twenty-six developing countries[1] are operating or building research or power reactors of one kind or another today. Twenty-five of these countries (i.e., all except India) are operating a research LWR and in 12 of them a small research LWR is the only nuclear plant of any kind (see Appendix III).

The main reason why the LWR is relatively simple to safeguard has already been referred to; its fuel core is usually changed only at intervals of 12 to 18 months in an operation that involves opening the core of the reactor, changing the configuration of the fuel elements and replacing one-third of the spent fuel elements with fresh fuel elements. The process lasts as long as a fortnight during which the inspector can supervise the critical parts of the operation. After the fuel has been replaced the pressure vessel can be sealed. Because of the length of time needed to change the core, any unreported opening and removal of fuel can be relatively easily detected by surveillance instruments. In the case of research

47

reactors, realignment of the core may be more frequent but the standard type of research reactor which the USA supplied to many countries under the 'Atoms for Peace' programme of the 1950s and 1960s and which accounts for most of those mentioned in Appendix III was designed so that its total inventory of fissile material is considerably less than a 'significant quantity', that is, the amount needed to make an explosive.

The LWR has other safeguards advantages. Because of the length of time the fuel spends in the reactor (the high 'burn-up') the spent fuel contains a large proportion of the plutonium isotope ^{240}Pu. The high burn-up also makes the spent fuel very radioactive and difficult to reprocess while the high proportion of ^{240}Pu makes it difficult (though not impossible) to manufacture a reliable explosive of a predictable yield from this 'reactor-grade' plutonium. So far, at least, no proliferation has resulted from the use or export of a LWR nor has a LWR research or power programme been used as a cloak for developing nuclear weapon capacity—though it has been used to justify the need for enrichment technology.

The heavy water reactor (HWR)

The only other type of reactor which is today available on the commercial market for power reactors (and which has also been widely used for research reactors) uses natural uranium[2] as its fuel and is moderated by heavy water.[3] The main supplier of HWRs today is Canada, although FR Germany has also supplied 2 HWRs (under IAEA safeguards) to Argentina. The Canadian power reactor is known as the CANDU.

The chief difficulty in safeguarding the CANDU-type reactor arises from the fact that it is refuelled 'on-load', that is, fresh fuel is constantly being introduced into and spent fuel removed from the reactor while it is in operation. This obviously offers opportunities for clandestine removal of spent fuel or for the introduction of dummy elements. To surmount this problem Canada has spent much effort and money on developing 'bundle-counters' to monitor automatically the insertion of bundles of fresh fuel elements and removal of bundles of spent fuel. More frequent inspection—up to twice a month, instead of the three-monthly inspection of LWR power reactors—and more elaborate camera surveillance of spent fuel and stores will also help to reduce the risk of undetected diversion.

Because of its 'on-load' fuelling a CANDU reactor can also be more easily used to make a reliable nuclear explosive with a predictable yield (weapon-grade).[4] Spent fuel from such an operation is also easier to reprocess than that from a LWR.

CANDU proponents point out that, unlike the LWR, the CANDU does not require the operation of a 'proliferation-prone' enrichment plant for the production of its fuel, its technology is less sophisticated than that of the LWR and it is inherently somewhat safer, its operating records are on the whole a good deal better (or were until recently)[5] and its fuel can often be produced from domestic sources of uranium ore. They claim that it is, therefore, better suited than the LWR to the needs of developing countries.

The proliferation record of the CANDU power reactor and of the large Canadian research reactor (also an HWR but somewhat differently designed) is much worse than that of the much more numerous and widespread LWR. An unsafeguarded Canadian research HWR reactor produced the plutonium for India's 1974 nuclear explosion; a safeguarded CANDU power reactor might be the source of spent fuel for Pakistan's pilot reprocessing plant. A safeguarded CANDU power reactor and a Canadian research HWR would probably have served the same purpose in the Republic of Korea and Taiwan respectively, had the United States not forcefully intervened and persuaded both countries to abandon their reprocessing plans. Both countries (parties to the NPT) still operate these reactors. A safeguarded CANDU or a West German-supplied natural uranium/heavy water power reactor will probably serve as the source of spent fuel for the Argentine reprocessing plant. In the case of Israel an unsafeguarded French natural uranium-fuelled and heavy water moderated reactor also served as the source of unsafeguarded plutonium.

In short, four of the five NNWS operating unsafeguarded 'sensitive' plants (Argentina, India, Israel and Pakistan)—including, in each case, one or more reprocessing plants—have incorporated HWRs, which can easily produce weapon-usable plutonium, in their nuclear structures. Two NPT NNWS (the Republic of Korea and Taiwan), in another region of political tension, have also done so. Much earlier, the USA, the USSR, Britain and France used natural uranium reactors, moderated in most cases by graphite instead of heavy water, to produce their first military plutonium. Several of these reactors are still in use.

The fast breeder reactor (FBR)

The fast breeder reactor is just around the corner—just how far away it is has been a subject of much argument during the past 10 years or more. It is fuelled by plutonium. The prospect of widespread use of the breeder and therefore of reprocessing plants and of stores of plutonium and the transport of fresh and spent breeder fuel aroused much concern in the late 1970s. President Carter put the brakes on the US fast breeder programme in the hope that other nations would follow the US example (they did not) and the US Congress adopted a restrictive export law intended among other things to discourage the reprocessing by other countries of spent fuel originating from US supplies.

The IAEA's experience in safeguarding FBRs is still very limited (mainly to the British FBR at Dounreay in Scotland), but it does not appear that the reactor will offer any greater difficulties in achieving the IAEA's 'quantity' goal than those encountered at other types of reactor (although the absence of one element of FBR plutonium fuel could obviously have more serious implications than the loss of a similar weight of 3 per cent enriched LWR reactor fuel). A more serious problem would be whether the IAEA could reach its 'timely detection' goal. This is discussed below.

The main justification for the FBR is that without it more than 98 per cent of the energy potential of the world's uranium resources would remain untapped. The reserves seemed relatively small a few years ago and nuclear power using thermal (non-breeder) reactors was expanding rapidly. Since then vast new deposits of uranium have been discovered (chiefly in Australia, but also in Canada), while nearly all the nuclear power programmes of the West and of the developing countries have slowed down to such an extent that recent (1982) projections of the amount of nuclear power that will be in operation in the OECD countries by the year 2 000 *are less than one-quarter* of those of 1975[6] (see table 1). At the same time the technical development of the FBR is proceeding more slowly than foreseen. Only France and the USSR have prototype commercial FBRs in operation and only these two countries have firm plans for a second.[7]

In short the prospect of significant commercial use of the FBR has receded well into the 21st century. Even then it is likely to be confined largely to a handful of highly industrialized countries, namely, France, the USSR, the UK, Japan, FR Germany and perhaps India and the USA, four of which are NWS.

Table 1.   Forecasts of installed nuclear capacity in OECD countries. Figures are in GW

Region and country	Forecasts for the year 2000			
	OECD 1975	INFCE 1980[a]	OECD 1982[a]	IAEA[a]
Western Europe	798	341	214	160
France	170	96	86	
West Germany	134	63	34	
UK	115	33	31	
North America	1 115	384	173	145
Canada	115	59	22	
USA	1 000	325	151	
West Pacific	166	130	68	50
Japan	157	130	68	
Australia/New Zealand	9	0	0	
OECD total	2 079	855	455	355

[a] Figures are the averages of high and low estimates.

Sources: For OECD and INFCE estimates—Walker, W. and Lönnroth, M., *Nuclear Power Struggles. Industrial Competition Proliferation Control* (George Allen & Unwin, London, 1983), p. 49; for IAEA estimates—*IAEA Bulletin* (IAEA, Vienna, December 1984).

The high temperature gas-cooled reactor (HTGR)

The only other type of reactor in sight today is the high temperature gas-cooled reactor. One prototype 330-MW HTGR (Fort St Vrain) has been used since 1979 for power production in the United States[8] and another (Schmeehausen) is nearing start-up in FR Germany. The IAEA has little experience in safeguarding this type of reactor which, because of the fuel it uses (small spheres of a conglomerate of graphite and uranium oxide), would pose some novel accounting problems if the plant were ever to go into wide use.

All reactors

In all reactors in use today, except HTGRs, the fuel consists of separate, usually identical and often individually identifiable fuel rods. The rods can thus be verified by 'item' counting and there is no reason for any MUF. The inspector's goal will be to account for every element—in other words the detection goal will be a single fuel element which will normally be much less than a significant quantity of nuclear material.

Material accountancy at other types of plant

Applying safeguards becomes more difficult when the nuclear material is in bulk form, that is, in the form of fluids, gases, powder, pellets, wires or sheets. As in any comparable industrial process there are inevitably losses or discards. Measuring the flow of material in this form is also subject to some degree of uncertainty which may be of the order of 1 per cent or more depending on the inherent accuracy of the instruments, how well they have been calibrated, and so on. It is in the interests of the operator as well as the IAEA to minimize losses and uncertainties. Nevertheless, when the operator halts operations and takes a physical inventory of all nuclear material in the plant it is unlikely that the results will be precisely the same as those calculated by measuring material as it is cut and machined or as it passes through pipes, tanks or cascades while the plant is in operation. In other words, there is likely to be some MUF. If, however, the MUF exceeds an amount that can be explained by technical causes such as measurement uncertainty, the IAEA must consider the possibility of diversion.[9]

Measurement uncertainty and related problems can lead to situations in which the IAEA would not be able to detect the diversion of one significant quantity of fissile material—that is, the amount needed for a single explosive. In very large reprocessing and enrichment plants the normal measurement uncertainty is of the order of 1 per cent. If the plant is large enough, this uncertainty could be a correct and genuine explanation of a MUF of several significant quantities between two physical inventories. In other words, the IAEA could not be certain whether the apparent loss of material was due to a slight bias in measuring instruments or whether several significant quantities had in fact been diverted.

This problem has been known for a long time and it has received much attention, perhaps too much since the more pressing dangers of proliferation lie elsewhere. All the large bulk-handling plants in this category are in NWS. Only towards the end of this decade or in the early 1990s will a large reprocessing plant come into operation in one NNWS (Japan).[10] A medium-sized enrichment plant will soon be under construction in FR Germany.

Since material accountancy cannot always ensure detection of the diversion of a significant quantity at such large plants, the solution will have to be sought elsewhere—partly perhaps in more effective containment and surveillance measures as well as continuous inspection.

Measurement uncertainty and other factors have also made it necessary to set inspection goals of up to five significant quantities in a few large plants fabricating low-enriched fuel. It would be possible to reduce the inspection goal by taking more frequent physical inventories but this would seriously disrupt the work of the plant and would be unacceptable. However, any low-enriched fuel diverted from such large fuel fabrication plants would have to be further enriched before it would become 'weapon-usable'. (It could also be irradiated in a reactor but the plutonium so produced would, as already noted, be difficult to use for nuclear explosive purposes.) There would thus be additional opportunities to detect diversion and from this point of view the problem is less difficult than at large reprocessing or enrichment plants.

At this point it is worth recalling that, so far as is known, no large commercial reactor nor, in the NNWS, any commercial bulk-handling plant has been used to produce fissile material for nuclear explosives. The five NWS have each used a series of 'dedicated' facilities to make their nuclear weapons. The four 'threshold' NNWS—India, Israel, Pakistan and South Africa—have used research reactors coupled with unsafeguarded pilot reprocessing plants (India, Israel, Pakistan (?)) or pilot enrichment plants (South Africa, Pakistan (?)) to produce their unsafeguarded weapon-usable material.[11] If Argentina decides to produce such material it would also be with pilot reprocessing and possibly with pilot enrichment facilities. In short, if previous experience is a guide, the path to proliferation is more likely to lie through 'research' and pilot facilities than through plants at the top end of the scale.[12] The main reason is that it is cheaper, quicker, easier and less conspicuous to use this route than to build large plants and operate them in an obviously uneconomic and therefore suspect manner. This generalization must, however, be qualified—a large on-load-fuelled natural uranium power reactor can be used as a source of spent fuel for weapon-usable material without any serious disruption of economic operation.

The 'timeliness' element of material accountancy

While recognizing that material accountancy must be the basis of any comprehensive and systematic verification regime, one inherent limitation to this method of verification must be stressed. It is inherently *post factum*. Material accountancy by itself can only disclose what *has* happened some time previously—in many cases a considerable time previously. To give a concrete example, the model NPT agreement calls for a monthly report on changes in the inventory of each MBA. The report must be sent to the IAEA within 30 days of the end of the month in which the change occurred—in the case of the agreement with EURATOM this period is increased to 60 days. Thus, even within the deadlines set by the agreement the operator has nearly two, or in certain cases nearly three, months to report an inventory change that took place near the beginning of the month about which he is reporting. As is noted later, this period is, in practice, often exceeded. Moreover, the IAEA cannot draw a final conclusion about the correctness or otherwise of the report, or on the extent of MUF, until the operator takes the next physical inventory—which may be at six-monthly or even annual intervals.

Fortunately, material accountancy does not stand alone and the IAEA is not and need not be in the dark until the next physical inventory. As noted, in applying the other two safeguards measures, containment and surveillance, the inspector will check seals, review filmed records of the plant's operation and, in the case of the most sensitive facilities, be permanently present monitoring the plant's operation. In these ways the detection time can be made much shorter than it would be from the use of material accountancy alone.

Whether it can be made short enough to meet the requirements of every possible scenario (however improbable the scenario may be) is open to doubt. As is noted earlier, in attempting to quantify the 'timeliness' that safeguards should seek to achieve, the IAEA takes into account the length of time that would be needed to convert the safeguarded material into the metallic component of a nuclear explosive device. If the material is a natural or slightly enriched uranium fresh-fuel rod or if it is uranium and plutonium mixed with fission products in a spent fuel element, the time needed to enrich or reprocess the material so as to make it directly usable in a weapon may be of the order of months—up to one year in the case of fresh fuel.[13] On the other hand, if the safeguarded material is plutonium or highly enriched uranium and if the other parts of the explosive device have been tested and assembled, the time needed to complete the device may be of the order of 7–10 days or even less.

'Timely warning'

Obviously it would damage the creditibility of IAEA safeguards if the first news of a diversion came on the seismographs of neighbouring states or as the flash and fall-out from an atmospheric test, rather than in a report from the IAEA. But there are already a few plants in NNWS in which the conversion of an existing stock of highly enriched uranumum or plutonium could, theoretically, be an overnight affair. These are large critical assemblies containing tens of kilograms of metallic plutonium or the buffer stocks of plants fabricating highly enriched uranium fuel rods. In some circumstances, even continuous inspection might not be sufficient to ensure that the IAEA received a report of diversion before the diverted material was exploded, let alone to obtain a decision by the IAEA's Board of Governors.

Such a scenario is, however, very improbable, at least today. Significant stocks of separated plutonium or highly enriched uranium exist only in NWS and, under IAEA safeguards, in three NNWS, namely Belgium, FR Germany and Japan.

Quite apart from the fact that any move towards nuclear weapons would represent a momentous reversal of 40 years of post-war policy that could hardly be concealed from public, parliamentary and foreign observers, the political penalties to which any of these three countries would expose itself if it were to divert such stocks are quite out of proportion to whatever political or military advantage it might gain.

Nevertheless, in the mid-1970s, when concern developed about the adequacy of the non-proliferation regime, the argument was strongly pressed in the USA that the central purpose of the IAEA safeguards was neither to verify and certify compliance with international obligations ('confidence building') nor to deter diversion, but to give sufficient 'timely warning' *after* a diversion to afford the forces of diplomacy the opportunity to persuade the diverter not to explode the diverted material. This was of course a rather radical re-interpretation of the purpose of safeguards and the scenario on which it was based also seems improbable. It also sets IAEA safeguards an objective which, as noted above, they cannot be guaranteed to achieve.

The concept of 'timely warning' found its place in Section 303(b).2 of the 1978 US Nuclear Non-Proliferation Act (NNPA) as one of the main criteria against which any proposal for the reprocessing of fuel of US origin is to be approved or rejected.

II. Use and performance of containment and surveillance equipment

The two other safeguards measures, containment and surveillance, are usually lumped together as 'C/S' and, as noted, often overlap.

It has also been noted above that the shorter the detection time, the more the safeguarding authority is likely to depend on C/S to achieve its goals, and that detection times become particularly short in plants that handle or store large quantities of weapon-usable material.

Appendix II describes some of the instruments that the IAEA uses today or that are now being tested. The chief surveillance instrument is the twin tamper-resistant camera referred to in chapter 4. The twin cameras, of which about 200 are in operation, are slowly being supplemented by TV and video-recorders. Another important surveillance instrument gradually being installed at CANDU reactors is the 'bundle counter', described in Appendix II. The IAEA and the national laboratories assisting it are also testing instruments for measuring continuously the contents of streams of nuclear material (fluids and gases) moving through reprocessing and enrichment plants.

The chief *containment* device is a special tamper-indicating seal of which the IAEA is now applying about 8 000 (and verifying most of them) each year.

Mention should also be made of important safeguards instruments that do not fall under the heading C/S, for example, a portable instrument for measuring the energies and intensities of gamma-ray emissions from fresh and spent fuel in a non-destructive (ND) manner.[14] This instrument can be used to confirm the presence of plutonium and uranium and it can determine the degree of enrichment of uranium in fresh fuel. It can also make measurements on spent fuel which help to assess its plutonium content. Another ND instrument is the night vision device described in chapter 4, which is used to verify spent fuel by detecting its Cherenkov glow.[15]

The main problems that the IAEA encounters in regard to C/S and other safeguards instrumentation are:

1. Some critical equipment is not yet available in sufficient quantity. An example is the fuel bundle counter for CANDUs and other on-load-fuelled reactors.

2. Non-destructive assay techniques must be improved and more widely used in a more systematic and standardized manner.

3. The reliability of surveillance instruments has markedly improved but the failure rate is still high—between 3 and 4 per cent during each two or three months of operation, in the case of surveillance cameras in 1983 (as compared with 9 per cent in 1981).

4. Resistance by operators and other administrative problems are still an important factor.[16] The problems encountered in installing additional surveillance equipment in the Pakistan KANUPP reactor have received wide publicity but they are by no means isolated. In the UK there was initial resistance from the work-force at one plant who perhaps suspected that the cameras would be installed with other aims besides safeguards in mind! The three partners in URENCO have resisted any installation of camera surveillance units in the sensitive cascade area of their plants, for fear of compromising the secrecy of the process, and Japan will doubtless follow suit. (It must be conceded that in such cases there is a degree of conflict between the interests of effective safeguards and the risk of spreading a potentially highly 'proliferant' technology. Moreover, safeguards equipment is not directly productive and the plant operator may rightly ask that it be non-intrusive, interfere as little as possible with the working of the plant and only require the minimum service from him.)

5. The IAEA has also experienced difficulties in getting its samples to its laboratory as promptly as possible. Many states have not yet licensed the special air-transport container designed by the IAEA. As in the case of equipment failure, such delays increase the difficulty of meeting 'timely detection' goals.

6. In a few cases, governments refuse to allow films from surveillance cameras to be sent back to Vienna and insist instead that the films be developed and analysed locally.

In concluding this section, three points should be brought out. First, the IAEA's efforts to obtain new and better instruments have been greatly helped by the extensive research and development work carried out in about a dozen of its member states. Mention has already been made of Canadian work on instruments for CANDU reactors. Nearly all the research, development and testing of safeguards instruments is carried out in the national or regional laboratories and facilities of 10 countries (Australia, Belgium, Bulgaria, Canada, FR Germany, the German DR, Japan, the USSR, the USA and the United Kingdom) and of EURATOM.

Second, a steady improvement in performance as well as an increasing degree of ingenuity and sophistication can be expected in this field. But it must not be expected that even the best instrumentation will greatly diminish the need for human inspectors. It will, however, make safeguards more effective and enable the IAEA to reach more of its inspection goals more quickly and with greater assurance.

Third, although equipment problems have detracted from the IAEA's ability to reach its 'timeliness' goals and in one case (KANUPP) from its ability to give adequate assurance of compliance with the relevant safeguards agreement, they represent a less serious problem than those encountered in accrediting inspectors and in carrying out inspections.

Notes and references

[1] Including South Africa.

[2] Canada and Argentina are reportedly experimenting, or planning to do so, with very low-enriched uranium fuel (1 per cent enrichment).

[3] The LWR uses *slightly* enriched uranium (up to 3 per cent) in nuclear *power* plants. LWRs used for naval propulsion use *highly* enriched uranium; so do many light water research reactors.

[4] Because it is constantly receiving new fuel elements (and spent fuel elements are constantly being removed) it is much easier to move CANDU fuel elements around in the reactor so as to get the desired even, very low burn-up needed for weapon-grade plutonium. As noted elsewhere, the fuel of an LWR is normally only changed every 12–18 months and the configuration of the fuel elements, between such changes, is rigid.

[5] There have been reports of ruptures in the pressure tubes of some early CANDU plants in Canada, necessitating costly replacements and putting the reactor out of use for lengthy periods. It has been stated that these problems are unlikely to arise with later models. The operating records of *light water* power reactors differ rather widely from country to country. The proportion of the time they are in operation each year is high in Belgium, Bulgaria, the FR Germany, Sweden and Switzerland, rising in France and Japan, and comparatively low, on average, in the USA.

[6] Walker, W. and Lönnroth, M., *Nuclear Power Struggles. Industrial Competition and Proliferation Control* (Allen & Unwin, London, 1983), p. 48, quoting OECD projections. The OECD countries are: Australia, Austria, Belgium, Canada, Denmark, Finland, France, FR Germany, Greece, Iceland, Ireland, Italy, Japan, Luxembourg, the Netherlands, Norway, New Zealand, Portugal, Spain, Sweden, Switzerland, Turkey, the UK and the USA, in other words all the main 'free-market'

states. They accounted for 288 GW (75 per cent) of the 385 GW of nuclear plant in operation or under construction at the end of 1983.

7 Besides France and the USSR, the only countries operating or building smaller pre-commercial prototypes are the UK, FR Germany and Japan. By the year 2000, three or four commercial fast breeders may be in operation or nearing completion in Western Europe, two in France, and one each in the UK and FR Germany.

8 There are reports that it will soon be closed down.

9 Because of the possible slight imprecision of even the best instruments, the IAEA must accept in practice small MUFs within the range of measurement uncertainty. It is possible, though very unlikely, that a state would attempt a 'trickle' diversion over a very long period, within these "statistically acceptable MUFs". The larger the plant or the greater the measurement uncertainty, the better the possibility of a significant diversion.

10 Generally speaking, projects for building or expanding reprocessing plants are based on what has turned out to be an over-optimistic assessment of the economics of reprocessing, either to produce plutonium for breeders (or 'recycle' in existing reactors) or as a step to waste disposal. It is proving a good deal cheaper, in Swedish experience, to treat spent reactor fuel as waste and to dispose of it permanently instead of reprocessing it. However, much controversy still surrounds this issue.

11 It is not publicly known whether Pakistan has yet produced any unsafeguarded fissile material from the unsafeguarded plants it is operating or building. Leonard S. Spector in his book *Nuclear Proliferation Today. The Spread of Nuclear Weapons 1984* (Vintage Books, New York, 1984), pp. 95–96, maintains that partly because of US pressure there will be no reprocessing in Pakistan for the time being.

12 For a discussion of these questions see Walker and Lönnroth (note 6), p. 104. See also Fischer, D., *Nuclear Issues* (Australian National University, Canberra, 1981), and *International Safeguards 1980*, International Consultative Group on Nuclear Energy. The author believes that Dr Sigvard Eklund was the first to draw attention to the graver danger posed by smaller R&D plants.

13 SAGSI's estimate of conversion times for natural or low-enriched uranium is "about one year", presumably for the first explosive (IAEA/SG/INF/4, p. 29). Allan Krass, co-author of *Uranium Enrichment and Nuclear Weapon Proliferation* (Taylor & Francis, London, 1983) [a SIPRI book], challenges this in a personal comment on this chapter. Krass writes that if 3 per cent enriched fuel is diverted from a gaseous diffusion plant to a small clandestine centrifuge plant, it could produce highly enriched uranium for a nuclear weapon in one or two weeks. The present author is not able to contest the technical accuracy of this statement. However, he considers that the scenario is somewhat far-fetched. If a state has a clandestine centrifuge why should it take the risk of *diverting* from a gaseous diffusion plant? In any case the only countries known to be operating or building gaseous diffusion plants *and* gas centrifuges are the UK and the USA.

14 'Non-destructive' in that they do not require any samples of fresh or spent fuel to be taken for laboratory analysis.

15 See chapter 4.

16 The IAEA Deputy Director General for safeguards lists three main reasons why the IAEA has difficulties in reaching its 'timeliness' goals: (*a*) the failure of surveillance instruments; (*b*) insufficient manpower (hence less 'sensitive' plants tend to receive less inspection than foreseen); and (*c*) the long time needed to reach agreement with states

on the use of new safeguards equipment. He points out, however, that as long as a possible diverter cannot predict at which plant the IAEA might fail to reach its inspection goals, the fact that these goals are not being reached at *all* plants does little to diminish the deterrent effect of safeguards. See Tempus, P., 'Progress in safeguards: 1983 implementation', *IAEA Bulletin*, September 1984. See also Rundqvist, O. and Watkins, O., 'Improving safeguards techniques: instrumentation', in the same issue of the *IAEA Bulletin*.

Chapter 8. Problems with safeguards procedures

I. Design review

The prospect of having the design of one's plant examined by a body of foreigners, including perhaps engineers from competing plants, on contract as IAEA inspectors, gave rise to much apprehension in the late 1960s and early 1970s. In practice a design review has turned out to be a less sensitive matter than feared. The information to be given to the IAEA is confined to the minimum necessary for safeguarding nuclear material at the plant in question. If the country concerned regards the plant as particularly sensitive it may require (and in a number of cases it has required) the IAEA to examine the design information "on premises of the State"[1] instead of transmitting it to Vienna.

The country may also require the IAEA to establish a special material balance area around a commercially sensitive part of a plant, from which routine inspection is normally excluded, a so-called 'black-box'.

In practice, only two significant problems have arisen in arranging for design reviews and both have related to enrichment plants. The reason that South Africa originally gave for not submitting its pilot enrichment plant at Valindaba to IAEA safeguards was that to do so would compromise industrial secrets contained in the design of the plant. (The IAEA offered informally to negotiate the elements of a facility attachment for the plant which, the IAEA believed, would meet South Africa's concern to protect the secrecy of its process, but the offer was not taken up.[2])

Problems also arose in connection with the gas-centrifuge enrichment plant at Almelo in the Netherlands and the same kind of plants in operation in the United Kingdom and under construction in FR Germany, Japan and the USA. After several years of discussion a 'hexapartite' committee, consisting of experts from the countries most interested, and from the IAEA and EURATOM, agreed in 1983 on the safeguards approach to such plants. According to press reports the cascade area of the plants will be subject to a special regime. Frequent brief unannounced visits of inspectors will be permitted—seals may be attached on flanges and valves—but there will be no photographic surveillance equipment in the cascade areas.

II. Records and reports

As noted, states are required to report changes in the inventory at each material balance area in the country and to do so no later than 30 days (60 days in the case of EURATOM), after the end of the month during which the changes took place in the 'book' inventory or 30 (60) days after the physical inventory was taken. Delays in the latter reports usually mean commensurate delays before the IAEA can strike a material balance and thus verify, by accounting, that there has been no diversion.

Though there has been some improvement over the years, these requirements continue to be honoured more in the breach than in the observance. Delays of three months and more are still quite common and more than half the reporting states are consistently late in submitting inventory change reports.

There are several causes for delay, including (diminishing) unfamiliarity with the IAEA's reporting procedures, and computer and other mechanical or electronic breakdowns. An important factor is that reports do not go direct from the operator to the IAEA; all are sent via the authority concerned in the national government. This procedure is probably inevitable and it has the advantage of making the state responsible for accurate reporting. Unfortunately, it also inevitably leads to delay.[3]

The quality and scope of reports have gradually improved over the years but still leave much to be desired. The important reports sent to the IAEA after inventories have been taken present a particular problem. They often fail to give information on the precision of the operator's measurements (measurement uncertainty). These data are essential to determine how much uncertainty attaches to the estimates of material unaccounted for.

A useful source of information (and pointer to any possible diversion) comes from the reports that the exporting and importing countries send to the IAEA about material sent from one to the other. The reports on a particular transaction should, of course, show that the amount received was the same as that shipped. Since collusion between two countries is unlikely (though not impossible) any shipper/receiver differences point to some MUF and this discrepancy must be explained. However, it is essential that the reports from both sources should be sent in a standard or at least in a compatible form so that the IAEA can make a valid comparison between them. The IAEA has made a number of recommendations in this regard but many states still do not observe them.

Although it is improbable that the IAEA will ever reach the happy state where all deadlines are met and all reports are complete, precise and accurate, a slow but fairly steady improvement can be expected as the procedures of reporting become routine, as national techniques and systems of information handling become more efficient and as the IAEA and its staff improve their own procedures and techniques.

The delays that result from such procedures may be partly offset in time by better surveillance and containment instruments, such as those that transmit information in 'real time' to Vienna, that is, virtually immediately and perhaps also by an international satellite monitoring system should it prove possible to realize this idea.

III. Inspections

As noted, the credibility of the entire safeguards operation depends in the final analysis on adequate and effective on-site inspections.[4] Acceptance of the principle of such inspections by 132 NNWS[5] and 4 NWS has been an important breakthrough in international relations and is hopefully a precedent for wider measures of arms control. It is here too that the entire safeguards system is most dependent upon the help and good will of the state in which inspection is to be carried out and it is here too, by the same token, that the system is most vulnerable.

Chapter 4 refers to the complex restrictions that states, acting collectively through the IAEA Board of Governors, have placed on the freedom of action of inspectors, especially in NPT NNWS (the elaborate designation procedures, the requirements for advance notice, the states' rights to have the inspectors accompanied by national officials, the restrictions on routine access, the limits on frequency and number of inspections, and the explicit itemization of what the inspector may and may not do when he inspects a nuclear plant).

Limits on the amount of IAEA inspection

Besides the limits that INFCIRC/153 thus sets upon the number and frequency of routine inspections, some leading NNWS have required that the document that describes in detail the safeguards regime for each plant, the 'facility attachment' (FA) described in the section on design review in chapter 4, must contain an estimate of the routine inspection effort (expressed in man-days) that the IAEA will carry out at the plant—the actual routine inspection effort or 'ARIE'. Sweden was the first NNWS to insist on such estimates. In the course of negotiations with EURATOM the latter insisted that in practice the ARIE should also be the *maximum* routine effort at each plant. After protracted negotiations, the IAEA accepted EURATOM's proposal on condition that the maxima should only apply if EURATOM fully discharged each of a series of its own obligations under the agreement. The IAEA/Japanese agreement contains similar clauses. Estimates of routine inspection effort are now made in all agreements concluded with NPT states, but not in safeguards agreements concluded under INFCIRC/66/Rev. 2.

It cannot be denied that all these constraints are a far cry from the forthright language of the IAEA Statute. As has been noted, the Statute lays down that one of the rights that the IAEA shall have is to send into the territory of the state "... inspectors, designated by the Agency after consultation with the State or States concerned, *who shall have access at all times to all places and data and to any person* who by reason of his occupation deals with materials, equipment, or facilities which are required by this Statute to be safeguarded . . ."[6]

A layman may also be forgiven if he forms the impression that the IAEA inspector must go around with a book of rules in his hand and in constant anxiety lest he transgress any of them.

However, these constraints have done less to blunt the edge of safeguards than one might at first expect.

In practice, for instance, the IAEA has found it difficult to carry out all the routine inspection effort prescribed in the various NPT facility agreements (i.e., the aggregated ARIEs),[7] let alone reach the much higher hypothetical maxima set by INFCIRC/153 itself. In no case so far has the ARIE set for a particular plant proved inadequate though conceivably difficulties might arise at certain research reactors where the prescribed ARIEs and maxima are low. In general, too, the NPT restrictions on access for routine inspections have not proved to be unduly onerous, as shown below.

Limits on access by inspectors

The problem of access is to ensure that IAEA inspectors have adequate freedom of movement at and in a safeguarded plant. The limitations that NPT safeguards agreements place on routine access, which is essentially confined to 'strategic points', have already been noted. Defining inspectors' access has in fact been one of the knottiest points in most negotiations on the facility attachment for each plant—particularly in plants that produce or process weapon-usable material. The problem of access to one group of plants in this category, the gas-centrifuge enrichment plant, has already been mentioned. For reprocessing plants the problem is somewhat different. Operators are loath to undertake complete inventories at these plants since these may mean cleaning out all tanks in the plant, an expensive and time-consuming operation which requires the plant to be shut down.

With the best will in the world, operators are unlikely to agree to more than two complete inventories a year—that is, a 'timeliness' of six months. However, without a complete inventory, the IAEA is unable to strike a material balance and reach a definitive conclusion about the amount of nuclear material unaccounted for at the plant. Long delays between full inventories thus detract from the goal of 'timely detection' of any possible diversion.[8] And the time that would be needed to convert plutonium from a reprocessing plant into the charge for a nuclear explosive is, as has been noted, rather short: of the order of a week or two.

In an attempt to get around this problem the IAEA carries out frequent partial inventories at reprocessing plants. In certain cases continuous inspection by resident inspectors may be required. The IAEA is also looking into the possibility of using instruments and techniques that would give better access to the rough, 'in-process', inventories or calculations that the operator makes so as to ensure the safety and efficiency of the plant. These procedures are necessarily more intrusive than those at less sensitive plants and this has led to certain difficulties in getting operators and governments to agree to the extent of access the IAEA requires.

Nevertheless, once the safeguards regime for the plant has been agreed upon most problems of access become less serious. Thirteen years have passed since the first NPT safeguards agreement came into force (in 1972) and eight years since the major agreements with EURATOM and Japan (in 1977). During the entire period, the IAEA has never considered it necessary to invoke the NPT safeguards agreement procedures for special inspections and thus gain (or rather negotiate) the additional access foreseen under those procedures. The implication must therefore be that the limited access provided under routine inspection procedures is adequate for the types and sizes of plant that the IAEA has so far safeguarded.

The impression that the agreed amounts of routine inspection and the agreed degree of routine access have so far been adequate is strengthened by the annual conclusion on the results of the safeguards operation.

Designation of inspectors

The routine work of inspectors brings the IAEA into close contact with the operators of nuclear plants. In general, these working contacts have been harmonious and cases of friction have been uncommon.

The interface at the political level between the IAEA and governments in obtaining the latter's consent to the designation of inspectors has been much more difficult and has impaired the overall efficiency of the operation. With the exception of a few neutral and smaller countries, almost every government concerned has at one time or another refused to accept individual inspectors or categories of inspector.

The procedure for obtaining the consent of the government concerned derives from the normal diplomatic practice of *agrément* and is intended to enable the government to reject any inspector who was personally unacceptable. However, with the passage of time governments have increasingly followed the practice of making it clear that they will not accept whole categories of inspector.

The most common explanations given, if any are given at all, are that the government will only accept:

1. Inspectors who are nationals of countries that have themselves accepted safeguards. In many cases this has amounted to a rejection of inspectors of Soviet nationality—and it was doubtless so intended. This policy will thus no longer achieve the intended effect after the Soviet–IAEA safeguards agreement comes into force.
2. Inspectors who are nationals of a country that has ratified the NPT.
3. Inspectors who are not nationals of specified countries.
4. Inspectors who speak the language of the 'accepting' government. This

requirement has been more frequently advanced by Spanish-speaking countries, on the grounds that Spanish is one of the working languages of the IAEA.

5. Inspectors who are nationals of countries with which the 'accepting' state has diplomatic relations.

In addition a handful of countries have imposed unofficial limits on the number of inspectors of a particular nationality—or on the total number of inspectors they will accept. The EURATOM NNWS present special difficulties. Each proposal by the IAEA has to be cleared with every government concerned and if one reaction is negative, the inspector will not be accepted by the Community as a whole. Each new member of the Community thus means another 'veto-right'.

By 1983 nearly three-quarters of the states in which the IAEA was carrying out inspections were applying one or other restriction relating to nationality, linguistic qualifications or numbers.

For maximum efficiency, flexibility of operation and economy in travel and other costs, all of the inspectors in each of the IAEA's three regional divisions should be designated to all the countries in the region in which inspections are carried out (the total number of inspectors was about 200 at the beginning of 1985).

These restrictions lead to a waste of manpower, inefficient deployment of inspectors who are specialists in particular types or makes of plant, additional and unnecessary expenses, the unbalanced deployment of certain nationalities which may lessen the credibility of the operation in certain countries (one of the Israeli charges in justification of its attack on the Tamuz 1 reactor was that the IAEA inspectors designated to Iraq all came from the same region—Eastern Europe). They also increase the complexity of administering safeguards and depress the morale of the Inspectorate which is thereby constantly exposed to political discrimination on grounds of nationality—a discrimination which is hardly consistent with one of the basic principles of international organization. Inspectors of 'difficult' nationalities, moreover, may have to wait at headquarters for months while endeavours are made to accredit them and some—for example, among the large Soviet contingent—may have to be kept more or less permanently on headquarters work.

The remedy for this situation foreseen in the model NPT agreement (INFCIRC/153) unfortunately does not fully meet the problem. It envisages that the Director General will bring to the Board's attention "the repeated refusal of a state to accept the designation". It thus foresees Board action only at the end of an iterative process in which the Director General proposes one name (or a list of names) and the proposal is rejected, the Director General then puts forward an alternative proposal which is also rejected, and so on.

The system does not usually work this way. States make it clear *in advance* that they will not accept inspectors in one or more of the categories referred to above and they are thus spared the need, in most cases, of having to reject a particular designation.

The Director General has often brought these problems to the Board's attention, but in general terms and without naming the states that are causing difficulties. The annual Safeguards Implementation Report now also contains a section analysing the difficulties that have arisen but also without 'naming names'.

The Board has made little response to the Director General's appeals. The Board now consists chiefly of diplomats who are probably well aware of their own government's restrictions, are loath to throw stones at those of other governments and are well versed in the traditional procedure of *agrément*, in which another state's acceptance of a diplomatic envoy is discreetly sought and a rejection is rarely questioned.

The heart of the problem is, of course, that many states see IAEA inspectors not as the agents of an international body but as citizens (and possibly agents) of another state. It would be a pretence to claim that this perception is always wrong. In particular, inspectors from the superpowers may sometimes be seen as working for their own governments as well as for the IAEA. This impression was strengthened in 1982 when two former IAEA inspectors testified before Congress on the weaknesses of IAEA safeguards, as they saw them. Although their testimony showed that both men had been dedicated to their tasks, one of them disclosed that he had had regular contact with the US mission to the IAEA. This caused no surprise in Vienna. It is also well known that Soviet staff members regularly report to their mission to the IAEA and that staff members of many other nationalities have contacts with their embassies or missions.

Many inspectors are, moreover, on short-term leave of absence or secondment from their national authorities; this is often a prescription for divided loyalty.

The problems of designation could probably be reduced if:

1. The proportion of inspectors from the NWS were kept as low as possible. Problems sometimes arise in designating such inspectors to countries in the 'other bloc'. Because of this, there is some tendency to assign them to countries that are allied with or friendly with the NWS of which these inspectors are citizens (US, British and French inspectors to EURATOM, Japan, Canada, Australia, etc., and Soviet inspectors to Eastern Europe and India).

2. The proportion of inspectors were increased from those countries that are universally regarded as neutral and aloof from international conflicts and that have renounced nuclear weapons, for example, Austria, Sweden, Switzerland, Finland, Mexico. They are normally easy to 'place' but only constitute about 6 per cent of the total accredited inspectorate.

3. The IAEA were to move forward to a dedicated career inspectorate. The present Director General is taking steps in this direction and already many of the most experienced and effective inspectors are career men.

Increasing the proportion of inspectors from neutral NPT NNWS would not be easy. There is a constant argument in the IAEA as well as in other UN organizations about the number of posts 'assigned' to various countries, about the share of the Third World in Secretariat posts, and even about individual appointments. As noted, moreover, each appointment of an inspector has to be approved by the Board. Salaries in most of the neutral countries tend to be high and international careers are not necessarily financially attractive unless there are good prospects of promotion and eventually of moving out of the inspector's job, which tends to pall with time.

A few years ago the IAEA also began to appoint 'inspection assistants', qualified and experienced technicians fully able to do routine inspection work, sometimes better, and considerably more cheaply, than inspectors having professional status (i.e., university graduates with several years of relevant experience). This experiment has proved successful and deserves to be more broadly applied.

Notes and references

[1] INFCIRC/153, para. 8 (see Appendix V).
[2] At the end of January 1984, South Africa announced that it was prepared to negotiate a safeguards agreement to cover its semi-commercial, but not its pilot, enrichment plant.
[3] The system of reporting via the national authority rather than direct from operators is anchored in the structure of each NPT agreement which requires the state to set up and maintain its own system of accounting for and control of all nuclear material within its territory. The EURATOM safeguards system collects information directly from all nine Common Market states and it is expected to check and process the information before transmitting it to Vienna.
[4] See Szasz, P., *The Law and Practices of the International Atomic Energy Agency* (IAEA, Vienna, 1970), p. 599.
[5] That is, the 121 NNWS that have adhered to the NPT (1 January 1985), Colombia which has full-scope safeguards under the Treaty of Tlatelolco and the 10 NNWS in which non-NPT safeguards are being applied.
[6] IAEA Statute, see Appendix I.
[7] It is understood that in 1983, the 'best' year so far, the IAEA carried out about three-quarters of the total planned ARIEs.
[8] It is also at these sensitive plants where nuclear material is in fluid (bulk) form that most of the samples are taken for analysis in the IAEA's laboratory near Vienna (about 1 100 samples in 1983). 'Timeliness' of detection at these plants is affected by administrative problems and delays that the IAEA encounters in transmitting the samples to Vienna. However, the average shipment delay fell sharply in 1983.

Chapter 9. SAGSI and SIR

I. SAGSI

SAGSI (the IAEA Standing Advisory Group on Safeguards Implementation) has its roots in a 1971 Japanese proposal for an "oversight" safeguards committee of the Board. The Director General of the IAEA appoints the members of SAGSI after consulting the governments concerned; in fact he often asks the government to put forward a name (much the same practice is followed in appointing the members of most other advisory committees of the IAEA and other UN expert groups).

As a result SAGSI became a meeting of national experts, representing their governments' views. This has some advantages. When SAGSI gives its advice it is giving the consensus or majority view of the governments that have the greatest stake in safeguards. (Today, SAGSI is composed of experts from the USA, the USSR, the UK and France (four of the five NWS), FR Germany and Japan (the most safeguarded states), Canada and Australia (major uranium exporters), Czechoslovakia (to give an extra voice to Eastern Europe), Yugoslavia, India and Brazil (leading Third World nuclear nations, the last two unfortunately often critical of safeguards). No doubt China will soon be added.)

However, this type of arrangement also means that behind the web of technical arguments most members are trying to advance their governments' views and interests and not necessarily the best interests of IAEA safeguards, except where the two coincide. Very soon the lines drawn in SAGSI were much the same as those in the 1970 Safeguards Committee that drew up the model NPT agreement. Thus, for instance, the USA, the USSR, the UK, the GDR (later replaced by Czechoslovakia), Canada and Australia all pressed to ensure the most stringent safeguards—sometimes going unrealistically far. FR Germany and Japan sought to keep the 'burden', 'intrusiveness' and cost of safeguards as low as they could and (in the case of FR Germany) advanced EURATOM's rather than the IAEA's interests.

With such divergencies it became difficult to obtain advice on the practical issues that the Secretariat was dealing with every day—what should be set as detection goals, significant quantities, conversion times, detection probability, and so on. Some experts displayed a wish to review the basic premises of the Secretariat's approach before tackling bread-and-butter questions.

The situation changed considerably after the main issues between the IAEA and EURATOM were solved. France, FR Germany and Japan, though still concerned about safeguards costs and 'intrusiveness', have a growing stake in effective safeguards, particularly on their own exports. It seems likely that a decisive majority of SAGSI members can today be expected to support reasonable policies needed for effective safeguards. It should be possible to make more constructive use of SAGSI than in the 1970s.

SAGSI might thus be made into an instrument for expert consideration of the safeguards operation, particularly if the Board itself becomes more politicized.

II. SIR

The size and responsibilities of the IAEA safeguards operation grew rapidly in the second half of the 1970s. Governments and the public wanted to know whether the IAEA could in fact detect diversion. It became essential to create mechanisms and procedures for evaluating safeguards systematically, for analysing their strengths and weaknesses and seeing what could be done to correct the latter.

The Director General therefore established an evaluation unit (now a Division) in the safeguards secretariat to ensure continuing, independent, internal evaluation. On US initiative, the Board asked the secretariat to submit a detailed annual report, the 'Safeguards Implementation Report' (SIR) on how the system was working.

These measures to ensure critical self-examination, and especially the SIR, are among the most useful internal steps taken by the IAEA in the field of safeguards since 1975. The value and quality of the SIR have improved with time and it now provides the Board with a systematic analysis of the operation, and the steps needed to improve it.

The SIR is classified (like all Board documents until they are made public) as 'Restricted' and 'For official use only'. The pros and cons of this quasi-confidential approach are discussed in chapter 8.

Chapter 10. Regional safeguards systems, EURATOM and Japan

The following is a brief sketch of the two main regional systems in operation today—those applied under the Treaty of Tlatelolco and by EURATOM—and how they differ from IAEA safeguards.

I. The Treaty of Tlatelolco

The Treaty of Tlatelolco envisages two types of safeguards. All parties to the Treaty are required to conclude agreements with the IAEA for the application of safeguards to their nuclear activities.[1] In addition, provision is made for 'special inspections';[2] if a state believes that another party is carrying out nuclear activities prohibited by the Treaty it may arrange for the Organization for the Prohibition of Nuclear Weapons in Latin America (OPANAL) to carry out a special inspection at the state's expense to investigate the activity. The 'suspect' state may not refuse such an inspection. A state may also request such an inspection to confute allegations that it is violating the Treaty.

Of the Tlatelolco countries that have concluded safeguards agreements with the IAEA, all except one (Colombia) are also parties to the NPT, and the safeguards agreements with them are slightly modified versions of the standard NPT agreement.

Neither OPANAL nor the IAEA has articulated procedures for carrying out 'challenge inspections' and none has been performed so far. Nevertheless, the concept is an interesting one that might also find application if it becomes possible to establish nuclear weapon-free zones in other regions, such as the Middle East.

There are several important differences between the Treaty of Tlatelolco and the NPT in regard for instance to duration (the Treaty of Tlatelolco is of indefinite duration) and withdrawal and in the way they deal with the 'peaceful' uses of nuclear explosives and permitted military uses. However, these differences have not, so far, required any departures, in the safeguards agreements concluded under the Treaty of Tlatelolco, from the normal IAEA approach in model NPT safeguards agreements.

II. The EURATOM system

The EURATOM system is based on the Rome Treaty concluded in 1957 between the then six members of the European Economic Community. It applies now to all 10 members (Belgium, Denmark, France, FR Germany, Greece, Ireland, Italy, Luxembourg, the Netherlands and the UK).[3] Although much of the relevant language of the Rome Treaty is similar to that of the Statute of the IAEA (both reflecting strong US influence), EURATOM safeguards differ from those of the IAEA in the following respects:

1. Unlike those foreseen in the IAEA Statute, EURATOM safeguards do not formally prohibit the military or non-peaceful use of safeguarded nuclear plant and material. They simply verify that the material is being used in conformity with the purpose stated by the user or with agreed supply conditions. This was to accommodate France, a nuclear weapon state in embryo, which could obviously not give a peaceful-use undertaking for all material in France. However, since the ratification of the NPT by all EURATOM NNWS and the conclusion of the IAEA–EURATOM safeguards agreement, there has been no difference between the aims of the two safeguards systems in EURATOM NNWS.

2. EURATOM safeguards apply automatically to all nuclear material in the member states of the Community. They were thus the first full-scope safeguards. The IAEA's safeguards apply only to the extent specified in agreements with the states concerned (which are not necessarily IAEA members). In the case of NPT NNWS the IAEA's agreements are of course also 'full-scope'.

3. EURATOM safeguards cover uranium ore, at least in principle. IAEA safeguards begin when nuclear materials have been further processed. In the case of non-NPT safeguards, uranium concentrates or yellowcake are subject to all safeguards procedures including inspection. NPT-type IAEA safeguards begin to apply fully even higher up the fuel cycle, with uranium metal or oxide or UF_6 (uranium hexafluoride, the gas which is fed into enrichment plants). However, NPT NNWS are required to *inform* the IAEA of shipments of nuclear material that have not reached this stage of the fuel cycle.

4. In certain cases, EURATOM permits its officials to serve as inspectors in the state of which they are nationals. The IAEA does not designate any national of a state to serve as inspector in his own country.

III. The special treatment of EURATOM

By 1970 when the NPT entered into force, EURATOM had built up a safeguards organization comparable in size and scope to that of the IAEA and using much the same techniques and procedures as those that the IAEA applied under INFCIRC/66/Rev. 2 safeguards agreements.[4]

In the 1950s and 1960s all the Western suppliers of nuclear plant and fuel (the USA, Canada, South Africa and Australia) accepted EURATOM safeguards, but the Soviet Union and its allies maintained that they were no more than self-inspection by a small group of NATO countries, lacking international credibility. The USSR eventually succeeded in ensuring that the NPT should only recognize IAEA safeguards. The NPT did not, however, insist upon an individual safeguards agreement with each state. Instead it recognized that this agreement might be concluded by 'a group of states', a phrase chosen to accommodate EURATOM.

The NPT also required both NWS and NNWS parties to ensure that IAEA safeguards were applied to their nuclear exports to NNWS. This meant that after becoming parties to the NPT the USA, Canada and Australia could no longer legally export to EURATOM NNWS until the latter accepted IAEA safeguards.

When they signed the NPT in 1970, the EURATOM NNWS made it clear, however, that they would not proceed to ratify it (and thus be forced to accept IAEA safeguards) unless the IAEA and EURATOM first concluded a satisfactory agreement that would take full account of EURATOM's own safeguards system. FR Germany and Italy were particularly insistent on this point. Japan, for its part, made it clear that its ratification would be contingent upon Japan receiving treatment equal to that gained by the European Community. The stage was thus set for some complicated negotiations.

The negotiations between the IAEA and EURATOM (together with its five NNWS) began in November 1971. Although the text of the agreement was approved by both organizations before the end of 1972 and signed in the spring of 1973, it only entered into force in 1977 after protracted and difficult exchanges between both organizations about the most minute details of safeguards arrangements.

EURATOM's opening position in 1971 was that EURATOM would continue to be the only organization applying safeguards in the European Community and that the IAEA's role would be limited to that of making 'spot checks' on a random basis to verify that EURATOM was doing a good job; in other words, the IAEA would verify the application of safeguards by EURATOM and not apply its own safeguards. It would carry out one 'spot check' to every 10 EURATOM inspections.[5]

This was naturally unacceptable to the IAEA. In the compromise eventually reached it was agreed that both organizations would apply their own safeguards in the European Community, that the main part of the agreement should consist essentially of the standard NPT model but that there would be a protocol setting out the special procedures for co-ordinating both systems. Under their respective systems neither side could or would 'delegate' any important activity to the other, each would be required to reach its conclusions on the basis of its own work. Both organizations would agree to carry out specified amounts of routine inspection at each facility, but EURATOM's inspection effort would always exceed that of the IAEA. Whenever it could so achieve its purposes the IAEA would carry out its routine inspections by 'observing' the work of EURATOM inspectors (the so-called "principle" or "concept of observation"), but this principle/concept was subject to a number of conditions and exceptions set in extremely convoluted language. There would be no limitations on the IAEA's 'special' inspections.

The EURATOM countries concerned ratified the NPT in 1975. The two agencies then negotiated detailed facility attachments. It was agreed that for the more sensitive facilities—that is, those handling large quantities of fissile material—the two organizations would form joint teams of roughly the same size (the IAEA's team always being slightly smaller) and that the "principle" or "concept of observation" would not apply. The facility attachments might be reviewed after a trial period.

The joint team is a sensible arrangement; it significantly reduces the manpower that each organization would need if it were to work separately instead of jointly. It has worked well in practice, both organizations benefiting from working together. The "principle" or "concept of observation" on the other hand, has caused a good deal of friction and has led to much sterile and sometimes absurd discussion of precisely what it means in practice and what the IAEA inspector is or is not allowed to do.

In a more rational world one might have expected that in the interests of economy and common sense, once the Common Market countries had accepted IAEA safeguards and inspectors they would have sought to reduce their own safeguards operation to the minimum compatible with the Treaty of Rome and would have encouraged their inspectors to move over to the IAEA. They have not done so. On the contrary, EURATOM's safeguards staff has kept growing and is not far short today of the size of the IAEA inspectorate with its world-wide responsibilities.

An outsider can only speculate why the more rational course was not followed. Apart from Parkinson's Law, two possible reasons suggest themselves.

First, the NWS of EURATOM, and especially France, consider that EURATOM safeguards give added security at relatively little cost against any possibility, however remote, of a West German move towards nuclear weapons, as well as a 'fall-back' if the IAEA should falter. The relative power of France (and the UK) in EURATOM is, of course, much greater than in the 112-member IAEA.

Second, the NNWS of EURATOM regard its safeguards as a means of ensuring the application of the 'equality of misery' principle[6] in the two NWS, that is, of ensuring that France and the UK have to bear the same 'burden' of inspection and reports, and run the same risk of leakage of commercially valuable information as Belgium, FR Germany, Italy and the Netherlands. Although in recent years the IAEA has begun to apply safeguards in the UK and in France, the IAEA's effort in these and other NWS is kept as low as possible so as not to divert costly manpower from more important tasks that directly serve non-proliferation. EURATOM on the other hand treats the peaceful nuclear activities of the NWS in the same way as those of the NNWS.

Whatever the reasons, the duplication[7] that results from expanding the

EURATOM operation makes diminishing sense as the size of the European Community increases. With each new member, EURATOM has to take over or, rather, duplicate some of the work previously carried out by the IAEA alone. When Denmark, Ireland and Greece joined the impact was small. If and when Spain joins the amount of additional EURATOM inspection will have to be larger. The prospect of introducing the complexities of the IAEA–EURATOM agreement in yet another country with nuclear power and research and development plants will not please the IAEA Secretariat.

More serious, however, than this waste of manpower in a profession where experienced operators are still at a premium, has been the diversion of political and diplomatic energy. There are few, at least in the West, who regard any EURATOM state as a serious proliferation risk today. Nevertheless, much of the attention and energy of the IAEA's Board and senior staff, as well as that of the national authorities concerned, was diverted for nearly 10 years from considering more serious risks to the non-proliferation regime. Similarly, EURATOM, which might have been more profitably engaged in trying to harmonize the nuclear-supply policies of its leading members and to minimize the type of export competition that has favoured proliferation in the past and may do so again in the future, has instead focused most of its safeguards concern on keeping to a minimum the role of the IAEA.

NPT safeguards agreements remain in force as long as the NPT itself. If the latter were to expire soon after the 1995 Conference (which will decide upon the future of the NPT), the EURATOM and Tlatelolco Treaty NNWS would, it seems, be the only states legally bound to continue to accept full-scope safeguards (those of EURATOM in the first case and of IAEA in the second). The two groups of countries have therefore a rather special interest in the outcome of the Conference.

IV. Japan

Even before the IAEA–EURATOM agreement had been approved, Japanese officials made it clear that there was no prospect of Japan ratifying the NPT unless it were offered a similar agreement.[8] The agreement eventually negotiated with Japan in 1973 is very similar to the EURATOM agreement, with the important exception that Japan will only be granted treatment comparable with that of EURATOM when it has set up and maintains a national safeguarding apparatus that is as effective and as "functionally independent" (using the language of Article 81 of the model NPT safeguards agreement) as that of EURATOM. The task of establishing such an apparatus was subsequently undertaken by the Japanese Ministry of Trade and Industry. In practice there have been far fewer difficulties in implementing the agreement with Japan, there being much less of a vested interest to protect.

Notes and references

1 Article 13 of the Treaty of Tlatelolco. The formula used is "... agreements with the IAEA for the application of its safeguards to its [the state's] nuclear activities". Clearly *all* nuclear activities of the state are implied and the Article has been thus interpreted by the IAEA and the countries concerned in all agreements concluded pursuant to the Treaty of Tlatelolco. The Treaty is reproduced in Goldblat, J., *Agreements for Arms Control: A Critical Survey* (Taylor & Francis, London, 1982), pp. 162–70 [a SIPRI book].

2 Article 16(1)(b) of the Treaty of Tlatelolco (note 1).

3 The OEEC (Organization for European Economic Cooperation), now the OECD (Organization for Economic Cooperation and Development), agreed on a safeguards system in 1956 which entered into force in July 1959. The system reflected the same technological, economic and political assumptions as those that inspired the IAEA and EURATOM systems. The OECD subsequently suspended its safeguards operations.

4 In fact, EURATOM safeguards were 'full-scope' in all countries of the Community except France where they did not, of course, apply to the military programme. Those of the IAEA were only legally full-scope in Mexico (under the first Tlatelolco agreement, based on INFCIRC/66 and later replaced by an NPT/Tlatelolco agreement based on INFCIRC/153) though in practice they covered all the nuclear activities in many countries, including Japan.

5 When the IAEA Board established its 1970 safeguards committee to work out the standard model for the NPT safeguards agreements (INFCIRC/153), it first proposed to work out two models—one for individual states and the other for "groups of states", that is, EURATOM. It soon became clear that this would be politically impossible and that only a single model could be negotiated.

6 See chapter 3.

7 Since the entry into force in 1977 of the IAEA–EURATOM safeguards agreement, the safeguards 'philosophy', methods and procedures that EURATOM applies in the eight EURATOM NNWS have become almost identical to those of the IAEA. Both agencies are in effect applying the technical provisions of INFCIRC/153, supplemented by arrangements for co-ordinating their work and defining what and how much each must do. The same is true of the safeguards they both apply at those plants in the EURATOM NWS (France and UK) that the IAEA selects for routine inspection.

8 And in 1971 the IAEA cautioned EURATOM that any privileged treatment which is obtained would also have to be accorded to Japan; otherwise Japan would not ratify the NPT.

Chapter 11. Defects of the safeguards documents

Some of the problems the IAEA has run into are due, as has been noted, to the approach taken by the two safeguards documents (INFCIRC/66/Rev. 2 and INFCIRC/153), or to deficiencies in them. Before analysing these deficiencies it should be said that both documents, and particularly the NPT safeguards agreement set forth in INFCIRC/153, are remarkable achievements. Their texts are reproduced in Appendices IV and V.

I. INFCIRC/66/Rev. 2

The pre-NPT approach reflected in the main part of INFCIRC/66/Rev. 2 and drawn up in 1965, five years before the model NPT safeguards agreement, results in a much shorter, more generalized and less technical document. As noted earlier, INFCIRC/66/Rev. 2 was designed chiefly to outline the safeguards that would apply to various types of supply arrangement. Those vary from situations in which a country asked for the IAEA's help in obtaining a particular plant or even a single fuel loading, to comprehensive arrangements under which an exporter contracts to supply over many years most of the elements of an entire fuel cycle (reactors, reprocessing plants, enrichment plants, etc.) and the fuel required. In view of the wide variety of situations which this document had to cover it was not feasible to develop a standard model.

The clauses of INFCIRC/66/Rev. 2 are normally incorporated into individual agreements by 'reference' instead of being reproduced *in extenso* in the text of the agreement. Besides these references to INFCIRC/66/Rev. 2, each non-NPT safeguards agreement deals with several other technical, legal, administrative and political matters not treated by INFCIRC/66/Rev. 2 (e.g., the basic undertakings of the government and the IAEA, procedures for notifications to the IAEA and for listing of safeguarded material in "inventories", sanctions (those specified in the IAEA Statute) for breach of agreement, procedures for settlement of disputes, entry into force and termination, financial and liability clauses).

The main part of INFCIRC/66/Rev. 2, drawn up in 1965, contained explicit guidance only for safeguarding reactors. The Board extended the system in 1966 and 1968 to cover reprocessing and fuel conversion and fabrication plants, by adding two short annexes. There have been no further extensions of the system since 1968, but in 1973 the Board approved a document (GOV/1621, reproduced in Appendix VI) giving more detailed guidance on the duration of INFCIRC/66 agreements. NPT parties needed this guidance so as to ensure greater uniformity in the nuclear export agreements they concluded with non-NPT NNWS under Article III.2 of the NPT.

Defects of INFCIRC/66/Rev. 2 and related documents

Besides lacking detailed guidance and comprehensiveness, INFCIRC/66/Rev. 2 and agreements concluded under it until the mid-1970s have four main defects.

Banning all nuclear explosive uses

The stated purpose of the document is to establish a system of control to comply with the obligation in the IAEA Statute that items under safeguards "are not used in such a way as to further any military purpose". The quoted term was used in non-NPT safeguards agreements concluded until 1975.

The NPT, on the other hand, expressly proscribes the acquisition of "nuclear weapons or other nuclear explosive devices". Consequently all NPT safeguards agreements forbid the use of safeguarded material to make any kind of nuclear explosive. Why is INFCIRC/66 not explicit on this point?

When the IAEA Statute was drafted in 1954–56 no one would have suggested that a state could begin to carry out nuclear explosions without thereby "furthering a military purpose", whether the ostensible object of the explosions was to make holes in the ground or to test the charges for a nuclear weapon. In both cases the essential technology is the same. In fact, the first nuclear explosion carried out by an incipient nuclear weapon power is that of a nuclear explosive 'device' which is far from being a deliverable weapon, but which pre-eminently serves a military purpose. Accordingly it would have seemed quite superfluous in the mid-1950s to specify that all nuclear explosions, whatever their object, were banned by the 'no military purpose' clause or that IAEA-safeguarded nuclear material must not be used in any kind of nuclear explosive.

In the 1960s, both superpowers carried out numerous explosions "for peaceful purposes" and vigorously promoted the technology which, they hoped, would be used to build canals, excavate harbours and dams, make cuttings through mountains, release reservoirs of underground gas and help mine ore. The USA has long since abandoned its peaceful nuclear explosion (PNE) programmes and there have been reports that the USSR may be curtailing its main projects, but the barrage of publicity which PNEs received in the 1960s whetted the desire of many other countries to carry out their own PNE projects and bolstered the arguments of those who maintained that the language of the IAEA Statute does not preclude the use of IAEA-safeguarded material to carry out PNEs. Ambiguity in this matter is perpetuated and aggravated by the Tlatelolco Treaty which, in Article 18, expressly permits its parties to carry out explosions of nuclear devices for peaceful purposes. However, Article 5 of the Treaty appears to define a nuclear weapon in such a way as to include (and thereby prohibit) any "peaceful" nuclear explosive device. Moreover, Article 13 requires each party to conclude a safeguards agreement with the IAEA covering its nuclear activities. All agreements that the IAEA has negotiated under the Tlatelolco Treaty expressly forbid the use of safeguarded material in any kind of nuclear explosion.[1]

In the light of Tlatelolco's unfortunate precedent, the drafters of the NPT apparently decided to avert any possible ambiguity by using the phrase already referred to—no "... nuclear weapons or other nuclear explosive devices..."

All INFCIRC/66/Rev. 2 (non-NPT) agreements concluded since 1975 have also eliminated any possible ambiguity by requiring that safeguarded material must not be used "... for the manufacture of any nuclear weapon or to further any other military purpose or for the manufacture of any other nuclear explosive device..." In other words this defect in INFCIRC/66 has been 'negotiated out' of all recent agreements, but not without much resistance from the non-NPT states concerned.

Subsequent generations of fissile material

INFCIRC/66/Rev. 2 deals only in a very vague and unhelpful manner with the important question of applying safeguards to fissile material produced from the material originally placed under safeguards. It merely states that "... it is desirable that safeguards agreements should provide for the continuation of safeguards... with respect to produced special fissionable material..." Following the 1973 decision of the Board of Governors[2] on the duration of safeguards agreements (see Appendix VI), this defect has also been negotiated away, but again not without resistance from the states concerned.

The need for subsidiary arrangements and facility attachments

INFCIRC/66/Rev. 2 also lacks any specific requirement for the conclusion of subsidiary arrangements and facility attachments (the need for which was not fully grasped in 1964-65) or for keeping abreast of technological developments or for installation of the containment and surveillance instruments described in previous chapters. This defect has also been remedied in more recent agreements. So, too, has the absence of any provision for safeguarding plant or equipment built on the basis of technology transferred by the supplier—e.g., by replicating the plant originally supplied (for instance, India has replicated, without safeguards, power reactors supplied by Canada).

Safeguarding enrichment and heavy water plants

INFCIRC/66/Rev. 2 also gives no explicit guidance on the safeguards to be applied to enrichment plants or to plants for the production of heavy water.

Negotiating problems

Since the IAEA Secretariat must use INFCIRC/66/Rev. 2 as the basis for proposed non-NPT safeguards agreements the deficiencies in that document often place the IAEA delegation in a difficult negotiating position. The Secretariat, therefore, makes as much use as possible of helpful precedents that it has been able to negotiate into non-NPT safeguards agreements since the mid-1970s. Its hand is usually strengthened if the supplying country takes part in the negotiation and becomes party to the eventual agreement and can lend support to the Secretariat's proposals instead of leaving it to the Secretariat to 'hammer out' a bilateral agreement with the importer. France invariably takes part in the negotiation of agreements under which it is the supplier, the USA sometimes does so while FR Germany usually and the USSR invariably prefer to 'leave it to the Secretariat'; although the USSR may lend a hand informally behind the scene.

The supplying state may feel that it has played its part in securing good safeguards when the Board approves the safeguards agreement. However, there is still much to be done. The IAEA Secretariat must get the agreement of the importing state to the subsidiary arrangements and to the facility attachment for each plant supplied, or built on the basis of supplied technology. As the KANUPP case and experience with EURATOM have shown, the contents of the facility attachment may determine just how effective safeguards will be at the plant; how many times a year the IAEA may inspect it and how many man-days the inspectors may spend at the plant, what access the inspector will have and what equipment he may install.

Ideally the supplying state should not transfer any plant until the IAEA and the importing state have agreed on the facility attachment for it. In many cases, however, this may not be practical. The more important safeguards agreements may cover years of supply and even later replications (e.g., the agreement covering supplies from FR Germany to Brazil). But the Secretariat's negotiating position would be somewhat stronger if future INFCIRC/66/Rev. 2 agreements were to contain a clause to the effect that the IAEA will inform the supplying state, and perhaps the Board of Governors, when satisfactory facility attachments have been agreed to for the plants supplied. In the case of INFCIRC/153 agreements such a clause could be included in the commercial contract between the supplier and the importer and the IAEA could be requested to send the notification.

Such arrangements would not help the Secretariat in negotiating facility attachments for plants that an NPT NNWS builds in its own country. For several years the IAEA's annual report, in listing all plants under safeguards, has shown in each case whether the facility attachment has been concluded. The Secretariat might take this further by a special report in the SIR on overdue or difficult facility attachments. This might bring some pressure on the governments concerned to conclude satisfactory arrangements.

Some advantages of INFCIRC/66/Rev. 2

In a few respects INFCIRC/66/Rev. 2 provides the basis for more extensive or effective safeguards than the later model NPT safeguards agreement. For instance, unlike the latter, INFCIRC/66/Rev. 2 foresees full safeguards on yellowcake (uranium concentrate); it authorizes safeguards on plant and equipment as well as nuclear material; and in some cases INFCIRC/66/Rev. 2 agreements permit the supplier to play a direct and most helpful part in ensuring the effective application of safeguards by authorizing or requiring it to notify the IAEA of transfers to the importing country and by giving it the right to inform the IAEA of plant built in the importing country on the basis of supplied information. (As noted in chapter 3, in the one case where this provision was put to test, namely the reprocessing plant in Pakistan, it did not come out with flying colours.) INFCIRC/66/Rev. 2 also permits much higher frequencies of inspection and more untrammelled access than the model NPT safeguards agreements.

II. INFCIRC/153 (the model NPT safeguards agreement)

INFCIRC/153 prescribes a two-tiered safeguards system. The lower tier is a *national* system (or, implicitly, a regional or multilateral system) for keeping account and control of all nuclear material in the state's fuel cycle.[3] The upper tier—IAEA safeguards—is elaborated in considerable detail and depends on the effective operation of the lower tier to provide most of the data and facilities that it needs.

INFCIRC/153 is divided into two parts. The first sets forth the main political, legal and financial rights and obligations of the state and the IAEA; the second describes in detail the technical rights and obligations of the IAEA, the state and the operator. The document is comprehensive; no important element is omitted and there are few ambiguities or inconsistencies. This is all the more surprising in the light of the fact that the document was the product of a committee of some 45 delegations representing the conflicting interests of NWS and NNWS, North and South, supplier and consumer.

This achievement is a tribute to the intellectual reach and grasp and the diplomatic skill of the delegates and the members of the IAEA staff who drew up the document. It was, however, only possible because of political and technical circumstances that may not be repeated, namely, detente coupled with a waning but still very effective superpower domination of the world's affairs and with an increasing convergence of their interests in matters of non-proliferation, and the even more dominant position of the two superpowers (backed up by the UK) in both the peaceful and the military uses of nuclear energy.

The proponents of the NPT (in particular the superpowers, the UK, Canada, the Scandinavian countries, the Netherlands and the USSR's allies in Eastern Europe) deliberately set about to make NPT safeguards less "burdensome" than those of INFCIRC/66 so as to encourage acceptance of the NPT. They did this chiefly by setting additional limits to the authority and freedom of action of the

IAEA. They also had to make many concessions in order to obtain a consensus.

The lines were drawn chiefly between the three NWS parties to the NPT (USA, USSR and the UK) on the one hand and the leading Western industrial NNWS who were likely to experience the full impact of safeguards (FR Germany, Italy, Japan and, to some extent, Sweden). The latter were suspicious of the super-powers and of the IAEA Secretariat which, they felt, was too often dominated by the former. The non-NPT states that took an active part in the committee's work (Argentina, Brazil, India, Pakistan, South Africa and, at that time, Australia) generally supported any proposal to limit or 'soften' safeguards.

Most of the weaknesses of INFCIRC/153 can be traced to these concessions and to the consequent compromises at the cost of safeguards coverage and intensity and of the IAEA's authority.

As noted, INFCIRC/153 is more complete and clear-cut than INFCIRC/66/Rev. 2. In fact, its very comprehensiveness makes it much more difficult to negotiate improvements than in the case of INFCIRC/66/Rev. 2.

Defects of the NPT model

Safeguards on nuclear materials only

The safeguards concept reflected in the Preamble of the NPT is ''. . . the principle of safeguarding *the flow of source and special fissionable materials* by the use of instruments and other techniques at certain strategic points''. Reflecting this concept, the model agreement provides for safeguards only on nuclear materials. Some of the consequences of this concept have been examined in previous chapters; it is, for instance, the basis for many of the restrictions on inspection access. It also leads to some ambiguity about the safeguards status of plants that are reported to be shut down or not to contain any nuclear material. Does the IAEA have the right to inspect them?

A more serious problem following from this concept is that the IAEA has no right to obtain information about any new plant at a reasonably early date.[4] Thus, for instance, the IAEA had no official information about the hot-cell facility that (NPT) Italy supplied to (NPT) Iraq and that was one of the factors which, according to Israeli statements, led Israel to bomb the Tuwaitha (Tamuz 1) reactor. In fact, under NPT safeguards, an entire reprocessing or enrichment plant could be exported to an NPT country (such as Iraq) without any notification to the IAEA. An NPT country can similarly construct such a plant on the basis of imported technology without notifying the IAEA. As we have seen, the IAEA must be brought into the picture only ''as early as possible'' before the operator introduces nuclear material into the plant.[5]

In practice this might mean that the IAEA is less informed about certain matters important for effective and credible safeguards in an NPT NNWS than in, for instance, a non-NPT NNWS such as Brazil. A mosaic of INFCIRC/66 agreements still covers virtually the entire national fuel cycle and requires Brazil (and in some cases its suppliers) to provide full information about all transfers of plant and technology and about all replications of plant or other uses of supplied technology.

This is not of course an argument against the NPT or NPT safeguards, which give much greater assurance than any combination of non-NPT safeguards in force today. It is rather an argument in favour of seeking ways to improve the flow of information under NPT rules.

'Permitted' military uses

A matter which attracted some concern in early days is that both the NPT and the model safeguards agreement permit (or rather do not proscribe) the non-explosive military use of nuclear material in NPT NNWS. This was chiefly at the insistence of some industrial countries, in particular Italy, which at that time envisaged using a nuclear-powered engine in a naval supply ship. As a result the model agreement contains a clause permitting certain nuclear material to be withdrawn from safeguards but only in accordance with a series of procedures designed to ensure that the IAEA will be able to keep reasonable account of the material so withdrawn and that it will come under safeguards again as soon as it returns to the peaceful fuel cycle for reprocessing or for other, inherently non-military, industrial treatment.

In fact the Italian nuclear ship was not built and no NNWS has sought to make use of this 'military' option. If any country were ever to do so the procedure it would have to follow would be fairly complex. In the first place it would have to show that the material was not subject to any prohibition against all military uses. All material of US origin and much other nuclear material in peaceful fuel cycles throughout the world today is subject to such a prohibition and it is inextricably mingled with other nuclear material. It seems likely, therefore, that the state wishing to use the option would have to obtain 'new' (for instance, freshly-mined) uranium, then process it, enrich it (probably to the very high level of enrichment needed for submarine fuel) and perhaps fabricate it, all under special supervision, so as to demonstrate that it was exempt from any 'no-military-use' clause.

Pre-eminence of material accountancy

A more technical criticism sometimes made of the model NPT safeguards agreement is that it puts too much stress on material accountancy and not enough on containment and surveillance. As has been shown, accurate accounting must be the basis of any system designed to verify the peaceful use of nuclear material and it can produce quite satisfactory results for most types of reactor and other plants using low-enriched material but it has considerable shortcomings if the 'diversion time' for the material is short. If the model agreement does not say much about containment and surveillance, it does recognize that they are important and nothing in the model agreement stands in the way of using them to the fullest possible extent.

Smaller plants may be more 'dangerous' than larger ones

Both INFCIRC/66 and the model NPT safeguards agreement set the upper limits to inspection frequency on the basis of the capacity of the safeguarded *plant* (incidentally illustrating the inconsistency of the NPT concept that safeguards apply only to nuclear *material* and not to plant). Plant capacity is measured by its 'throughput' or maximum inventory, taking into account the degree of enrichment of the uranium or quantity of plutonium that the plant handles. The larger the plant and the more 'dangerous' its material, the higher is the permitted frequency of inspection. This is, of course, quite correct for the more 'dangerous' materials, that is, those that have a short diversion time—highly enriched uranium or plutonium. But many of the plants that have caused most concern are relatively small or use unenriched uranium—or meet both descriptions. We have already noted the 'proliferation-prone' combination of *natural-uranium*-fuelled *research* reactors and small or pilot reprocessing plants in India, Israel and Pakistan and of a small enrichment plant in South Africa. In all cases the throughput of the reactor is smaller, by a couple of orders of magnitude, than that of generally much less dangerous though much larger commercial reactors. The maximum frequency of inspection is therefore set much lower for the smaller but more dangerous plant. Fortunately, it has so far been set sufficiently high to be more than adequate.

In short, the curve of 'proliferation proneness', seen from a political point of view, may be at its peak in the middle ranges of plant size and does not go on rising in the manner implied by the maximum frequencies of inspection set by the two safeguards documents.

Storage of separated plutonium

Neither of the two documents attempts to make provision for the IAEA to exercise its statutory right to call upon governments to 'deposit with it' surplus amounts of separated plutonium so as to prevent governments from building up national stockpiles of weapon-usable material.[6] A good opportunity might therefore have been missed when INFCIRC/66 was drawn up and there was much less civil plutonium about at that time.

At what point does diversion begin?

Probably deliberately, neither system addresses the related and difficult question of the point in the processing or fashioning of nuclear material at which a diversion to 'military use' begins. In an extreme example of excessive devotion to material accountancy and of obsession with MUF, it has even been argued that under the NPT safeguards document INFCIRC/153 it would be quite in order to manufacture, under the eyes of an inspector, the components of a nuclear explosive device, provided that all nuclear material was accurately accounted for. However, Article II of the NPT as well as common sense make it clear that this would be a violation of the Treaty.

States' rights *versus* the IAEA's rights

A more serious shortcoming of both systems but particularly of the model NPT safeguards agreement has already been thoroughly examined, namely their excessive concern with states' rights and the restraints they consequently impose upon inspectors and related matters such as designations.

Secrecy

Another consequence of this concern is the somewhat excessive secrecy with which the IAEA conducts the safeguards operation. It has already been noted that both safeguards documents require the IAEA to protect the confidentiality of industrial and commercial information that it acquires while applying safeguards. There is no requirement in either document to be secretive about what the IAEA itself is doing and how effectively it is doing it. Nevertheless, there is a need for some operational confidentiality. An inspector is likely to be less frank in his report to his superior if he believes that the report may be read by the government of the country in which he operates—and that government is likely to become even more particular about those designated to inspect its plants if it believes that the inspectors' reports will promptly become available to other governments.

It would also be counter-productive to point a finger at a particular government for a relatively minor safeguards transgression or in regard to a minor anomaly that has not yet been resolved. The co-operation of governments is essential to the operation and it should not be lightly jeopardized. The charge of non-co-operation should only be made when the government's performance seriously impairs the ability of the IAEA to verify that no diversion is taking place. Moreover, there are so many minor transgressions and anomalies that naming names in public would soon lose any positive effect!

On the other hand excessive secrecy can be counter-productive, reducing the effectiveness of the safeguards operation and the support of governmental or parliamentary bodies like the US Congress, the media and the public at large.

It is also well-nigh impossible to keep an important secret within an organization whose staff includes the citizens of over 70 states, most of whom are on fixed-term contracts and will return to their national service. Because of this it is very unlikely that any government or plant would entrust any truly valuable industrial or commercial information to the IAEA. When states have something they want to protect from the eyes of other states they put a special material balance area or metaphorical 'black box' around it and exclude inspection (as in effect they intended to do with gas centrifuges), or they require the information to be examined "on the premises of the state" as they often do with design data.

A balance must therefore be struck between conflicting interests. It seems to have been struck on the side of excessive secrecy by both the Board and the Secretariat. An example of this is the annual Safeguards Implementation Report. While it does contain a good deal of implicit criticism of states it "names no names"[7] and it is chiefly an exercise in self-criticism by the IAEA itself and particularly by the safeguards secretariat. It certainly contains no confidential commercial or industrial information. A copy of the document goes to each of the 112 member states of the IAEA so that it can hardly be regarded as highly classified. Yet when the Director General suggested that the document should be released to the public and the press (which obtains leaked copies anyhow) there was a decisive majority in the Board against his suggestion, only the USA and a couple of other like-minded delegates favouring publication.

III. Should amendments be attempted?

It must be stressed that despite a concern with states' rights that may seem excessive today but was necessary in 1970 to gain acceptance of full-scope safeguards and ratification of the NPT by leading industrial NNWS, the model NPT safeguards agreement has stood the test of time and has provided the basis of a remarkably workable system of safeguards.

For reasons that are explained later in this book, it is unlikely that any amendments, however desirable they might seem to be, can now be made. And even if it did prove possible to revise the document, to be meaningful any changes would require renegotiation of some 50 NPT safeguards agreements concluded since 1970 and, in particular, the agreements with EURATOM and Japan.

If meaningful amendment is not in prospect there are nevertheless other ways in which desirable changes can be made. For instance, NNWS suppliers could agree to keep the IAEA better informed of exports of nuclear plant and technology to NPT as well as non-NPT NNWS. The problems encountered in designating inspectors could be brought more out into the open and a more detailed and less anonymous analysis of the problem could be put to the Board, with explicit recommendations.

The Board could also take *ad hoc* decisions to interpret or supplement the model agreement as it has done in one case with INFCIRC/66 (its 1973 decision on the duration of safeguards is reproduced in Appendix VI). But to be meaningful such 'additions' would also require renegotiation of existing agreements.

It should be remembered that there is a risk that if proposals for changes were introduced, they themselves might be amended in such a way as to put even more restrictions on the safeguards operation. In particular there is no practical prospect today that the majority of the Board would agree to change the balance of rights and duties in such a way as to favour the IAEA at the cost of states.

As for INFCIRC/66/Rev. 2, it has been shown that most of its major defects have been remedied in agreements concluded since 1975.[8] Some pre-1975 agreements will lose their practical importance with the passage of time or if the country concerned ratifies the NPT or concludes a new comprehensive safeguards agreement (e.g., Spain). A few others may continue to cause some trouble but there would be little prospect of renegotiating them. The deficiencies of INFCIRC/66/Rev. 2 in regard to enrichment and heavy water plants could be remedied if the Board were prepared to approve new Annexes to INFCIRC/66/Rev. 2, but they are more likely to be taken care of in a pragmatic way in facility attachments for particular plants. This point is further discussed in chapter 12.

IV. What would happen if NPT safeguards came to an end?

NPT safeguards agreements remain in force while a NNWS remains party to the NPT. NPT safeguards would thus cease to apply if: (*a*) the 1995 Conference decided to extend the NPT for a single fixed period with no further arrangements for extension; (*b*) the NPT ceased to be viable, for example, because of a large number of withdrawals; (*c*) the NNWS concerned withdrew from the NPT; or (*d*) the IAEA ceased to be able to apply effective safeguards.

All these contingencies are most unlikely but none can be totally excluded. In the last case only non-IAEA safeguards would still continue (e.g., bilateral 'fall-back' safeguards foreseen as an ultimate contingency in US and some French supply agreements, EURATOM and OECD safeguards, Soviet requirements for the return of spent fuel and the 'special inspections' of OPANAL).

If the IAEA remained viable but the NPT basis were removed, IAEA–Tlatelolco Treaty safeguards agreements would remain in force and so would most INFCIRC/66 safeguards agreements. They would cover many existing nuclear plants and much nuclear material, for example, in Japan and many developing countries. IAEA safeguards would not apply, however, in many industrial countries (e.g., they would no longer apply to most plants in EURATOM, or to any plants in East European NNWS). Moreover, as time goes on, more and more material will be produced or plants built in NPT NNWS that would not be covered by INFCIRC/66 or by any other 'fall-back' safeguards arrangement. What was left of the non-proliferation regime would be a disparate and weakened structure, full of gaps at crucial points, having lost much of its international credibility. The aggregate safeguards coverage would be much less than in 1969 before the NPT came into force. It might be worth undertaking a detailed study of what would be lost and what would be left. One point that clearly emerges is that INFCIRC/66 safeguards would once again become very important.

Notes and references

1 Three agreements were negotiated with Tlatelolco states to give effect to their obligations under that Treaty only. Two of the states (Mexico and Panama) subsequently became parties to the NPT and, as noted elsewhere, Mexico's 'Tlatelolco only' safeguards agreement was later replaced by a NPT–Tlatelolco agreement. By 1 January 1984 Panama had ratified neither its 'Tlatelolco only' agreement nor the NPT–Tlatelolco agreement negotiated later. The third state, Colombia, is not a party to the NPT and its 'Tlatelolco only' agreement is in force. As of 1 January 1985, 14 NPT–Tlatelolco agreements were in force, including the one with Mexico.

2 Fully analysed in SIPRI, *Safeguards Against Nuclear Proliferation* (MIT Press, Cambridge, MA and Almqvist & Wiksell, Stockholm, 1975), p. 16.

3 Again largely designed to accommodate EURATOM which had such a (multinational) system in operation in the Community.

4 Design information is to be provided "... as early as possible before nuclear material is introduced into a new facility" (see INFCIRC/153, para. 42, in Appendix V), a vague phrase susceptible to many interpretations. INFCIRC/66/Rev. 2 uses much the same language. However, since INFCIRC/66/Rev. 2 safeguards agreements may apply directly to plants, whether or not they contain any nuclear material, and since most INFCIRC/66/Rev. 2 safeguards agreements do in fact relate to a transfer to a non-NPT NNWS, these agreements require that the IAEA be informed, usually in advance, of the transfer of plants and major components as well as of nuclear material. IAEA safeguards agreements with the NPT NNWS on the other hand require only that the IAEA be informed of the exports of nuclear material.

5 Under Article III.2 of the NPT, an NPT exporter is obliged to ensure that IAEA safeguards apply to such exports—but not to notify the IAEA (see Appendix IX).

6 The relevant clause of the IAEA Statute (Article XII.A.5) is reproduced in Appendix I.

7 Except for a table showing how many plants of different types are under safeguards in each state.

8 Para. 8 of INFCIRC/66 provides that its principles and procedures "... shall be subject to periodic review ...". There has been no such review.

Chapter 12. The IAEA's interfaces with states

I. Government attitudes towards safeguards

There has been a considerable evolution in the attitudes of governments towards safeguards and the positions they have taken in the Board.

As the chief sponsor of the IAEA, the USA has always been a strong and vigorous proponent of safeguards, supported effectively by the UK and Canada, the Scandinavian countries, the Netherlands, usually by Australia and by Japan, which has the distinction of being the first country to accept IAEA safeguards. Initial Soviet opposition swung around to full support in 1963 and has been steadfast since then. France, originally lukewarm if not hostile, became increasingly supportive in the early 1970s.

The attitude of other major industrial countries has changed according to their NPT status. As is pointed out earlier, Belgium, FR Germany and Italy generally supported any move in the 1970 committee (which drew up the model NPT safeguards agreement) to water down safeguards but started to become more positive as they entered the process of ratifying the NPT. Their attitude towards the IAEA safeguards operation is, however, still somewhat tempered by their prevailing interests in EURATOM and a general tendency, which they share with France, to regard with some suspicion any safeguards initiative taken by the USA, particularly since the transatlantic differences that arose when President Carter attempted to stop the development of the fast breeder reactor.

In safeguards matters at least, the apparent solidarity of the Group of Seventy Seven (G-77) masks wide differences of view, also often a reflection of the NPT status of the country concerned. Since 1955 when they joined the Washington discussions on the IAEA Statute, a group of countries led by India has consistently sought to constrain the development of IAEA safeguards. In addition to India, this group now includes Pakistan, Argentina, and Brazil (all non-NPT states), in other words four[1] out of the nine developing members of the IAEA that are operating or building nuclear power plants. What lends even more power to their voices is that Argentina, Brazil and India are 'permanent' members of the Board and Pakistan serves on it two years out of every three.

The NPT countries among the G-77, while siding with Argentina, Brazil, India and Pakistan in most North–South issues, usually differ from them if a safeguards issue is put to the test, although they are much less unequivocal in their support for safeguards than the other four are in their opposition.

Most of the remaining developing countries take relatively little interest in the NPT and safeguards which they seem to regard as of remote concern compared with, say, the size of the technical assistance budget or political issues. The attitude of the African states and the Middle East may in part be conditioned by South Africa and Israel, and by the failure of 'the West' as they see it, to bring into the non-proliferation regime the two states that they most distrust.

II. The role of the Board of Governors

In view of its crucial role in all aspects of IAEA safeguards, the Board's ability to get things done quickly and efficiently has been vital to the success of the operation. This ability depends on the competence of its chairman and members, on the political balance within the Board and, above all, on its harmonious operation based on a shared conviction of the importance of safeguards. To give a negative example, when in the early days the Board was riven by the Cold War it was quite unable to bring forth a meaningful safeguards document.

The disputes of the Cold War also led to very inefficient operation of the Board with frequent, lengthy and sterile meetings. The arrival of detente around 1964 brought an immediate improvement. It became possible in 1964 and 1965 to reach agreement with remarkably little dissent on the text of INFCIRC/66. From then on until the mid-1970s there emerged what sometimes seemed to be a superpower condominium in the Board, reflecting the convergence of US/Soviet interests which, in Geneva, was bearing fruit in the NPT itself. In 1973, following the ratification of an amendment to the Statute (in this case against strong Soviet opposition), the Board's membership increased from 25 to 34 countries. The amendment was an Italian initiative and it was designed to give Italy[2] and FR Germany permanent seats on the Board, perhaps as part of the price to be paid for their eventual ratification of the NPT and in compensation for the safeguards 'burden' that FR Germany would have to accept. The sudden leap in the size of the Board was to have implications for its effectiveness, which was at its peak in the late 1960s and early 1970s.

With a few notable exceptions (Argentina, Brazil, Egypt, India and Pakistan) Third World countries played a relatively minor role[3] in the Board until the mid-1970s. The 1973 expansion significantly increased their representation (to about one-half of the total membership) and the arrival of other UN organizations in Vienna brought an influx of Third World diplomats. The Group of Seventy-Seven, which was already a power in other UN bodies, began to make its weight felt in the IAEA and a pattern of bloc voting emerged. North–South political issues also became more prominent with the expulsion in 1977 of South Africa from its previously permanent seat on the Board and its replacement by Egypt. Under G-77 pressure the Board rapidly increased the size of the IAEA technical assistance programme. It also virtually froze the contribution of developing countries to the IAEA safeguards budget. The pressure for larger developing country 'representation' in the Secretariat became stronger. Since 1977 there has also been constant pressure to increase the number of African and Middle Eastern countries on the Board, but no agreement has yet been reached on this issue which would tip the balance of the Board decisively towards the Third World.

The Board's role in developing the safeguards system

The Board's work in drawing up the first safeguards documents (culminating in INFCIRC/66/Rev. 2 and the model NPT safeguards agreement) is described in chapter 4.

It has already been noted that the prospects for any significant further evolution or amendment of the model NPT safeguards agreement are small. Much the same could be said of INFCIRC/66/Rev. 2.

There are several reasons for this. The most important one is political. The 1973 expansion of the Board, the waning influence of the superpowers, the emergence of the G-77 and of bloc voting and, most recently, the entry of China into the IAEA have changed the political balance of the late 1960s and early 1970s and the prospects for major initiatives. As a consequence, the proponents of safeguards are now reluctant to do anything that might open Pandora's box. In particular they are chary of any initiative that might lead to the creation of a new safeguards committee, a committee that might have a rather different composition and outlook from those that drew up INFCIRC/66 and the model NPT safeguards agreement. Whether or not these fears are justified, they are a potent factor against change.

It should be noted that in the last instance in which the views of the Board were put to the test by vote, safeguards emerged as the clear 'victor'. The question at issue was whether to include in agreements for technical assistance a pledge by the recipient not to use the assistance for the development of nuclear explosives of any kind.[4] The Board sided with the 'pro-safeguards' faction by a decisive majority including most of the developing country members. Argentina, Brazil, India and Pakistan strongly opposed the inclusion of the pledge and, rather than subscribe to it in future agreements for technical assistance, Argentina and India affirmed that they would take no further technical assistance from the IAEA.

There is another more mundane but quite cogent reason for leaving both safeguards documents undisturbed at present. Almost all the important NPT safeguards agreements have already been negotiated and concluded, and the same may be largely true of INFCIRC/66/Rev. 2 agreements.

The Board's progress on other safeguards fronts

Despite the absence of systems evolution, there has been much progress in the Board on other matters. As noted, the question of the non-proliferation commitment to be made in order to obtain technical assistance has been clarified. The need for safeguards agreements to cover technical assistance in major and particularly sensitive nuclear technologies has been established—it has apparently discouraged requests for help in these fields to such an extent that there has been no occasion to conclude any such agreement!

More important has been the success achieved in enlarging and improving the safeguards operation itself. The safeguards budget has grown from US$1.2 million in 1970 to US$39 million in 1985. The organization of the safeguards department and its management have been improved at least in certain respects. The number of inspectors has grown from 48 in 1970 to 200 in 1985. The annual Safeguards Implementation Report and its annual review by the Board have provided a much needed opportunity to examine the way in which the system works and what should be done to improve it.

Because of the 'negotiated' improvements in INFCIRC/66/Rev. 2 agreements and the inherent merits of the model NPT safeguards agreement, the Board's 'immobility' may not cause serious problems for several years to come. But it may have significant implications in the longer term. For instance, it may no longer be realistic to look to the Board to adapt the safeguards system to technological or other developments that might require new safeguards approaches or offer new opportunities for safeguards. To give an example: it might become possible for the IAEA to verify (as a result of access to satellite information or of other developments) that all significant nuclear *plants* in an NPT NNWS had been declared to it.[5] It might then become desirable to amend the model NPT safeguards agreement so as to require NPT NNWS to make an initial declaration of all their nuclear plants as well as all nuclear material and to notify the IAEA of all subsequent construction or imports of nuclear plants. (In fact, even now, there is a lot to be said for such an amendment.)

More serious perhaps are the implications of the Board's failure, so far, to make progress after seven years of discussions in setting up an international plutonium storage system, which the IAEA Statute foresees as an integral and important part of the safeguards system. Unless progress is made fairly soon, one may have to conclude that it is unrealistic to look any longer to the Board for important measures to strengthen the safeguards system.

Approval of individual safeguards agreements

Although the Secretariat has sole responsibility for negotiating agreements, the Director General must submit each agreement to the Board for its approval. The resulting endorsement by the Board of improvements in INFCIRC/66/Rev. 2 agreements has created a valuable series of precedents, despite the ritual statement by countries which did not like the Secretariat's 'innovations', that they were approving the agreement on the understanding that it did not constitute a precedent!

With the exceptions of EURATOM and Japan, all NPT agreements are virtually standard and no significant problem is encountered in negotiating them or securing Board approval.

There are still numerous NPT NNWS that have not yet concluded the required safeguards agreement with the IAEA. While this is regrettable, none of them have any nuclear material or plant that would attract safeguards. The only countries that might be regarded as possible prospects for significant new NPT safeguards agreements are 9 of the 10 non-NPT NNWS that are building or operating nuclear plants (Argentina, Brazil, Chile, Cuba, India, Israel, North Korea, Pakistan and South Africa), but unfortunately the possibility of their adhering to the NPT seems remote in most cases. (If the tenth country in this category, Spain, were to adhere to the NPT, it would be covered by a full-scope variant of the existing IAEA–EURATOM agreement.)

The demand for INFCIRC/66/Rev. 2 agreements is also diminishing, chiefly because few if any new orders for nuclear plants are at present in prospect in the main non-NPT NNWS. The Brazilian/West German supply agreement can provide all the nuclear hardware that Brazil could absorb during this century. No orders are expected in the near future from Argentina, Cuba, Israel or South Africa. There is a slight possibility that India and Pakistan will each order a nuclear power plant from abroad. But the only expanding or new nuclear power programmes in the Third World are in NPT countries—South Korea, Taiwan[6] and perhaps Egypt and Turkey. Of course there is always the possibility that some, not yet identified, non-NPT country will enter the market for a nuclear plant. For instance, Algeria has considered importing a research reactor. Such meagre prospects would not justify the effort of revising INFCIRC/66.

A more interesting project might emerge as a result of developments in Argentina. For several years there were desultory discussions with the previous military government for the conclusion of a full-scope safeguards agreement under the Treaty of Tlatelolco. They did not get very far, chiefly because Argentina insisted on retaining the option of using safeguarded nuclear material (of local origin) to make a 'peaceful' nuclear explosive, which it considered was permissible under the Treaty of Tlatelolco. It was made clear that Argentina would not ratify the Treaty and bring it into force until the contents of the safeguards agreement were settled. The IAEA had already negotiated safeguards agreements, under the Treaty of Tlatelolco *alone*, with Colombia and Panama as well as several agreements under *both* the NPT and the Tlatelolco Treaties with other states parties to both treaties. Argentina flatly rejected the idea of using these agreements as a model for its own, maintaining that they were no more than slightly adapted copies of the standard NPT model and took little account of the singularities of Tlatelolco. The Argentinians came forward with a text of their own which was equally unacceptable to the IAEA.[7]

If the civilian government is ready to modify Argentina's attachment to peaceful nuclear explosions (PNEs)—which have long since ceased to have any practical meaning—a way may be found out of the impasse. And if it were possible to clear the way for Argentinian ratification of the Treaty of Tlatelolco without compromising the principle that no IAEA safeguarded material may be used in any kind of nuclear explosive, it would be a major step forward, not only for Argentina and Latin America but for the prospects for non-proliferation throughout the world. Argentinian ratification would have much impact on Brazil and Chile, both of which have already ratified the Treaty but have refrained from taking the final step needed to bring the Treaty into force for themselves. If these three leading Latin American countries came into the fold, Latin America would become the world's first major region bound by Treaty to outlaw all nuclear weapons and nuclear explosives. It is true that there would still be one important absentee, Cuba, but there is little prospect that Cuba would turn to the manufacture of nuclear explosives.[8]

As indicated, it is improbable that the Board would take any action to draft a model Tlatelolco Treaty safeguards agreement to serve as a basis for negotiation with Argentina, Brazil, Chile or any other Latin American country that has not yet accepted full-scope safeguards (a number of smaller Latin American states have ratified the Treaty of Tlatelolco and sometimes also the NPT, but have not yet concluded the required safeguards agreement with the IAEA). If progress were to be made on such a model agreement it would have to be in negotiations between the Secretariat and the governments concerned.[9]

A similar 'delegation of responsibility' to the Secretariat might be needed if progress were to be made towards a Middle East nuclear weapon-free zone. It has already been shown that the standard NPT safeguards agreement and standard IAEA safeguards do not give sufficient confidence to some of the states chiefly concerned[10] about the purely peaceful character of their neighbours' nuclear activities. Special arrangements might have to be made to supplement IAEA safeguards such as 'challenge' inspections, as well as for reinforced sanctions and for the selection of inspectors. Most of these matters would probably fall outside the scope of IAEA safeguards but some might affect the nature and scope of the agreements to be concluded with the states concerned or with the organization set up to oversee a zonal agreement.

Expanding the coverage of INFCIRC/66/Rev. 2 agreements

The INFCIRC/66/Rev. 2 agreements approved in recent years are adequate as far as they go. The problem is that they do not go far enough, that the obligations they impose leave the door open to construct unsafeguarded facilities, a door through which Israel, India, South Africa and Pakistan have long since passed (the first two before INFCIRC/66 and its extensions existed).

Over time it has been possible to extend the scope of INFCIRC/66/Rev. 2 agreements. The principle is now well established that not only the safeguarded plant or fuel but everything derived from it must come under safeguards—all other plants based on the same design as the safeguarded plant and, in some cases, on similar technology and all succeeding generations of fissile material.[11] All nuclear material that passes through a safeguarded plant is likewise thereafter safeguarded for all succeeding generations.[12] If safeguarded heavy water or a safeguarded major plant component is introduced into a plant, the plant itself comes under permanent safeguards.[13] Many roads to the acquisition of unsafe-guarded plant or material left open by earlier INFCIRC/66/Rev. 2 agreements have thus been blocked. But in the absence of a formal undertaking by the government to accept full-scope safeguards it is impossible to block them all.

There is one way in which the IAEA could attempt to force the issue. The Board could declare that it was no longer prepared to approve any except full-scope safeguards agreements.[14] But there is no prospect of such a declaration. It would arguably conflict with the IAEA Statute, but even if it did not there is no possibility that the leading supplier states, let alone the importers, would agree to it.

In practice, therefore, the chances for mandatory full-scope safeguards lie in the hands of the suppliers and not of the IAEA, but there is no consensus on this point among the countries concerned.

The following is a brief review of the Board's other safeguards roles under the Statute of the IAEA.[15]

The safeguards budget

Under the Statute the Board submits the budget of the IAEA to the General Conference for approval. If the General Conference does not agree with the estimates, it may not change them but must return the budget to the Board with its recommendations.

In practice of course it is the Director General and his staff who draft the budget and submit it to the budgetary committee of the Board, which invariably recommends some cuts when it transmits the document to the Board. After approval by the latter, the Director General transmits the budget to the General Conference where he and his staff (and not the Board) defend it.

So far the General Conference has accepted unchanged all the 28 annual budgets recommended by the Board. The Board, for its part, has approved every increase in the safeguards budget formally recommended by the Director General (although in a few cases he has had to reduce his preliminary proposals).

Part of the price that the proponents of safeguards have had to pay for the large growth in the safeguards budget has been a comparable increase in the IAEA's technical aid so as to maintain, in the words of many Third World delegates, "a balance between promotion and regulation". Another part of the price has been to divide the budget[16] into two parts and to freeze the contributions of developing countries to the safeguards part at about US$473 000 or one-seventieth of the total. While this has not prevented *pro forma* complaints by some developing countries about the annual increases in the safeguards budget it has put an end to any real opposition. The freeze has been extended until 1986 and there has been some discussion of new formulas.

Future prospects of adequate financing are good although if the size of the Board continues to grow the price to be paid in development-oriented programmes may go higher.

The Board's role if an agreement is violated

The sanctions that the Board could impose if a safeguards agreement were violated are fully analysed in Part II.[17]

In considering whether a state was in breach of its obligations the Board would be exercising a semi-judicial function. For states to have full confidence that safeguards agreements will be fairly administered the Board should enjoy a reputation for impartiality and for strictly respecting the IAEA's own basic law, namely its Statute. There have been a few lapses in the past. For instance, the replacement of South Africa by Egypt on the Board in 1977 was hardly consistent with the statutory requirement that the Board must designate the member state in Africa "most advanced in the technology of atomic energy including the production of source material" and it led to a division of the Board on political lines. The procedure followed by the Board in deciding to halt technical assistance to Israel was also legally questionable.

The Board is becoming more political and any further expansion of its membership is not likely to reverse this trend. If the need should ever arise it might become increasingly difficult to obtain a finding of non-compliance against a member of a large bloc—or too easy to do so in the case of an isolated, unpopular country.

This risk should not be overstated. On the whole, the Board's record over 28 years has been good, as good as could realistically be expected in view of the powerful political winds that blow through all UN organizations. And although Pakistan is one of the leaders of the G-77 in the IAEA, Board members from all blocs including the G-77 supported the Director General when he warned the Board on several occasions that the IAEA would not be able to give assurances against diversion until Pakistan agreed to additional safeguards measures, and thereby implicitly asked the Board to put some pressure on Pakistan.

Some further observations are relevant. The first is that the Board has never had occasion to invoke sanctions and perhaps it never will; the matter may remain academic. Second, if the Board were to make a partisan finding against any country such a finding might damage the Board more than the 'convicted' state. Nevertheless, actions of dubious legality against Israel and South Africa do not improve the prospects of bringing them into the non-proliferation regime and give arguments to the opponents of the NPT in those countries. And it is particularly important for the Third World's perception of the extent to which safeguards serve its interests that Israel and South Africa be brought fully into this regime.[18]

III. The role of other bodies

Most of the energies of the IAEA's General Conference, which normally completes its work in the unusually short time of one week, are taken up by a

'General Debate', which is not a debate at all but a series of 50 or more statements by delegates of their governments' nuclear achievements, their views on the IAEA's programme and budget (including safeguards), and on topical political issues. The General Conference's powers of decision in regard to safeguards are confined, as already shown, to approving the annual budget (or sending it back to the Board), and approving the scale of contributions of member states to the budget, including a separate special scale for safeguards costs.

The IAEA submits its annual report to the UN General Assembly, where it is presented by the Director General. The Assembly also discusses in its First (Disarmament) Committee those parts of the report that deal with safeguards and thus have a bearing on international security. The Assembly has fallen into the habit of adopting a lengthy resolution on the IAEA's annual report. The resolution is traditionally adopted by consensus and it therefore skirts around any controversial issues.

Since the Third World has an even more commanding majority in the UN General Assembly than in the General Conference of the IAEA, the G-77 has occasionally used the Assembly to launch political initiatives, such as the proposed UN conference on promotion of international co-operation on the peaceful uses of nuclear energy,[19] which would have less chance of being approved by the IAEA's governing bodies.

IV. The future of the Board

Of the uncertainties that lie ahead for IAEA safeguards one of the greatest is that of the future evolution of the Board.

Since the decolonization of the 1950s the executive bodies of UN organizations have moved in one direction only—towards greater and greater representation of the Third World. This has been accomplished by a series of sizeable increases in the number of countries serving in the executive bodies. Some UN agencies, like the FAO and Unesco, are now run mainly by the G-77 to serve its economic, social or political interests; its pressure in this direction being curbed only by the fact that the budgets of the agencies are still largely paid for by the industrialized countries, which might withdraw if they feel unfairly exploited.

If the size and composition of the IAEA Board change again in the future (and sooner or later they are likely to) it must be assumed that it will go in the same direction and that the present more or less equal balance will be tilted even further towards the G-77.

As noted above, the G-77's attempts since 1977 to give additional seats on the Board to Africa and the Middle East have so far not been successful. First, because the G-77 itself has not been able to agree on an amendment that would be acceptable to all developing regions and, second, because the Socialist and Western industrialized countries have jointly set their faces against any change.

The G-77 is today almost in reach of the two-thirds majority needed to adopt an amendment in the General Conference. But to enter into force the amendment would have to be formally ratified by two-thirds of the IAEA's 112 members, a much longer and more uncertain process. This probably means that in order to succeed any amendment would have to have the support of a sizeable segment of industrial member states.[20]

The new actor on the scene is the People's Republic of China, which became a member of the IAEA in January 1984. It is generally agreed that China must have a permanent (so-called designated) seat on the Board, but this can only be arranged by replacing or changing the status of one of the present 'permanent' members or, in the long run, by changing the Statute. China's entry is therefore precipitating an amendment of the Statute.[21]

Senior Chinese officials have indicated that there has been a considerable evolution since Mao Zedong expressed his outspoken dislike of the NPT, that China is now opposed to any further proliferation and will not do anything to promote it. But it remains to be seen how this changed attitude translates into the practical politics of the IAEA.

What would the impact be on safeguards if the G-77 were to gain control of the Board? This depends upon how it perceives that the IAEA can best serve its interests. Obviously the 'North' fears that safeguards would be down-graded and development aid or development-oriented activities expanded at the cost of safeguards. This fear is strengthened by the position taken in the past by many of the leading G-77 spokesmen, by the apparent 'North–South' polarization of views in several IAEA forums, by the attempts made by a group of Third World countries to bring pressure on the IAEA through the forthcoming UNPICPUNE Conference (and through the Third NPT Review Conference), at which they will ventilate their aspirations and grievances about the policies of the supplier states and about developments in the IAEA.

But, as previously mentioned, the matter is much more complicated than 'bloc' positions suggest and under the surface there is a wide divergence of Third World views. Many Third World initiatives such as the proposed United Nations Conference have been little more than reactions against United States nuclear export policy and against the 'Guidelines' of the Suppliers' Group. Unfortunately that group consisted exclusively of industrialized countries and tended to identify safeguards as a 'Northern' interest in the 'North–South dialogue'.

Moreover, Third World perceptions may well be changing. Much of the bloom has come off the nuclear peach in recent years and some of the enthusiasm for holding the UNPICPUNE Conference seems to have waned. It was originally planned for 1983 but will now not be held before 1986.

The Third World's perceptions of the IAEA are examined later in more detail. In the meantime, note may be taken of some of the consequences of present trends. The less the Board is able to launch bold initiatives of the kind it undertook in the late 1960s and early 1970s, when it produced two entire safeguards systems in a span of five years, the more will responsibility devolve upon the Secretariat and its advisory bodies, or on states and groupings of states outside the framework of the IAEA. The latter tendency is reflected in the work of the London 'Suppliers' Club', the US Nuclear Non-Proliferation Act, the International Nuclear Fuel Cycle Evaluation and (in reaction against the first two) the proposed United Nations Conference—all of which took shape or will take shape under non-IAEA auspices.

The tendency of the Secretariat to take initiatives in matters of policy that were once the province of the Board has already been evident for some time in the negotiation of safeguards agreements and, to an even greater extent, in the development and refinement of safeguards philosophy, approaches and practices. This is a natural consequence of the evolution since 1970, which gradually made the IAEA Secretariat the world's most experienced and authoritative body in the art of applying safeguards, but it has been hastened by the growing immobility of the Board.

The Secretariat operates within strictly defined boundaries. It must work within the framework of the two safeguards systems (or at least without formally amending either document), and its main initiatives only bear fruit if they are ratified by the Board. Nevertheless, the choice of key officials in the Secretariat is vitally important. The Secretariat did most of the groundwork for the 1965 and 1970 safeguards systems. It is solely responsible for negotiating safeguards agreements. It normally has sole responsibility for negotiating *and concluding* subsidiary arrangements and facility attachments (which are not submitted to the Board). Under the very broad (and not always clear-cut) guidance of the Board and of SAGSI, the Secretariat alone bears the burden of transforming the safeguards documents into a complex and generally effective operation for safeguarding the nuclear industries of most NNWS.

Notes and references

1 Of the remaining five developing members having nuclear power programmes, four (Egypt, South Korea, Mexico and the Philippines) are parties to the NPT and Mexico was the originator of and still is the chief force behind the Tlatelolco Treaty. The fifth, Cuba, tends to be reticent on safeguards issues.

2 The West European countries recently agreed to rotate the seat held by Italy so as to give a turn to other West European countries at least as far advanced as Italy in nuclear matters.

3 Although India (with Soviet and other support) was able to water down and weaken the first safeguards 'document' or system (INFCIRC/26), later replaced by INFCIRC/66 and the Inspectors' Document GC(V)INF/39, Annex. Some of the early defects have persisted right through, even into INFCIRC/153.

4 In many technical assistance projects insistence on this clause can verge on the absurd. Almost all IAEA technical assistance relates to the use of nuclear science techniques in medicine, hydrology and especially, agriculture, and could not possibly be used to make nuclear explosives. But the same countries that opposed the NPT language had been quite prepared to give the earlier version of the pledge, i.e., not to use the help to serve any military purpose, which is hardly less absurd. More seriously, technical

assistance can help in the transfer of quite sensitive unsafeguarded technology and has probably done so in the past; for instance, help in developing reprocessing capacity may have been provided unwittingly under the rubric of "assistance in nuclear waste disposal".

5   As, note, satellite monitoring might not detect small plants.

6   Taiwan's ratification of the NPT (as the 'Republic of China') was accepted by the USA, one of the three depositaries of the NPT (the others are the USSR and the UK).

7   For instance, it permitted the withdrawal of safeguarded material for use in PNEs, and it foresaw the type of IAEA 'observation' of PNEs referred to in Article 18 of the Tlatelolco Treaty. This is quite the opposite of the "appropriate international observation" foreseen in Article V of the NPT, and subsequently elaborated by the IAEA Board of Governors. Under the concept approved by the IAEA Board the aim of "appropriate international observation" is to ensure that there is no significant transfer of nuclear explosive technology from the NWS that carries out the PNE to the NNWS in which the PNE is carried out. Metaphorically speaking, the international observers keep an eye on the NNWS rather than on the PNE.

8   The USSR has provided Cuba with a research and two power reactors, all under IAEA safeguards. It is assumed (but not yet certain) that the normal Soviet policy applies to these transactions—that the spent fuel and its plutonium will be returned to the USSR. Cuba affirms that it will not ratify the NPT or the Treaty of Tlatelolco while the USA retains the Guantanamo base, but it is not clear how firm this position would be if Cuba became the only abstainer.

9   The Director General of the IAEA held some exploratory discussions during a visit to Argentina in late 1983, shortly after the change of government.

10 Iran as well as Israel was reported to have attacked the Iraqi nuclear research centre and Iran has claimed that Iraqi planes attacked the uncompleted nuclear power plant at Bushehr. Iraq and Iran are both parties to the NPT, Israel is not.

11 The agreements are therefore potentially of infinite duration (while states have the right to withdraw from the NPT under Article X.1). The question of how long the NPT will be extended by the 1995 Conference is also moot.

12 The Secretariat once attempted but failed to negotiate the converse principle that once safeguarded nuclear material passed through a plant—e.g., an unsafeguarded reprocessing plant—that plant would henceforth fall under permanent safeguards. There were too many precedents in the opposite sense.

13 Heavy water is thus treated as a major plant component.

14 This position could also be taken by the NPT members: a possible though not accepted interpretation of Article III.2 of the NPT is that it requires full-scope safeguards on all nuclear activities of the importing country (and not merely on the imported items and its products)—the latter is the interpretation reflected, for instance, in the London Guidelines.

15 The Board also approves the appointment of inspectors (after looking at their curricula vitae) and considers the SIR, special safeguards reports and the safeguards part of the IAEA's statutory annual report, and thereby gives general policy guidance. Except for the annual report, these functions are not however statutory requirements.

16 The 'regular' or assessed budget. There is also a voluntary (misleadingly named 'operational') budget chiefly used to pay for technical assistance.

17 Under INFCIRC/66 safeguards agreements—following the language of the Statute—the Board may impose the statutory sanctions for unrectified non-compliance

with any part of the agreement—not only for violation of safeguards. The model NPT safeguards agreement limits the application of sanctions to circumstances relating to diversion, i.e., to a possible breach of the state's basic undertaking not to divert nuclear material. As we have seen, the model NPT safeguards agreement does not, however, require that the diversion be proved (which might be very difficult). The Board simply has to determine that the IAEA is not able to verify that no diversion has taken place—see Part II.

18 Although the UN family and most states no longer recognize Taiwan as a state, it ratified the NPT (while it was still recognized by the USA), has a large, fully-safeguarded nuclear power programme and may also be vulnerable to unfair decisions.

19 The proposed Conference has the unwieldy acronym UNPICPUNE (United Nations Conference for the Promotion of International Cooperation in the Peaceful Uses of Nuclear Energy). For different reasons neither the states promoting the conference nor the IAEA Secretariat wanted it under IAEA auspices; the first because of the still strong voice of the suppliers and the superpowers in Vienna, the second because it (the Secretariat) did not wish the IAEA to have responsibility for an avowedly political conference.

20 Although the amendment to increase the size of the Board from 25 to 34 was supported at the General Conference by the Western industrial states (Western Europe, the USA, Canada, Japan, Australia, New Zealand) as well as by the developing member states it still took two and a half years to gain a sufficient number of ratifications to bring it into force. The negative attitude of the Socialist countries—nine in all—was the chief cause of the delay.

21 Each year the Board designates the countries "most advanced in the technology of atomic energy including the production of source materials" to sit on the Board for the following year. Nine are designated without regard to geographical distribution, the remainder (three up to 1984) are designated in such a way as to ensure that all major regions are represented in the Board by designated members. Although the designations are for one year only they have, with a few exceptions, become permanent seats. In June 1984 the Board designated China a member, thereby increasing the number of designated seats to 13, without amending the Statute. There are some doubts about the legality of this action. For complex reasons it could only be achieved in accordance with the Statute by 'demoting' India from the 'top' nine, 'down' to the group of regional members, but the Chairman of the Board explicitly stated that there had been no change in the status of any designated state. At the same time the Board recommended a Statute amendment to increase the 9 'top' seats to 10.

Chapter 13. Trigger lists, the London Club and INFCE

I. Export controls—the Trigger List

Several developments outside the IAEA are shown to have had an impact on IAEA safeguards. The most important in recent years have been two far-reaching attempts to control nuclear exports, the London or Suppliers' Guidelines of 1977 and the US Nuclear Non-Proliferation Act (NNPA) of 1978 as well as international reaction to the Guidelines and the policies inspiring the NNPA.

But the first successful step towards multinational agreement on detailed nuclear export controls was spurred by the NPT itself.

Under Article III.2 of the NPT, each state party:

> ... undertakes not to provide: (*a*) source or special fissionable material, or (*b*) equipment or material especially designed or prepared for the processing, use or production of special fissionable material, to any non-nuclear-weapon State for peaceful purposes, unless the source or special fissionable material shall be subject to the safeguards required by this Article.[1]

Source and special fissionable material are defined in the IAEA's Statute. For NPT countries to know on what other items they should apply export controls it was necessary to define more amply what was meant by the "equipment or material especially designed or prepared for the processing, use or production of special fissionable material" that should not be exported to a NNWS except under safeguards. The definition is important. In many cases the exporting country provides only some key components of the plant, the rest being manufactured locally. The local manufacturers' share tends to grow in most importing countries. But if the key components are under safeguards the entire plant comes permanently under safeguards too.

A committee of most of the main suppliers, under the chairmanship of Professor Claude Zangger of Switzerland, met in the early 1970s to draw up a 'Trigger List' of the materials (other than source and special fissionable material), equipment and components that would require the application of safeguards, and completed its task in July 1974.[2] In August 1974, 10 of the leading NPT countries informed the IAEA of the steps they were taking to carry out their obligations under Article III.2 of the NPT. By the same letter they formally communicated to the IAEA copies of the Zangger Trigger List, which they had agreed to apply to their nuclear exports, reserving the right to add to it.[3]

But events were taking place that raised doubts as to whether the export regime foreseen in Article III.2 of the NPT would be adequate to prevent further proliferation. Among the developments that gave concern was the Indian test of 18 May 1974 and French and West German negotiations to export reprocessing plants and technology to Pakistan, South Korea and Brazil (as well as West German enrichment plant and technology to Brazil). All these plants—and for the first time the technologies themselves—were to be under IAEA safeguards, but doubts were growing about the ability of those safeguards to give 'timely warning' of diversion from plants where large amounts of separated plutonium or highly enriched uranium were available. Moreover the countries to which the plants would be sent were causing concern. Brazil and Pakistan were not parties to the NPT. In the wake of the Indian explosion, but suspecting India's nuclear plans, Prime Minister Bhutto had said Pakistanis would "eat grass", if necessary, to catch up with India. South Korea, although an NPT party, was also obviously a sensitive place in which to build a plant capable of making nuclear weapon-usable material. At the same time, it was becoming clear that South Africa would be able to make highly enriched uranium from a process which owed some debt to West German technology. As already noted, because of US pressure and second thoughts in Paris, the Franco–Pakistani agreement went off at half-cock. For similar reasons the South Korean sale was cancelled. The USA failed, however, to persuade FR Germany to drop its sales of sensitive plant to Brazil.

II. The London (Suppliers') Guidelines

Beneath these events, deeper changes were taking place. Chief among them was the oil crisis which, it was expected, would lead to a rapid spread of nuclear energy especially in the Third World and to politically tense or unstable areas (it did not), the erosion of the US commanding position as a nuclear supplier and, more profoundly, of its ability to determine the course of international events, as well as the deepening North–South divisions. All in all the USA considered it essential to put stronger brakes on nuclear exports, expecially to 'unstable' countries.

On Dr Kissinger's proposal the London Suppliers' Club began in 1975 to seek agreement on more stringent controls. In 1978 the agreement the suppliers had reached was made public. It consisted of a set of Guidelines for Nuclear Transfers (attached as Appendix VIII) rather than a formal agreement. The Guidelines incorporated the Zangger Trigger List (adding heavy water and heavy water production plants to the items that should trigger safeguards) and spelled out in greater detail how the list would be applied. It was agreed that the duration and coverage of safeguards should conform to the Board's decision of 1973 (GOV/1621, see Appendix VI).

The main new features of the Guidelines (which only apply to exports to NNWS) were that: (*a*) safeguards should cover technology and plants replicated by the importing country as well as items of hardware already on the Trigger List; (*b*) suppliers should "exercise restraint" in the transfer of sensitive technology, plants and weapon-usable materials ('sensitive technology' covered enrichment reprocessing and, apparently, heavy water production); (*c*) supplier nation consent should be required before any supplied enrichment plant (or one based on supplied technology) was designed or operated to produce uranium enriched to more than 20 per cent; (*d*) suppliers should endeavour to obtain agreement that their consent would be sought before supplied material or material from supplied facilities was reprocessed (the so-called "prior consent" clause); (*e*) supplier's consent should be required before re-export of sensitive plant or material; (*f*) effective physical protection (against theft, sabotage, etc.) would be required for all Trigger List items; and (*g*) suppliers should regularly consult with each other about the implementation of the Guidelines and should promptly consult if safeguards were breached or a nuclear test took place.

The Guidelines were intended not only to put a brake on the transfer of sensitive technologies but also to prevent the erosion of safeguards by unregulated competition. Their main achievement was to bring a degree of order and consensus among suppliers, to ensure relatively uniform minimum standards and uniform interpretation of NPT obligations and to bring France into the 'Club', even though it was not an NPT party.

Despite the adverse reactions they provoked, particularly in the Third World, which were voiced at length at the second NPT Review Conference in 1980, the Guidelines are not very restrictive. They place no embargo[4] on the export of the technologies that can be directly used to make nuclear explosives, enrichment and reprocessing. They do not require full-scope safeguards in the importing country as a condition of supply.

III. The US Nuclear Non-Proliferation Act (NNPA)

The Guidelines did not go far enough for President Carter's Administration or for the US Congress. In 1978 the Congress passed the Nuclear Non-Proliferation Act which, among other matters required (*a*) *de facto*[5] full-scope safeguards as a condition for US supplies; (*b*) US prior consent to reprocessing, in all cases including the EEC countries (most US supply agreements already required such prior consent; that with the EEC did not); (*c*) a cut-off of US military and economic aid to any country that built or received a reprocessing plant under less than full-scope safeguards (Symington Amendment); and (*d*) the renegotiation of all existing US supply agreements. At the same time the Carter Administration made it clear that it would like to put a stop to civilian reprocessing everywhere (thus implying that "prior consent" to reprocessing would be hard to obtain). As an indication of its intentions and to set a good example the US government effectively halted the construction of the only civilian reprocessing plant in the USA (the Barnwell plant), and the Congress eventually cut off funds for the US demonstration breeder reactor at Clinch River.

The NNPA and the Carter policy were welcomed by a few like-minded suppliers but provoked as hostile a reaction in France, Japan, FR Germany, the UK and Switzerland as they did in the Third World. As a result, the USA has since considerably modified its policy without, however, amending the NNPA. Many supply agreements have been renegotiated but the main one with the Common Market has not. The USA has given prior consent to the reprocessing of Japanese fuel of US origin and has made it possible for a recently completed first Japanese reprocessing plant at Tokai Mura to begin operating. It has also given its prior consent in several other cases and, under President Reagan, has made it clear that it will do so on a 'programmatic' rather than a case-by-case basis for countries whose nuclear intentions it has confidence in.

IV. INFCE

In 1977 President Carter took the initiative of launching a full-scale International Fuel Cycle Evaluation (INFCE). The intention was in part to calm the concern raised by his Administration's nuclear policies but it was also hoped that INFCE would reveal a less 'proliferation-prone' fuel cycle than that which the nuclear energy industry had planned since the 1950s (under which the present generation of thermal reactors will be succeeded by the 60 times more energy-efficient breeder, burning a mixture of uranium and plutonium and producing more plutonium than it burns).

INFCE turned into a two-year discussion of the technical, economic and institutional aspects of nuclear trade and technology. It was unable to identify any particular fuel cycle as less proliferation prone. "No single judgement can be made about risks of diversion from different fuel cycles that is valid both now and in the future" is how the INFCE Summary Report rather opaquely put it.[6]

INFCE produced a vast amount of data and its findings take up eight volumes. However, the projections it made about the growth of the nuclear industry, the demand for uranium, the relatively early exhaustion of cheaper uranium reserves (and hence the early need for breeder reactors and for reprocessing) tended to reflect the hopes and aspirations of the nuclear community and soon proved unrealistic. While INFCE debated, the nuclear industry was slumping. It has continued to slump since then, and uranium demand has followed it down. Mining output has declined while large new reserves of uranium have been discovered in Australia and Canada. As the costs of fresh fuel fell those of recovering plutonium (by reprocessing) have risen sharply.

As noted earlier, these trends and events have pushed back the large-scale commercial use of the breeder reactor well into the first quarter of the 21st century. They have thus largely eroded the commercial justification for reprocessing. They have not prevented France, the UK, FR Germany and Japan, as well as the USSR, from going ahead with their breeder demonstration programmes. But they have probably encouraged closer and less duplicatory West European co-operation in breeder research and development. They have also taken much of the brightness out of the present commercial breeder picture. Only one commercial breeder is under construction in the West at this time, the Super-Phénix in France which is expected to begin commercial operation in August 1985.[7] Only one commercial reprocessing plant for the standard reactor fuel (light water fuel) is in operation, also in France, at La Hague.

Contrary, perhaps, to the expectations of the Carter Administration INFCE thus had little effect on IAEA safeguards. It did, however, succeed in taking a good deal of the heat out of the controversies which the US Administration's policies had generated.

As already mentioned, one of the first reactions to those policies and to the London Guidelines was the idea, originally proposed at the General Assembly by Yugoslavia and Pakistan, of a UN Conference to discuss the political aspects of international co-operation in the peaceful uses of nuclear energy—UNPICPUNE.

V. *Non-proliferation through co-operation* versus *non-proliferation through denial*

In discussions of supply policies the advocates of the 'softer' line point to the fact that both the very restrictive 1948 UN Macmahon Act, and President Carter's approach in the later 1970s, failed to stop proliferation. They argue that more can be gained through a co-operative policy and from the resulting ability of the supplier to exercise a moderating influence on the authorities of the country with which it has established mutually beneficial links. This approach, which is attractive to those who see science as a blessing to be shared, inspired much of the 'Atoms for Peace' policy of the 1950s and early 1960s. Unfortunately, as we have seen, the supplying countries, despite close technical or political relationships, were unable to prevent the construction of unsafeguarded sensitive plants in four or five NNWS—Argentina, India, Pakistan, South Africa (in the case of Israel, the supplying country made no attempt to arrange for safeguards)—or to prevent the Indian nuclear test of 1974.

No one gainsays the fact that 'policies of denial' have marked disadvantages or that their effectiveness is eroded by time. As we have seen, however, even the proponents of 'softer' supply policies have become stricter as the years passed. In the 1950s and early 1960s some supplies were made without any safeguards at all. In fact some importing NNWS, such as India, then regarded imposition of any IAEA safeguards on the item supplied as a 'policy of denial'. Today IAEA safeguards are the minimum norm and the 'soft' policy suppliers (France and FR Germany as well as some other West European countries) have agreed to further restrictions in the London Guidelines. The first two countries have gone even further in deciding not to export reprocessing plants "for the time being"—which has lasted nine years—and would probably not export enrichment plants except to 'reliable' NPT NNWS. In short, the meaning of a 'policy of denial' has changed with time and the differences between the Western supplying states have diminished *in practice* to the point where the only significant matters at issue today are whether or not to require full-scope safeguards as a condition of supply (and, in the case of the USA, the requirement that US consent be obtained before reprocessing, etc.) and how to strengthen the *de facto* embargo on the export of sensitive technologies. These matters will be examined in the next chapter.

VI. Physical protection

'Physical protection' is the term used to describe the measures that governments take to protect nuclear plants and materials against criminal acts: sabotage, hijacking, terrorist attack, forcible seizure or theft.

As in the case of nuclear safety it is governments (and not the IAEA) that can and must take responsibility for measures of physical protection. However, the IAEA has given guidance to governments on the minimum requirements for protecting various types of nuclear plant and material. This guidance reflects the consensus of national experts from the countries with most experience in dealing with the problem.

Obviously the more dangerous the plant or material, the more strict and elaborate must be the measures taken to protect it. Despite media reports to the contrary, putting together a nuclear weapon, even with highly enriched uranium or plutonium at hand, is no easy matter; if it were the world would be even more dangerous than it is already. But this is not a risk with which a responsible government would take any chances. And even if the nuclear material cannot be easily used to make an explosive, the prospect of highly radioactive material falling into the wrong hands is one that the authorities will do their best to guard against.

The protective measures themselves consist of the normal means of guarding dangerous and valuable material such as armed guards, alarm systems, physical barriers such as fences and walls as well as specially designed containers. At this point the requirements of physical protection, safety and safeguards may converge. Adequate containment of a nuclear plant helps to make both clandestine diversion and theft or seizure more difficult. Robust containers for spent fuel are not only essential for safety, they also hinder any tampering with the fuel. The system that signals a breach of containment may be indicating a criminal act.

The risk of such acts, especially hijacking, is clearly higher when nuclear material is being transported during international transport. It is desirable that there should be agreed and uniform rules about the measures that governments will take when nuclear material passes through their territories or is flown from one country to another. Such rules should also define the responsibilities of each government concerned and the arrangements for covering stolen material and for extraditing hijackers.

After two years of preparatory work at the IAEA, a number of the most interested governments reached agreement on an International Convention on the Physical Protection of Nuclear Material in 1979–80. By 31 December 1984, 38 states and EURATOM had signed the Convention, but only 10 states had ratified it. The Convention will enter into force after 21 ratifications. This would happen automatically once EURATOM and its members ratified.

The 1977 London Suppliers' Guidelines also provide that all items on the Trigger List, in other words, all supplies that prompt the application of safeguards, should be placed under effective physical protection "taking account of international recommendations" (i.e., those of the IAEA) and that there should be agreement between the supplier and the recipient states on the level of protection to be applied. Several recent IAEA safeguards agreements have also required the state or states concerned to apply the IAEA's own guidelines as a minimum to the items being safeguarded.

In these various ways good progress is being made in reaching world-wide agreement on the measures that should be taken to protect nuclear materials. These measures are most effective if the would-be thief or terrorist does not know in advance precisely what they are, in short, if there is a degree of secrecy. They are not the type of activity that can be verified or monitored by an international organization. The IAEA's role is thus essentially limited to that of giving guidance to governments and encouraging them to follow such guidance and to ratify the Convention.

Notes and references

1 NPT Treaty, Article III.2 (see Appendix IX).
2 The work of the Zangger committee and the events leading up to it are described more fully by Ben Sanders in SIPRI, *Safeguards Against Nuclear Proliferation* (MIT Press, Cambridge, MA and Almqvist & Wiksell, Stockholm, 1975), pp. 17–19.
3 The Zangger Trigger List is reproduced in IAEA document INFCIRC/209, and SIPRI (note 2), Appendix 1, pp. 61–64.
4 In 1977 France and FR Germany declared that they would not export reprocessing technology "for the time being". There is no such self-denying ordinance on the export of enrichment technology, though none has been exported since the Brazilian–West German agreement (see Walker, W. and Lönnroth, M., *Nuclear Power Struggles: Industrial Competition and Proliferation Control* (Allen & Unwin, London, 1983), p. 148. This chapter owes much to that book).
5 The term "*de facto* full-scope safeguards" is used if all nuclear plant and material in the country concerned happens to be under IAEA safeguards because of a complete mosaic of individual safeguards agreements. "*De jure* full-scope safeguards" are applied if the country has concluded a single comprehensive safeguards agreement covering all present and future nuclear activities (e.g., an NPT or Tlatelolco safeguard agreement).

[6] Library of Congress, *Nuclear Proliferation Factbook*, 96th Congress, 2nd Session (US Government Printing Office, Washington, D.C., 1980), p. 455.

[7] IAEA, *Nuclear Power Reactors in the World, April 1984 Edition* (IAEA, Vienna, 1984), p. 42.

Chapter 14. New institutions

After confidence in the existing NPT regime declined in the mid-1970s there were several suggestions for changing the regime. They ranged from proposals to abolish the IAEA in its present form to less far-reaching concepts for supplementing the present system of safeguards.[1]

I. Abolish the IAEA?

On the face of it a body which seeks both to promote and to regulate a particular technology must suffer from a built-in conflict of interest. Concern about the effects of such a conflict has led many governments to reorganize the national atomic energy authorities they created in the immediate post-war years. In the case of some of the NWS these were set up to manage the production of nuclear weapons. Some governments have taken regulatory (i.e., safety) responsibilities away from the nuclear authority and assigned them to another authority (e.g., the UK, which has assigned them to its factory inspectorate); others have merged the nuclear authority into a body of broader scope dealing with all forms of energy (e.g., the US Energy Research and Development Agency and the Department of Energy).

Is it not time to do the same with the IAEA? Does not its aim of spreading nuclear technology around the world come into direct conflict with that of trying to stop the spread of nuclear weapons?

A priori the case may seem incontrovertible. But practical considerations point the other way.

It might be enough to say, correctly, that a reallocation of *international* responsibilities for nuclear energy and nuclear safeguards is politically unthinkable today and likely to remain so. But such a reallocation has been proposed by persons and groups who are expert in international affairs and concerned about effective safeguards. It deserves serious examination.

First, the analogy between the IAEA and national nuclear authorities may mislead.

The 'promotional' work of the IAEA is in fact quite different from that of national nuclear energy bodies. The IAEA has neither the mandate, nor the staff, nor the financial resources which national bodies deploy in large-scale research and development designed to promote the use of nuclear power.

Most of the IAEA's 'promotional' aid to the Third World relates to ingenious by-products of the main use of nuclear energy. These are isotope and radiation techniques applied in medical and agricultural research and development, medical diagnosis and treatment, plant breeding, food irradiation, controlling insect pests, and so on. They have nothing to do with proliferation.

The difference between national and international nuclear authorities is reflected in the IAEA's internal structure. Of its 15 technical divisional units, seven deal with safeguards, two with nuclear safety and waste management, two with isotope applications and only one with nuclear power and reactors.[2] As for nuclear power itself, the IAEA's aid to developing countries is now chiefly directed to safety and waste management.

In fact, the IAEA contends that the dichotomy between 'promotion' and 'regulation' is a false one in the international context and that effective safeguards (as well as adequate nuclear safety and waste management) are pre-conditions for the further spread and growth of nuclear power in the countries to which the IAEA gives assistance. In this sense safeguards are also 'promotional'.

Another misleading analogy between national and international nuclear bodies concerns the nature of the regulatory work that each performs. Unlike its national counterpart, an international body cannot legislate safety or non-proliferation and it has no powers to enforce its rules. It must depend upon the freely given co-operation of governments. One reason it has gained this co-operation is that the national nuclear authorities of developing countries have generally looked to the IAEA as their benefactor, as a fount of information, advice and assistance in all branches of nuclear science, responsible for the specialized training of many of their scientists and engineers and as the body to which many of them would turn in the event of a nuclear accident. Even those countries that are most critical of IAEA safeguards maintain collegial relations with other parts of the organization. This scientist-to-scientist relationship has done much to facilitate the acceptance of safeguards and the NPT. It is doubtful whether a purely 'policing' agency would have been able to gain the confidence and co-operation of governments.

If an analogy is to be drawn it should not be between national nuclear energy agencies and the IAEA but rather between the IAEA and other international bodies, such as the International Civil Aviation Organization, to which governments have found it appropriate to assign both regulatory and certain limited promotional functions.

Rather than dismantle the IAEA there is an argument to be made for extending its mandate so as to cover new and renewable sources of energy. There is no world-wide body today which deals specifically with such forms of energy, although one aspect or another is sporadically dealt with by half a dozen agencies.[3] It would simplify the problems of developing countries if there were only a single competent body to turn to for advice and help in their energy programmes. The IAEA already operates an energy data bank covering all sources of energy; it is well-suited by its own technical orientation to take on the extra tasks with a very modest increase in staff and costs. It would also enhance the IAEA's appearance (and practice) as an impartial source of advice on energy matters if it were not confined to nuclear energy. A change in the IAEA's terms of reference would also set a good example for national nuclear energy commissions. Some nuclear commissions in the industrialized countries are already expanding their mandates to cover other 'new' energy sources.

There are also certain options for separating the safeguards operation itself more sharply *within* the IAEA from some of the other IAEA programmes and perhaps better isolating it from unrelated political issues. This separation began in fact when the IAEA decided that the scale of states' contributions to the cost of safeguards should be very different from that towards other expenses. Although this differentiation has not formally been made permanent it seems likely to become so for all practical purposes.

There would be no justification at present for separating the safeguards secretariat from the other services of the IAEA; on the contrary such a separation would result in unprofitable duplication.

It might, however, be desirable to move towards separate and more specialized political control. The options range widely. The most modest would be to establish another standing specialized committee of the Board[4] (the Board already has such a committee to deal with technical assistance, now renamed 'technical co-operation'). Such a committee would be subject to the Board's authority and would report directly to it. Past experience indicates that it would be difficult to restrict membership in any way; in principle the committee would have to be open to any state sitting on the Board. But states could be asked to send safeguards specialists to such a committee and if they complied this would result in a relatively small committee. The body could also serve a useful purpose by providing a forum for expert review of the entire safeguards operation—the annual Safeguards Implementation Report, the appointment of inspectors, the organization of the safeguards department, the approval of agreements, the need for system changes or additions, the safeguards budget, and so on.

The risk is that all members of the Board would elect to sit on the committee and send to it their junior diplomats under the guise of safeguards experts. This would lead to even greater political intrusion into the safeguards operation and would simply cause delay and uncertainty by adding one more hurdle on the track of policy decisions.

At the other end of the spectrum would be the creation of a statutory committee or commission of the Board (or of the IAEA itself), membership being limited to states having a substantial interest in safeguards (e.g., Board members that are operating or building nuclear power plants or are major exporters of nuclear materials). Decision-making authority in all safeguards matters would be delegated by Statute to such a committee. Some technical agencies of the UN family do in fact entrust vital safety questions to statutory committees of this kind, but these committees were foreseen in their constitutions from the start (e.g., the Maritime Safety Committee of the International Maritime Organization in London).

Such a far-reaching separation of authority might also have advantages for the IAEA. It would transfer all responsibility for safeguards to a small committee of truly interested states. It would, however, require such extensive amendment of the IAEA Statute as to make it extremely difficult to achieve today.

The creation of such a committee might conceivably be part of a major North–South 'deal', the other part being substantially to enlarge the Board (divested of its safeguards responsibilities) in such a way as to place it under G-77 control and, at the same time, formally extend the IAEA's mandate to include all advanced or all renewable energy technologies, as well as nuclear fission and fusion energy. The IAEA Director General and Secretariat would thus in effect serve two distinct, differently composed but related governing bodies. An analogy of sorts exists in the World Bank Group in Washington where the same secretariat serves the World Bank itself and the International Development Authority.

II. Multinational fuel cycle centres (MFCC)

There was much interest in the mid-1970s in the concept of a limited number of states pooling their resources in a single centre to provide fuel cycle services. The participation of states (other than the host state) might take the form of contributing funds to capital and running costs, as Italy, Spain and Belgium do to the EURODIF gaseous diffusion plant operated by France to help meet its own needs and those of the other contributors, for enriched nuclear fuel. Or there might be joint planning and pooling of research and development while each of the participating countries builds and operates its own plant as is the case with the URENCO enrichment consortium set up by FR Germany, the Netherlands and the UK. But the most discussed concept was (and still is) that of a multinational or regional reprocessing plant built, owned, managed and staffed by the interested governments and their personnel. The plant might be linked with another to fabricate fuel from the products of the reprocessing plant.

In the second half of the 1970s, the IAEA, with much US encouragement, carried out a detailed study of the concept of a multinational fuel cycle centre of the latter type. The study showed that such an undertaking would have obvious advantages compared with the alternative of a number of smaller, national fuel cycle plants; advantages of cost (economies of scale), safety and of reducing the number of weapon-usable material factories (in fact the concept had its ancestry in the 1945–46 Baruch Plan for international ownership and control of all sensitive nuclear facilities).

Despite these advantages no government (or governments) has come forward with a concrete proposal for such a centre. The complexities of multinationally managing and operating a commercial undertaking may have alarmed the technically advanced countries. In any case they chose to go ahead (if they went ahead at all) with their own separate reprocessing projects. There were initially a few flickers of interest in Western Europe[5] when some of these national projects ran into strong environmentalist opposition but when this opposition was overcome—or when it had succeeded in drastically downgrading the national nuclear power plan, the interest died away.

The countries to which the concept was principally addressed, namely those Third World countries that are perceived to be tempted by the nuclear weapon option, showed no interest at all and went ahead with their own reprocessing and enrichment programmes. And in the USA itself, where the concept had originated, President Carter turned against it on grounds that it would 'legitimize' the production of plutonium.

Aside from considerations of this sort, there is clearly some danger that a centre operated by personnel from all participating governments might hasten rather than retard the spread of the technology concerned. This is to some extent what happened in the 1960s after 13 West European governments had pooled their reprocessing research and development in the Eurochemic plant at Mol in Belgium. The scientists and engineers who worked at Mol doubtless played a part in the subsequent reprocessing projects of FR Germany and Italy and other West European countries.[6]

Although the merits of the multinational fuel cycle centre concept may outweigh its drawbacks, it is probably too late for it to have any significant non-proliferation effects today. Almost all the countries that are (or seem to be) keeping the nuclear weapon option open have by now completed their own reprocessing or enrichment plants (or both) or are at an advanced stage of constructing them (Argentina, Brazil, Israel, South Africa, India and Pakistan). Only in the Far East could such a centre still play a useful non-proliferation role as an alternative to building a reprocessing or enrichment plant in the Republic of Korea or Taiwan. But the political constraints are still sufficiently powerful in these cases to rule out the use of sensitive technology. Moreover in today's market there is little prospect that such a centre would be profitable. Governments do not invest large sums of money simply to promote non-proliferation.

It may still be possible to launch more modest versions of the multinational fuel cycle centre. Thus, growing nuclear co-operation between Argentina and Brazil could conceivably open the way to bilateral commercial ventures in enrichment or reprocessing. But the economic justification for such ventures is very small today and it is of course impossible to reverse those developments as a result of which both countries have already acquired both technologies.

III. Multinational spent fuel centres

As an alternative to multinational reprocessing or storage of separated plutonium the Carter Administration encouraged the idea of multinational spent fuel centres. Most experts regarded the idea as politically unrealistic because of the difficulty of persuading any country to store other countries' spent fuel indefinitely or permanently on its territory. The first few tentative soundings appeared to confirm this view. There was decisive opposition in Cairo when it was learned that Egyptian officials were discussing the possibility of accepting spent fuel from Austria and it is understood that there were similar reactions in Iran (the Austrian nuclear power programme subsequently collapsed, the main technical reason being the difficulties that the government encountered in finding means of spent fuel disposal).

Prospects for this type of project may since have changed. In the West only France has so far succeeded in operating a large commercial plant (at La Hague) for reprocessing light water reactor spent fuel. Another is under construction in the UK (at Sellafield, formerly Windscale). Most countries with nuclear plants in operation are having to store steadily accumulating quantities of unreprocessed spent fuel. It is possible that over long periods of time these stores may present a proliferation hazard as a potential source for plutonium. They also present considerable safety problems and are fairly costly to build and operate. There would be advantages in reducing their number.

One way of doing so would be for suppliers of nuclear reactors and their fuel to offer or to require that the spent fuel be returned to them.

Further encouragement for the idea of multinational spent fuel storage came in January 1984 when it was reported that utilities in FR Germany or Switzerland were negotiating an agreement for the storage of spent fuel in China.

IV. An international nuclear fuel authority

Another proposal of the second half of the 1970s was to create an international nuclear fuel authority (INFA). Its purpose would be to guarantee the supply of nuclear power plant fuel to countries that adhered to the NPT and that also abjured any intention to acquire national reprocessing or enrichment plants.[7] The INFA concept was codified in the 1978 US Nuclear Non-Proliferation Act which asked the President to ''negotiate binding international undertakings'', and which set aside an interim stockpile of US fuel to provide fuel assurances to qualifying states pending the arrival of an INFA.

The INFA failed to materialize, however, perhaps partly because uranium, both natural and enriched, is in over-supply. Moreover, the growing number of suppliers of both commodities now makes it impossible for a single supplier to threaten the disruption of another country's nuclear power programmes (by cutting off fuel) as the USA itself did in 1977–79 in an attempt to discourage the spread of reprocessing.

Even if the idea had borne fruit only a limited number of countries would have been eligible to benefit from it, and most of them have shown no interest in reprocessing or enrichment. The 'eligible' countries would have been Canada (hardly likely to import fuel!), Sweden, Finland, the Philippines, the Republic of Korea, Iran (before its own nuclear power programme collapsed), Egypt (if its nuclear power plan is realized), Yugoslavia and Mexico. All other countries operating or building nuclear power plants would be disqualified either because they do not accept full-scope safeguards or because they were planning or building the proscribed plants (or were members of a group (EURATOM) that was doing so), or were not eligible for political reasons (Eastern Europe).

V. International plutonium storage (IPS)

This concept was intended to animate a dormant provision in the IAEA Statute (Article XX.A.5) which authorizes the IAEA to require the 'deposit' with it of surplus plutonium so as to prevent stockpiling (see Appendix I for the full text of Article XII.A.5 of the IAEA Statute). After eight years of discussion the matter is still under study in the IAEA. Essentially three groups of states have emerged. The strong supporters of the project include Australia, Canada, the Netherlands, Sweden, the UK and the USA. The latter helped to launch it, turned against it during the years of the Carter Administration (again on the grounds that it would 'legitimize' the production of plutonium) and subsequently resumed its support, provided that the controls exercised by the IAEA over the subsequent release of plutonium deposited with it were sufficiently rigorous. The opponents (chiefly Argentina, Yugoslavia, India and Pakistan) probably have no intention of participating in any scheme that would exercise any meaningful control over any plutonium they produce. The stance of the 'middle' group, which includes countries like FR Germany, Japan, and Italy, might be summed as a willingness, albeit reluctant, to accept a minimal scheme. Their attitude was expressed informally in more or less the following terms: the non-NPT countries will not join an IPS, only countries like ours, that have already renounced nuclear weapons, will do so; why should we accept additional obligations and let the IAEA get between us and our own plutonium? The implication was that they would only consider joining if the USA significantly relaxed its export policies and provided that their own plutonium would be promptly released to them as soon as they said they needed it.

At all events the differences between the three groups are so wide as to preclude any immediate hope for a meaningful agreement, that is, an agreement that would put separated plutonium under international custody, that would have the right to question requests for separated plutonium if it considered them unsound, unsafe or suspect, that would verify that released plutonium was used under IAEA safeguards and only for the purposes declared by the country to which it was released and that would also be accepted by the main plutonium producers and users.

In the long term the prospects for an IPS may improve. The situation foreseen in Article XII.A.5 of the IAEA Statute is now beginning to take shape. A number of countries that have nuclear power plants in operation have sent their spent fuel for reprocessing to La Hague in France or Sellafield in the UK. As a result some of them are becoming the owners of separated plutonium for which they have no immediate use. It might suit them to have the plutonium stored under international auspices. At the same time it would suit the French and British reprocessors to have an agreed and uniform international regime under which they could store or release the plutonium for further peaceful use, the actual use being verified by the IAEA. More remotely, if it should prove possible to reach agreement on a cut-off of the production of fissile material for military purposes, an IPS could be useful as a system for absorbing surplus plutonium from military stocks.

A major defect of IPS as well as the other three concepts is that it does not directly address the main risk of proliferation, namely the existence of unsafeguarded plants, particularly those that make or could make weapon-usable material. Each concept, if realized, is likely to attract only those countries that have already accepted full-scope safeguards.

Another problem of all four concepts is that they require new intergovernmental agreement at a time when the climate for such agreements is, to say the least, not propitious. In the case of the Multinational Fuel Cycle Centres, deferral is likely to diminish their prospects still further as new national reprocessing plants come into operation.[8]

An important lesson for the future is that no matter how attractive a new concept may seem on the drawing board, it should not be allowed to distract attention from the main means of curbing proliferation, namely ratification of the NPT or the Treaty of Tlatelolco coupled with full-scope safeguards. This overriding objective sometimes seemed to be brushed aside by the proponents of new institutional arrangements in the late 1970s in their eagerness to put a stop to national reprocessing or, later, to any form of civilian reprocessing.

Notes and references

[1] For a full discussion of many of these proposals, see SIPRI, *Internationalization to Prevent the Spread of Nuclear Weapons* (Taylor & Francis, London, 1980).

[2] The other responsibilities of the remaining three technical divisions are 'Research and Laboratories' (which includes certain applications of isotopes), 'Scientific and Technical Information' and 'Technical Assistance and Co-operation'.

[3] The UN Centre for Energy, Resources and Transport (New York), Unesco, the World Meteorological Organization, the World Bank, UNIDO and the IAEA itself.

[4] A Japanese proposal on these lines in the early 1970s was not accepted but eventually led to the creation of SAGSI.

[5] The former Director General of the IAEA (Dr Eklund) informally explored the possibility of Austrian–Swiss–Swedish–Finnish co-operation. The Austrian programme subsequently collapsed and the Swedish one ran into severe difficulties. Representatives of a group of West European electric power companies also held some exploratory talks at the IAEA headquarters, but nothing came of them.

6 This might have been avoided if Eurochemic had been able to achieve its original aim of serving as a stepping stone towards a large West European commercial reprocessing plant. Because of the prospect of such a joint European plant, Sweden and possibly some other West European countries dropped their own plans to set up national reprocessing plants.

7 President Eisenhower's 8 December 1957 speech proposing the creation of the IAEA envisaged it serving as a bank or broker for the supply of nuclear fuel. Much of the Statute reflects this concept. In practice the IAEA's supply function has always been marginal.

8 Argentina, Brazil and Pakistan are the NNWS known to be building such plants. (FR Germany, Japan, India and Italy are already operating reprocessing plants, the first two are *pilot* plants for LWR fuel.) FR Germany has transferred reprocessing technology to Brazil but it is not clear whether construction of the Brazilian reprocessing plant has actually begun.

Chapter 15. The need for new perceptions

I. Introduction

Within certain inherent technical limits IAEA safeguards will be as effective
in deterring the further spread of nuclear weapons as the IAEA's member states
wish to make them. This in turn will depend upon how they perceive IAEA
safeguards as serving their own interests and contributing to their own security, in
other words how much importance they attach to the aim of limiting the spread of
nuclear weapons and to IAEA safeguards as a means of doing so. Two
perceptions are involved, the attitude of states to the acquisition of the nuclear
weapon option by themselves and their attitude to its acquisition by other states.

At present there are two categories of states that in certain cases place higher
priority on other security, foreign policy or commercial interests than on non-
proliferation. The first category is a sizable group of developing countries many
of which regard proliferation as a remote danger that hardly touches them. A few
will not, at present, accept any legal bar to their own acquisition of nuclear
weapons. The second category is a small number of Western industrialized
countries. All but one (France) have renounced the acquisition of nuclear
weapons for themselves. Nevertheless, their nuclear exports have in the past
substantially increased the risk that *other* states may be able to make nuclear
weapons. And their exports may do so again, chiefly because their domestic
nuclear industries may find it hard to survive without new foreign orders.

II. Third World perceptions

Is there any way in which these perceptions might change or be helped to change?
This question concerns particularly the perceptions of Third World countries,
since it is among them that the risk of proliferation seems highest today, and it is
they whose voices in the direction of the IAEA are becoming stronger.

The geopolitical position of each of the four or five developing countries that is
keeping the nuclear weapon option open (Argentina, India, Israel, Pakistan and
South Africa) differs greatly from that of the others. Any analysis of the
prospects of changing their perceptions would require a detailed and lengthy
study out of place in this book.[1] Except perhaps for Argentina which might still

ratify the Treaty of Tlatelolco, there seems to be little prospect of changing the hostile attitude of the members of this group towards the present non-proliferation regime and IAEA safeguards.

There are of course also great differences in the circumstances and perceptions of the other 65 or more developing countries that are members of the IAEA. Nevertheless, most of them see the IAEA as serving their interests chiefly as a source of technical aid for applying nuclear science and introducing nuclear power rather than as an important contributor, through IAEA safeguards, to their national security.

The accuracy of this perception may be questioned. Take the major nuclear technologies first. In the early 1970s there was widespread optimism (encouraged by the leading industrialized nations) about two nuclear technologies of which little or nothing is now heard—the civilian uses of nuclear explosives and the use of nuclear energy to desalinate sea water. In the early 1970s, following the five-fold increase in the price of oil, there was a similar wave of optimism that nuclear power would spread rapidly to smaller industrialized countries and throughout the developing world—to as many as 40 or 50 developing countries according to a 1974 IAEA survey—if the economically competitive size of power reactors could be scaled down sufficiently.

There was no such spread. Rapidly rising capital costs of nuclear power plants, rising interest rates, fears about safety after the Three Mile Island accident, as well as general economic recession and mounting foreign debts, have instead led to sharp cut-backs in the nuclear power programmes of the small number of developing countries that have launched into nuclear power. That number has remained static at about 10 countries since 1974, eight of which had nuclear power programmes which reached back into the 1960s.

Interest rates may come down, safety fears may subside, economies may recover and foreign debts be reduced to manageable proportions, but nuclear power is likely to remain a highly capital-intensive and very demanding technology, competitive with fossil fuel plants only in large units, and raising safety issues that only countries with a relatively sophisticated industrial infrastructure and well-organized, equipped and staffed nuclear safety system can contend with.

As a result, most experts believe that the future expansion of nuclear power in the developing countries will take place chiefly in those countries that have already surmounted the first formidable hurdles to its introduction. There are likely to be very few additions to that list, at least during this century. For the vast majority of developing countries nuclear power is likely to remain out of reach for the foreseeable future.

It is no coincidence that the IAEA is now, as it did in its early years, placing more emphasis on the transfer to developing countries of other more modest uses of nuclear science in agriculture, medicine, hydrology, and so on.

The size of the investment needed for even the large-scale use of such techniques is two orders of magnitude smaller than that needed for nuclear power (e.g., US$10–20 million for a centre using nuclear techniques in agricultural research or for the large-scale use of the radiation-sterilized insect techniques to control an insect pest, compared with US$1 000–2 000 million for a nuclear power plant).

Nevertheless, the use of such nuclear science techniques requires a level of scientific sophistication that is not available in the majority of developing countries. Moreover, except in medicine, the applications of these techniques are rather limited, they are usually in competition with a more conventional technique (e.g., for breeding new varieties of crop, controlling insects or preserving food) and the conventional techniques are often less capital-intensive and less scientifically demanding.

For many years, most of these nuclear techniques have been the subject of research and development or have been in practical use in the industrialized countries where they play a useful but modest role, so modest in fact that only the specialists are usually aware of them. There is no reason to expect that they will play a larger role in less scientifically sophisticated societies.

If one looks at other UN organizations, particularly the larger specialized agencies, the picture is completely different. The needs of the Third World for technical help in medicine, education, food and agriculture and for speeding up the process of industrialization are immense. This is one reason why the IAEA has encountered so little resistance when other UN agencies have perceived it to trespass jurisdictionally into their domains.

In short, the IAEA is unlikely for the foreseeable future to become a major source of assistance to the Third World. It can play a valuable role in helping 10 or so developing countries to deal with the safety and waste management problems that they are encountering in their nuclear power programmes (most of their other needs are taken care of by the companies supplying their reactors or by the export-financing institutions of the supplier country) and it can play a useful but essentially marginal role in helping the more scientifically sophisticated developing countries to use nuclear science techniques, but it cannot serve the Third World in the way that nearly all other specialized UN bodies do.

On the other hand the IAEA is quite unique among the specialized UN bodies in being designed and able to serve *the security needs* of the Third World as well as those of the industrial countries. The Third World would suffer from further proliferation as much as, if not more than, the industrial countries. If one of the major industrial countries obtained nuclear weapons the resulting political crisis—particularly if it were in the Far East—would perturb the Third World countries as well as those of the 'North'. Proliferation in any developing region would not only pose a grave threat to the security of all countries in the region but would lead to a squandering of one of the scarcest of all developing countries' resources—their best scientific brains—in a regional nuclear arms race.

Doubtless many developing countries perceive these dangers only too well, even if they say little about them. The Philippines must fear the possibility of further proliferation in the region and would certainly not be happy with

Japanese, Taiwanese, Indonesian, Vietnamese or Australian nuclear weapons; fortunately, all these countries have acceded to the NPT and accepted its safeguards. Indonesia would have similar concerns. Sri Lanka and Bangladesh would not relish the prospect of nuclear weapons in the hands of their more powerful neighbours. They have both acceded to the NPT relatively recently (1979), but their example has not been contagious. Egypt's concern is manifest not only in its 1981 ratification of the NPT but also in the initiatives it has taken to establish a nuclear weapon-free zone in the Middle East. In the mid-1960s, Mexico took the lead in promoting the Treaty of Tlatelolco and played a considerable role in the drafting of the NPT. The earlier nuclear rivalry between Argentina and Brazil has been replaced by bilateral co-operation, but there is little doubt that if either country acquired nuclear weapons (or explosives) the other would feel compelled to follow suit.

Changes in the Third World's perceptions of its interests in the IAEA are likely to be slow. To regard the IAEA as a source of greater security rather than of material and tangible assistance would run counter to longstanding and almost mechanical attitudes of the G-77 in all UN agencies. More technical assistance is also a platform on which all can unite and it is a price which the 'North' has been prepared to pay for more safeguards. As already noted in tracing the history of the IAEA Board of Governors, many countries in the North were equally slow to change their attitudes: the USSR began to see IAEA safeguards in a positive light only in 1963–64, and France, FR Germany and Italy swung around in support only in the 1970s.

III. The Western exporters

At the beginning of this chapter reference is made to another group of states, in this case a group of industrialized countries, whose export policies helped to sow the seeds of proliferation in the past. Their policies have become much stricter since the mid-1970s, but they are still deficient in two main respects.

Only Australia, Canada, Sweden and the USA require full-scope safeguards as a condition of supply to NNWS; Australia in fact will only supply to NNWS that are parties to the NPT and requires IAEA safeguards on its exports to NWS. The USSR and the UK support the concept of full-scope safeguards but in practice permit exports to countries that do not accept such safeguards. France has expressly distanced itself from the concept, on the grounds that to insist on safeguards on plant or material indigenously produced by a country would be to intrude upon its sovereignty. Belgium, FR Germany and Switzerland equally do not require full-scope safeguards and, as we have seen, the London Guidelines are silent on this matter. Japan is not yet an exporter of nuclear plant or fuel, but in safeguards matters it has often followed the lead given by the main Common Market countries.

The second deficiency relates to the export of sensitive plant and technology—namely reprocessing, enrichment and production of heavy water. The London Guidelines do no more than call for the exercise of 'restraint' in such exports.

It has been noted that in 1976 France and FR Germany announced that 'for the time being' they would not export any further reprocessing plants. But their concurrence on this point is based on ministerial policies and not on any firm agreement between exporters. There is no explicit embargo on the export of enrichment or of heavy water plants; for want of effective demand there has been no export of enrichment technology since the West German–Brazilian agreement, but Switzerland recently exported a heavy water plant to Argentina.

There will be no sound economic justification for any addition to commercial enrichment capacity during this decade and perhaps the next. As pointed out earlier, commercial demand for plutonium for breeder reactors (and therefore for reprocessing) is receding into the next century.[2] But there is a danger that the manufacturers of reactors faced with drastic reductions in domestic sales will try to persuade their governments to offer sensitive technology as a means of outbidding their competitors. This is what was done to promote sales to Brazil in 1975–76, to Argentina in 1981 and Mexico in 1982 (Mexico subsequently decided to postpone indefinitely its ambitious nuclear power programme).

It would of course be wrong to believe that supply policies alone can determine whether or not additional countries will place all their nuclear activities under safeguards or whether they will decide to develop sensitive technologies. But supply policies can still be effective. If they were prepared to devote the needed resources many countries could today engage in small-scale reprocessing and even enrichment. In contrast, the capacity to build a complete nuclear power plant without significant help from abroad is still limited to a handful of countries, the USSR, the USA, France, FR Germany, Japan, Sweden, the UK (which is not at present a supplier) and, perhaps, India for particularly Indian conditions (India maintains that its small (220 MW) reactors are economically competitive in the special economic circumstances of India). In the present state of the market, launching a new nuclear power plant construction company would moreover be regarded as economic insanity even if the country concerned possessed all the highly sophisticated technologies required.

Thus it is still possible for the plant manufacturing countries to offer importers a choice, either to expand their peaceful nuclear power programmes under full safeguards and with generous help from abroad or to take (or continue along) the road to unsafeguarded nuclear military capacity, but at the cost of any further expansion of their nuclear power programmes.[3] The ability of the suppliers to require such a choice will probably last for several years but it will not last indefinitely. What is now lacking is a consensus among them.

Another option still open in certain cases is to follow a policy akin to that of the USSR (and the USA in regard to certain research reactors), namely, to require the return of spent fuel when supplying a reactor and its fuel. Alternatively, the spent fuel might be sent to a mutually acceptable third country. Many smaller countries would regard such a policy as a godsend rather than a constraint. The problem of how to dispose of spent nuclear fuel was one of the main causes of the painful demise of Austria's nuclear power programme despite the fact that Austria had just completed a large and costly nuclear power plant. Similar problems have set back the Swedish and Swiss programmes and helped delay the introduction of nuclear power in other West European countries. A 'take back spent fuel' policy could therefore help to promote the peaceful use of nuclear energy, relieve smaller countries of the safety and technological problems of devising their own expensive spent fuel disposal facilities and impede the spread of reprocessing plant and of numerous stores of spent fuel.

Any attempt to develop a new consensus on supply policies should seek the support of at least some developing countries and thus avert or diminish the main political problem the London Guidelines have run into: Third World hostility.

IV. Policy support in bilateral relations

It is of course essential that in the normal course of relations and diplomatic contacts, the leading powers and other NPT countries should constantly encourage ratification of the NPT, full-scope IAEA safeguards and acceptance of other measures to increase the effectiveness of safeguards. As the two chief sponsors of the NPT, the USA and the USSR have a particular responsibility in this regard, but the EEC, China, Japan and smaller NPT countries can often play a useful and perhaps less suspect role than that of the superpowers.

This means NPT and safeguards considerations must be given a high priority among various and sometimes conflicting foreign policy objectives. The five threshold states are particular cases in point. Each of them has special relations with one or both superpowers. Though the latter have not been able to persuade any of the five to accept full-scope safeguards they have probably been effective in holding back South Africa, and perhaps Israel and Pakistan, from the climactic step of exploding a device, and perhaps have helped to restrain a repetition of India's 1974 test. As Argentina's most important customer today, the USSR might help to persuade Argentina of the importance of ratifying the Treaty of Tlatelolco. The effectiveness of a concerted action by the superpowers and the EEC was demonstrated when they jointly persuaded South Africa not to proceed with a nuclear test in 1977. In addition, the USA played a very useful role during the IAEA–EURATOM negotiations and the Soviet Union helped to persuade India to accept effective safeguards on Soviet-supplied heavy water and on any nuclear power plant into which it was introduced.

Conversely, US recognition of EURATOM safeguards in the late 1950s complicated the negotiation of the NPT and contributed to the defects in the IAEA–EURATOM agreement while the Soviet Union's failure to insist on NPT ratification, or at least full-scope safeguards, has added one more country (Cuba) to the list of Latin American countries having only INFCIRC/66 safeguards.

And the Soviet Union as well as France are discussing the sale of a light water power reactor to India. If this goes through it would further set back the already dim prospects for full-scope safeguards in India and Pakistan.

It is also essential that the three NWS (the USA, the USSR and the UK) parties to the NPT should take more seriously the commitment they made 14 years ago in Article VI of the NPT "to pursue negotiations in good faith on effective measures" for ending the nuclear arms race "at an early date" and for nuclear disarmament. Twenty-two years ago, in the Partial Test Ban Treaty, they pledged to seek to achieve the discontinuance of all test explosions of nuclear weapons for all time. On the better fulfilment of these commitments may hinge the long-term future of the NPT and, therefore, of IAEA safeguards.

Notes and references

1 Several studies have touched on the matter, for example, Kincade, W. H. and Bertram, C. (eds), *Nuclear Proliferation in the 1980s: Perspectives and Proposals* (Macmillan, London, 1982); Walker, W. and Lönnroth, M., *Nuclear Power Struggles: Industrial Competition and Proliferation Control* (Allen & Unwin, London, 1983); Fischer, D. A. V., *Nuclear Issues* (Australian National University, Canberra, 1982); Dunn, L. A., *Controlling the Bomb* (Yale University Press, New Haven, CT, 1982).

2 Reprocessing spent fuel to separate high-level nuclear waste (as well as to recover plutonium) has long been regarded as the second to last step in the fuel cycle before the final disposal of the high-level waste. For reasons of cost, among others, there is now a tendency in some countries to omit this step and to store unreprocessed spent fuel indefinitely—see chapter 7, note 10.

3 Such a policy is most unlikely to deflect any of the five 'threshold' countries (Argentina, India, Israel, Pakistan and South Africa) from the path they have chosen to follow, but it might have more effect on countries that have less pressing security or political motives for keeping the weapon/explosive option open and that are more deeply committed to nuclear power.

Chapter 16.   IAEA safeguards and arms control

I. On-site inspection—the breakthrough

Many schemes for disarmament have run aground (at least ostensibly) because of disputes about the means to verify that both sides (or all sides) are keeping their word. Satellite observation, being non-intrusive and hard to prevent, paved the way for the SALT I agreement; however, many other agreements may depend upon states being willing to accept each other's or international inspectors. The crucial accomplishment of IAEA safeguards has been to show for the first time that this is possible, that sovereign states are willing to accept international inspection—on a small scale and in a few countries at first, but now in almost every country that has made any industrial progress and in many that have not, and at some of the largest and most sensitive nuclear plants. Despite the many problems the IAEA has run into, regular on-site inspection by an international secretariat has been shown to work and to be accepted on a scale that few would have imagined possible 30 years ago.

This has led some arms control experts to ask how far the IAEA model could help to resolve a number of the verification problems that are obstructing progress. Support for this idea has come from an unexpected quarter. The USSR,[1] which for many years opposed the use of inspectors to verify arms control agreements, has referred in official statements to the IAEA's experience as a guide for other nuclear disarmament measures. In fact, certain elements of IAEA safeguards already appear in the (unratified) US–Soviet Threshold Test Ban Treaty and Peaceful Nuclear Explosions Treaty, for example, in their provisions for the exchange of information, on-site observation and on the rights and duties of observers which resemble those of IAEA inspectors.

In what way can IAEA safeguards measures and procedures be applied and to what extent could the IAEA's experience be useful in various areas of arms control?

II. Material accountancy

As we have seen, material accountancy is the main method the IAEA uses to verify that safeguards agreements are being observed. It could obviously be used, in fact it would be essential, if an agreement were reached to cut-off the

127

production of plutonium and highly enriched uranium for nuclear weapons and to ensure that they were being used only for peaceful purposes. The techniques and procedures that the IAEA is now applying at reactors and reprocessing plants in the NNWS already do precisely this. The IAEA is beginning to do the same at gas-centrifuge enrichment plants in the Netherlands, FR Germany, Japan and in one of the NWS, the UK.

The large gaseous diffusion plants, used by all the NWS to produce highly enriched uranium for their nuclear warheads, would present different but not insuperable safeguards problems. The first problem is technical. Plants of this type have very large amounts of enriched uranium 'in process' in their cascades. Verifying these 'inventories' may require a good deal of intrusive inspection. Such verification also runs the risk that the inspector might learn something about a still secret technology and could take this knowledge back home with him when he completes his service with the IAEA. However, the agreement recently reached on the methods for safeguarding gas centrifuge plants may help to solve the gaseous diffusion problem. Further guidance may be available if the IAEA and South Africa can reach agreement on techniques for safeguarding the stationary-walled centrifuge plant at Valindaba, which is believed to have large in-process inventories.

The second problem is that part of the output of gaseous diffusion plants is used as fuel for submarines and other naval craft. To continue to provide such fuel it may be necessary to animate the dormant provisions of paragraph 14 of INFCIRC/153 which, as noted earlier, have never been tested and, one might have hoped, would never need to be tested.

For a cut-off to be effective, full safeguards would have to be imposed on the entire nuclear fuel cycles of the NWS (as is done in all NPT NNWS) to ensure that no fissile material is diverted in *their* fuel cycles to nuclear weapons or other nuclear explosives. This would remove one of the elements of discrimination in the NPT. Safeguarding the entire nuclear fuel cycle of the NWS would require doubling or more the safeguards operation of the IAEA. This might take three or four years. It has been suggested that to avoid this delay, if and when a cut-off is agreed, (*a*) all NWS should follow the lead of the USA and the UK and immediately make *all their civilian nuclear plants* available for IAEA safeguards; and (*b*) the IAEA should gradually proceed to apply *full safeguards to all* plants made available by the NWS (and not, as it does now, to just a few selected plants on the 'eligible list').

Once the cut-off were agreed, the IAEA would be able, relatively quickly, to apply safeguards to those plants in the NWS that had been used to produce *military* fissile material. In this way, too, pending the cut-off, the NWS would be compelled to keep civilian and military fissile material entirely separate from each other, a separation which is symbolically important for NNWS and is already encouraged by the Australian policy of requiring IAEA safeguards on its exports to NWS.

Material accountancy (supplemented by containment and surveillance) might also be needed to verify an agreement to stop the production of chemical weapons (chemical warfare agents). The products of many of the plants concerned, like those of nuclear plants, can either be used in peaceful industry or as the lethal contents of weapons. There are, however, many factors that would make precise and accurate accounting more difficult at most chemical plants than at nuclear plants. The constant flow of radiation from fissile materials makes it relatively easy to detect them and to measure them precisely, much more precisely than most industrial chemicals. The high cost of certain nuclear materials and the danger of criticality oblige the operator of a nuclear plant to take very strict precautions to ensure that his measurements are as correct as possible and to keep meticulously accurate records of the stocks and of flow and production. This makes nuclear safeguards both easier to apply and more credible.

The IAEA has to apply safeguards only to a single and relatively scarce element, uranium, and to its product, plutonium, as it works its way through one of the two fuel cycles being used today. When safeguards began to be applied, nuclear materials were even scarcer and dearer than today and were confined to a handful of countries. It was and has remained relatively easy to track the flow of nuclear materials and to follow the spread of the plants producing, using and processing them.

Despite these differences there are enough features in common to make the IAEA's experience of interest for those concerned with the control of chemical warfare agents. Plants for converting uranium concentrates into uranium oxide or metal, plants for making the gaseous uranium hexafluoride, and nuclear reprocessing plants are, after all, no more than a special branch of the chemical industry.

Some elements of the IAEA system that might be of interest in safeguarding chemical warfare agents are:

1. The INFCIRC/153 requirement that the state should establish a national system for controlling and accounting for materials as well as the methods used by the IAEA to verify this accounting, in particular the system built around the concept of MUF. In arrangements for safeguarding civilian chemical factories the purpose would be to verify that no chemical warfare agents are being produced; this might also require routine visits and detailed material accountancy.

2. The requirement that the state should be responsible for declaring all material to be safeguarded and for reporting all changes taking place after its initial declaration.

3. The technical procedures that the IAEA employs (design review, records, reports and the various categories of inspection).

4. The legal and organic hierarchy of (*a*) a basic treaty, (*b*) an implementing agency, (*c*) a safeguards agreement with each state, (d) subsidiary arrangements and a detailed facility attachment for each plant, store, etc., and (*e*) methods and techniques for sampling and analysing materials, especially in bulk form.

5. The procedures followed by the IAEA to draw up and gain acceptance of its safeguards systems.

6. The internal organization of the IAEA Inspectorate and its supporting divisions.

7. The IAEA's experience in setting up and running an international safeguards laboratory.

Some of the problems the IAEA has run into should also serve as lessons, not only for controlling the production of chemical warfare agents but also for other schemes and areas of arms control. We have seen, for instance: (*a*) the problems of credibility that arise because of the IAEA's extremely limited right to look for undeclared plants or stocks; (*b*) the somewhat burdensome restrictions placed on the access of IAEA inspectors, particularly in the EURATOM countries; and (*c*) the difficulties the IAEA has had in designating enough inspectors in certain countries and in designating inspectors of particular nationalities.

III. Containment and surveillance

Accounting for materials is obviously a safeguards technique that is only applicable when the material being safeguarded is normally intended for peaceful industrial or research use but could be diverted to military ends. The techniques of containment and surveillance can be used for a much wider range of verification purposes. Seals can be used to secure a plant that has been closed down or mothballed or a store that has to be safeguarded while arrangements are being made to dismantle the plant, destroy the contents of the store or to convert either plant or materials to exclusively peaceful uses. Surveillance cameras, closed-circuit TV coupled with video-recorders and sensors could be used to verify that there had been no unreported entry into the plant (or into the critical parts of it) and to signal any tampering with seals. Containment and surveillance techniques and instruments could thus be used to help verify measures for nuclear, chemical and biological arms control should this prove necessary.[2]

IV. Nuclear arms control

Ironically, the means devised for safeguarding the peaceful uses of nuclear energy may, with the exception of containment and surveillance techniques, be only marginally useful in verifying agreements to limit or reduce nuclear armaments.

As paragraph 14 of INFCIRC/153 shows, safeguards end where permitted military uses of nuclear energy begin. No state would allow international inspectors into its nuclear submarines, onto its missile launching sites, or into the factories that make nuclear warheads. As is noted at the beginning of this chapter, it was the development of *non-intrusive* verification methods that overcame the obstacles obstructing the main nuclear arms control agreements. These 'national technical means of verification' gave each superpower confidence in its ability to monitor the other's nuclear armaments without sending inspectors into the other's territory.

If further nuclear arms control agreements are reached it seems likely that they too will rely chiefly on satellite observation (which is itself a C/S device—a form of instrumental surveillance). If the NWS, or at least those NWS party to the Partial Test Ban Treaty and the NPT, fulfil their pledges in those two treaties ''. . . to achieve the discontinuance of all test explosions of nuclear weapons for all time . . .'' a limited amount of 'human' inspection may be needed in cases where instruments are unable to determine whether the signals received come from a small nuclear explosion or a minor tremor or earthquake.[3] The IAEA's success in gaining acceptance of the principle of on-site inspection, especially by the NWS, might thus indirectly help to open the way to a comprehensive test ban treaty. But the inspections carried out under such a treaty would have little in common with the routine inspections of the IAEA.

Another feature distinguishing nuclear arms control from nuclear safeguards is that major measures of arms control are unlikely to be *internationally* negotiated and applied. The nuclear arms control agreements that go to the heart of the matter by imposing constricting limits on the number, size or other features of missiles and missile launchers, or the kilotonnage of weapon tests, are between the nuclear powers themselves (with the exception of the Partial Test Ban Treaty of 1963). The matters at issue are so vital to the national survival of both super-powers and so secret that neither is likely to allow outsiders to play any role in the verification of any agreements they may reach; except perhaps to admit other NWS, if they join such agreements. The roles of international bodies are likely to be limited, perhaps to that of verifying a ban on the production of fissile materials for nuclear weapons or of new nuclear warheads or, if an international satellite monitoring agency is set up, to provide corroboratory assurance to the states that join it. But the main players are likely to keep the game to themselves and the audience will have to watch it from afar.

This is not how the IAEA Statute foresaw it. President Eisenhower expected that the IAEA would syphon off nuclear material from the stockpiles of the NWS and would be responsible for impounding, storing and protecting the material. The IAEA would thus help to reduce nuclear armaments. Several Articles of the IAEA Statute (all dead letters today) foresaw the IAEA as the custodian of increasing stocks of material which it would then make available to its members for peaceful purposes. The IAEA is therefore enjoined in Article IX.H to store these materials ''. . . in such a way as not to allow concentration of large amounts of such materials in any one country or region of the world''.[4]

Could the IAEA still play this role; could it, for instance, establish repositories in the territory of each of the superpowers to store fissile material recovered from decommissioned warheads and from the stocks on hand at the time of a ban on new warhead production? The political evolution of the IAEA since 1957 has been such as to make it most unlikely that the superpowers would entrust it with such a vital task.

V. Summing up

The IAEA's experience in setting up and operating the world's first and so far only international system of verification can be of moral as well as practical value in finding means to halt and reverse the various arms races in which the NWS and other nations are each year running faster towards, what seems to many, an inevitable precipice.

The safeguards system of the IAEA could be applied forthwith to verify an agreement to stop the production of fissile material for nuclear weapons or to ban new warheads. With a good deal of adaptation similar systems could be used to verify that dual military-and-peaceful use products are not diverted to warlike ends. The chief example is the industry that produces chemical warfare agents.

Containment and surveillance devices of the type developed for the IAEA could be used wherever it is necessary to seal, moth-ball or otherwise keep out of use a plant, store or stockpile, including stockpiles of weapons. They could also be used to verify that recording devices are not tampered with.

The superpowers and other NWS are likely to depend chiefly on non-intrusive means, especially satellite observation, to verify agreements to limit or reduce nuclear weapons and other weapons being developed for use in outer space, and they are also likely to keep the game to themselves.

Notes and references

1 In 1982 a Soviet writer, R. Zheleznov, and in 1983 a Soviet representative at the General Assembly expressed the view that the experience of the IAEA could be used to verify specific nuclear disarmament measures. See Zheleznov, R., 'Monitoring arms limitation measures', *International Affairs* (Moscow), No. 7, July 1982, p. 82. The Soviet statement is in UN document A/C.1/PV.3, 17 October 1983, p. 71.

2 Biological weapons are banned under the 1972 Convention on the Prohibition of the Development, Production and Stockpiling of Bacteriological (Biological) and Toxin Weapons and on their Destruction, which does not, however, contain detailed procedures for verifying the ban.

3 By exploding a device in a large cavity ('cavity decoupling') its seismic signal is muffled and may be difficult to distinguish from background 'noise'. If the NWS were able to install seismic networks in each other's territory it is probable that "an evader would be caught attempting explosions with yields exceeding 5–10 kilotons . . ." (see Glen, L. A., 'Verification limits for test-ban treaty', *Nature*, Vol. 310, No. 5976, 2 August 1984, p. 359). The maximum test allowed by the 1974 US–Soviet Threshold Test Ban Treaty (observed though not ratified) is 150 kilotons. Glen writes that ". . . No monitoring technology can offer absolute assurance that very-low-yield illicit explosions have not occurred".

4 Their expectation that the IAEA would have large quantities of nuclear material in storage was one of the reasons why the USA and the USSR chose Vienna, a good, neutral and central location for its seat.

Part II

Sanctions

Paul Szasz

IAEA safeguards: sanctions

I. Introduction

Any examination of the IAEA safeguards system inevitably leads to the question of what the Agency can do if it concludes that a violation of a safeguards undertaking has occurred. Indeed, casual observers and even some expert commentators frequently express the view that this is the criterion or at least one of the principal criteria for judging the ultimate effectiveness of the Agency's system—though, for reasons explained below, this view cannot withstand serious analysis.[1]

Before going further it should first of all be recalled that various types of violation can be determined as a result of Agency safeguards. Graded in order of seriousness, such a violation may be an actual misuse, for a prohibited purpose, of materials subject to safeguards; the unauthorized and clandestine removal of such materials from the control system; some other violation of the control system that tends to mislead or obstruct that system; or some other violation, not directly safeguards-related (e.g., concerning health and safety) but detected as a result of the exercise of safeguards controls. Second, it should also be recalled that it is most unlikely that the Agency will ever be able to observe directly the misuse of any materials under its control—for even if a prohibited nuclear explosion were observed, it would not always be certain that the fissionable materials used therefor were ones supposedly controlled by the Agency (though obviously the inference would be strong in a non-nuclear weapon state party to the Non-Proliferation Treaty (NPT))—and that it is even unlikely that it will ever receive definitive proof that a significant quantity of controlled materials has been diverted. Rather, the Agency will infer, from an otherwise inexplicable obstruction of its safeguards functions (e.g., a large quantity of nuclear material unaccounted for (MUF); misleading records and reports; the exclusion of inspectors; tampering with instruments or seals) that some diversion is likely to have taken place or to be imminent.

Neither the IAEA Statute, nor the non-NPT safeguards documents (such as INFCIRC/66), nor the safeguards agreements based on them explicitly differentiate, in respect of sanctions, among these various types of violation or the means by which they may have been detected or inferred. In other words, a violation would in principle be sanctionable whether it constituted a clear misuse of safeguarded materials or a deliberate defiance of a control measure or perhaps even a

135

mere failure to observe a safety provision. However, while the instruments in question can and probably should be interpreted in that sense—since there is inevitably a substantial psychological element in the countermeasures available to the world community in responding to a safeguards violation, the measures decided on and the thoroughness of their implementation are likely to reflect the extent to which the violation in question is considered wilful, dangerous and certain—a state accused of any violation short of a proven military use of safeguarded materials would no doubt argue that treaty instruments must be interpreted restrictively so as not to allow serious sanctions for a mere violation of controls, no matter how difficult that might make the Agency's task.

Consequently, in drawing up the NPT safeguards document (INFCIRC/153) an attempt was made to relate the possibility of sanctions more precisely to the stated objective of safeguards—that is, the timely detection of diversion and the deterrence of such diversion by the risk of early detection[2]—by conditioning sanctions on a finding by the Director General "that the Agency is not able to verify that there has been no diversion of nuclear material required to be safeguarded".[3] It should be noted that this formula on the one hand clearly makes sanctionable conduct that prevents the Agency from carrying out effective safeguards, but on the other hand might be considered as violating at least the spirit of the statutory provision by allowing sanctions even if the Agency's inability to verify is in no way imputable to the state concerned (e.g., it is consequent on some internal failure in the Agency or on developments beyond the control of either the Agency or the state). It may, therefore, be assumed that under such circumstances no sanctions would or could actually be imposed, except possibly the cancellation of safeguards.

Whether the sanctions available to the Agency under its safeguards system, that is, the actions it itself can take or can induce other entities to take in response to a safeguards violation, are considered sufficient and effective depends on the function that the system is conceived to have. Obviously, if the safeguards system is expected to prevent violations, then only very strong and certain sanctions can accomplish that purpose; if the object is mere deterrence, a lower level of sanctions may suffice; and if it is merely expected that the Agency will prevent diversion from remaining clandestine, that is, that it will publicize any prohibited uses, then sanctions in addition to publicity may be unnecessary.

It is, therefore, in the light of the above considerations that the sanctions associated with the IAEA's safeguards system must be examined.

II. Sanctions foreseen in various legal instruments

The safeguards measures that the Agency may take are set out in a series of legal instruments: (*a*) the Statute, which briefly specifies all those measures that the Agency is in principle authorized to take; (*b*) safeguards documents, which specify, at greater length, what measures are to be included in particular types of safeguards agreements to be concluded with individual governments; and (c) individual safeguards agreements, which specify the particular measures applicable in the context of a particular set of arrangements between the Agency and a particular state or states.[4] Safeguards-related sanctions are among the measures that are so specified, for if these instruments were entirely silent on this point then the Agency would, under international law, have at most a limited and vague implied internal authority (i.e., as an international organization) and external right (i.e., *vis-à-vis* the countries concerned) to impose sanctions, and the obligation of governments to comply with the sanctions to be imposed on themselves or on others with their assistance would be similarly limited.

It is, however, somewhat indicative of the low status that characterizes the concept of sanctions in the actual implementation of the Agency's controls that—unlike other safeguards measures (e.g., records, reports and especially inspections), which are sketched briefly in the Statute but described in considerable detail in the safeguards documents and even more expansively in safeguards agreements and the related subsidiary instruments—in respect of sanctions the brief statutory description is for the most part merely incorporated by reference into safeguards documents and instruments, without any attempt at expansion or clarification. Thus a listing of the formal sanctions measures available to support IAEA safeguards necessarily starts and practically stops with the statutory provisions. However, each of the measures mentioned below is discussed at greater length in the following section (though their order and headings are slightly revised for functional reasons).

1. Notifications:[5] (a) of member states; (b) of United Nations organs.
2. Curtailment of nuclear assistance: (a) by the Agency; (b) by member states; (c) withdrawal of materials and equipment already provided.
3. Suspension of privileges and rights of membership.
4. Cancellation of safeguards.

Each of these measures, except for the last one, is specifically provided for in Article XII of the Statute. According to that instrument, these measures are to be taken in stages, with the indicated notifications to be made in every case in which the Board of Governors has found non-compliance to have occurred, the curtailment of assistance to follow optionally if the state concerned does not take corrective action, and with the suspension of membership rights to be considered only as a last resort.

Instead of this rather mechanical and therefore somewhat unrealistic automatic progression of steps, the NPT safeguards document attempts a somewhat more graduated and facultative set of responses, at least in those cases where the problem centres on the implementation of the Agency's controls. Implicitly the first step would be informal attempts by the IAEA Secretariat to resolve the matter with the competent national authorities. This might be followed by a demand by the Board that the state take certain measures—not because the state is accused of violating its safeguards obligations but because they are necessary to enable the Agency to ensure verification of non-diversion.[6] If this is then followed by a report by the Director General that the Agency is no longer able to verify non-diversion, the Board then may[7] make the statutory notifications, followed in due course by the other sanctions.

III. Analysis of various sanction measures

Report on non-compliance

According to Article XII.C of the IAEA Statute, the Board is to report to the Agency's members every instance of non-compliance which it finds to have occurred. Though the Statute itself provides no threshold for the seriousness of the non-compliance, in effect minor offences (e.g., a short delay or an unintentional mistake in a report) are likely to be screened out by the inspectors or by the Director General on the basis of a general, informal understanding that trivial deviations that do not appear to constitute part of a scheme for diverting nuclear materials should be resolved informally and without resort to the Board. Even if some such deviation were brought to the latter's attention, it might decline to find non-compliance, especially if it concludes that corrective action will be taken.

However, if the Board finds that non-compliance has taken place, and formally calls on the state(s) concerned to remedy it, it would seem to be obliged at the same time to notify all members of the Agency, as well as the UN Security Council and General Assembly. As pointed out above, the NPT safeguards document appears to make the notification facultative, depending on the Board's evaluation of "the degree of assurance provided by the safeguards measures that have been applied" and any "reassurance" furnished by the state concerned.

General publicity

Although it is not specified that the finding of non-compliance should be publicly announced (the Board of Governors holds closed meetings and its proceedings and documentation are basically confidential), and even if a report could be made on a confidential basis to the more than 100 member states of the Agency, the reports that must be made to the UN organs are perforce public since there are no arrangements, especially in respect of the General Assembly, that would make possible the submission of a report on any restricted basis. Thus, no later than when the Agency's report is published as a document of the Security Council or the General Assembly, the whole world would be apprised of the Board's finding of non-compliance. Indeed, the Agency's consideration of the matter would almost surely have been leaked (officially or otherwise) much earlier, probably as soon as the Director General submitted his first critical report to the Board.

It must be recognized that such a public accusation of a treaty violation by a competent and representative body, such as the IAEA Board of Governors, is, in itself, a powerful sanction. No government likes to be accused of a clear breach of an international legal obligation, and in the normal course will do a great deal to avoid being so charged. Indeed, it may be expected that when in the course of implementing safeguards the Agency finds itself impeded by non-co-operation, if that is due to factors other than an attempt to hide a diversion—for example, if it merely reflects resentment at the burden of safeguards or the desire to disguise a mistake—then the mere threat of a publicly revealed Board finding (or even of a leaked accusation by the Director General) of non-compliance is likely to result in a satisfactory resolution of the difficulty. Indeed, it seems so implausible that a state would willingly face widespread opprobrium merely in order to challenge some aspects of safeguards, that it can be assumed with some confidence that any unresolvable difference[8] relates to an actual or potential diversion. In this connection account should also be taken of the fact that safeguards are recognized as primarily a confidence-building measure, to which states submit voluntarily in order to assure their neighbours and their suppliers of their innocent intentions. Accusations of non-compliance are therefore the last thing that governments wish to provoke.

In addition to the general unease that any government feels at being accused of a deliberate treaty violation, a democratic regime is likely to be even more sensitive. In a popularly governed country a policy of nuclear abstinence is likely to reflect more than just external pressures by suppliers and neighbours but also a democratically taken and usually legally anchored domestic decision. Thus, evidence that the government is not able to satisfy an international control body that the country's nuclear energy programme is indeed solely peaceful may have serious political repercussions—even if a majority of the citizens may be inclined to support its own government against intrusive outsiders. On the other hand, if a democratic country decides to reverse an established anti-nuclear policy it could do so only after a public debate and decision, leading to a formal denunciation of the obligations that the safeguards are to control as well as of the safeguards themselves.

In actual fact, the publication of any formal accusation of non-compliance is likely to be preceded by leaks concerning the Director General's accusations, whether deliberately provoked by the latter, by some member of the staff or by any of the 100-odd governments to which all Board of Governors documents are automatically distributed. Unless the government concerned is very sure of its grounds, even such an unproven indictment may suffice, for the reasons stated above, to induce compliance or at least a willingness to approach closer to the Agency's position.

Reaction of states

The IAEA itself must notify all its members of any non-compliance with safeguards found by the Board. Similarly, all UN members would be informed through the General Assembly. Thus, all countries in the world would be alerted to the desirability of and possibly the need to react appropriately to this development.

It is instructive to consider what individual[9] action states can, may[10] and might take at this stage—that is, before either UN or Agency organs have called for any collective reaction to the violation. Again it should be recalled that though the initial notification from the Agency signifies a finding by the Board of some non-compliance or perhaps of some other obstacle to Agency verification of non-diversion, and such a finding requires that the Board shall have taken into account all mitigating factors, the accused state may still be willing and able to resolve the difficulty "within a reasonable time". Thus it is likely that the initial reaction of other states will, for the most part, merely be designed to encourage the taking of prompt remedial action—though perhaps some nations will immediately take a stronger line (if they consider themselves particularly threatened) while others may even support the violator (especially if tied to it through an alliance). It is, therefore, more interesting to consider what individual steps other countries might take later, in response to an apparently deliberate and persistent violation by a safeguarded state.

In the first place, evidently any state whose own nuclear policy depends in part on the presumed peaceful nuclear programme of the accused state will have to reconsider that policy. In particular, if it judges that threat to be a realistic one it may seek to terminate any restrictions on its own programmes. Whether it can do so depends, of course, on domestic political considerations, on legal or moral ties *vis-à-vis* other states,[11] such as mutual neighbours, and, above all, on its technical capabilities to produce nuclear weapons. If such a reaction is indicated by one or more countries rival or hostile to the violator, or indeed if such a reaction can be anticipated, this may be enough to persuade a state otherwise willing to flout safeguards to refrain from doing so. But, though potentially effective, the threat that one or more states could overtly abandon their non-nuclear weapon status is hardly one to be invoked lightly, because of the potential danger such a step would pose to unravelling an entire regional or world-wide non-proliferation regime.

Second, states that consider themselves particularly threatened or aggrieved by an apparent violation of safeguards by another might impose (or threaten) specifically nuclear trade or more general economic sanctions, either on an individual basis or collectively as part of a regional or other alliance. In particular, they may suspend financial, general economic or military aid or arrangements, on which more and more countries have become increasingly dependent. As the considerations relating to such sanctions are basically the same as those relating to the collective ones that might be called for by the Agency or by the United Nations, except for their potentially diminished effectiveness due to the lesser participation, they are considered below under the headings relating to collective measures.[12]

Third, states particularly interested in maintaining the integrity of the non-proliferation regime, including especially the two superpowers, may threaten to withdraw their nuclear umbrella or to cancel other security assurances they may have given—a loss of protection that could hardly be balanced by whatever nuclear weapons or threats thereof even a serious safeguards violation could produce.

Finally, a state that considers itself particularly affected by a safeguards violation and the potential nuclear weapon buildup it implies, may threaten or undertake military action to remove that threat or to force the offending state to restored compliance.[13] Obviously, whether such a threat or action is likely to be effective depends on the relative military situation of the countries and on the state of their alliances. However, it must be emphasized that, whether effective or not, the threat or use of individual military force is illegal under Article 2(4) of the UN Charter[14]: although that instrument does allow self-defence, it is permissible only to repel an armed attack and not to induce compliance with IAEA safeguards or even with the more weighty treaty commitments these controls are designed to guarantee.

Almost every non-nuclear weapon state has at least an Achilles heel, and most are quite vulnerable to external pressure when applied systematically by those states on which it normally relies. Firm and consistent action by one or more such concerned states may, given the weak structure of the international community alluded to below, on the one hand suffice to restore respect for the Agency's safeguards and on the other be more effective than any probably less forceful action that could be taken on a collective basis.

Reaction of UN organs

Though the Security Council and the General Assembly are to be notified as soon as the Agency's Board finds a safeguards violation, it appears most unlikely that either of these organs would consider taking any action before the state concerned has had an opportunity to comply with the Board's demands and before the Board itself has decided what to do in the absence of such compliance. Consequently, the types of sanctions that the United Nations might impose will be considered after those that might be decided by the Agency.

Curtailment of nuclear assistance

Though international law generally requires that punitive or 'disciplinary' measures such as sanctions be quantitatively proportional to the offence and to the requirements of an effective remedy, there is no such explicit requirement as to qualitative appropriateness—that is, that the punishment should fit the crime. However, for various reasons, including especially the network of treaty relations that govern most types of international interaction, it is usual to consider first of all sanctions measures that are functionally related to the offence. (For example, the shooting down of the Korean airliner in September 1983 was answered largely by short- or long-term restrictions on air communications with the Soviet Union.) This tendency is reinforced by the fact that collective sanctions, except for those imposed by the United Nations, fall mostly within the province of technical agencies whose oversight relates only to a particular segment of international intercourse, so that the agency that takes cognizance of a particular offence will only be in a position to respond in like coin.

It is therefore not surprising that the specific sanctions contemplated as part of the IAEA's safeguards system are nuclear in nature, that is, the suspension, cessation and even the withdrawal of nuclear assistance. There is, or was, however, another reason for that preference. When the IAEA Statute was being formulated, towards the end of the first decade of the nuclear age, almost no state (except for the two superpowers) could aspire to nuclear autarchy; to sustain a nuclear industry, whether for peaceful or military purposes, states would need to import nuclear materials, equipment or technology, and a cut-off of such imports would, sooner or later, bring the nuclear programme to a halt. Indeed, a dual effect of nuclear sanctions could be foreseen: a proposed military project could be halted or at least stunted, but even before that the production of nuclear power, on which it was assumed many states would soon become dependent, could be turned off. Moreover, as the number of nuclear suppliers was relatively limited, and all were to be encompassed by the new organization, it could be hoped that a punitive nuclear cut-off could really be made effective.

Over the past decades these initial assumptions have of course lost much, though not all, of their validity. More and more countries have attained a measure of nuclear self-sufficiency, and at the same time the number of suppliers of both nuclear materials and equipment has greatly increased. Indeed, in respect of at least certain types of nuclear materials there is a sufficiently open and free market that the flow of supplies can no longer be contained without extraordinary measures. In addition, few if any countries have yet become so dependent on nuclear power that a forced suspension of that energy source would bring them to their knees—or effectively coerce them into compliance with unwelcome safeguards if these are conceived as contrary to an overriding national interest.

Curtailment of assistance by the Agency

Legally and practically, the simplest measure for the Board of Governors to take is to order the reduction or cut-off of any assistance being provided by the Agency itself. All that is required is a decision subscribed to by a simple majority of the Board, with no possibility of any veto.

Unfortunately, however, the Agency itself provides almost no direct assistance, especially to nuclear power programmes, nor is it in a position to do so. The little assistance that the Agency normally provides is merely as a *pro forma* intermediary between a supplying and a receiving state if it is more convenient for them, from a legal or political point of view, not to deal directly with each other. This is so because the Agency never came into a position to fulfil the original main function foreseen for it: to become a "nuclear bank" into which the nuclear powers would deposit excess nuclear materials withdrawn from their weapon programmes, and on which other states could then draw for their own peaceful projects. Thus the Agency's safeguards, originally designed primarily as an adjunct to this nuclear 'banking' business, became instead first a control device for transactions merely brokered by the Agency and later for the quite independently assumed obligations of the Non-Proliferation Treaty.[15]

Not being effectively a nuclear supplier, the Agency is not in a position to impose any significant sanctions of its own.[16]

Curtailment of assistance by states

Article XII.C of the Agency's Statute also allows the Board to "direct curtailment or suspension of assistance being provided ... by a member". The first question therefore is whether the Board may *require* such a cut-off. To this it is not possible to give a conclusive answer. Though the word "direct" suggests a binding authority, it should be noted that the Statute contains no unambiguous language, such as Articles 25 and 48 of the UN Charter, requiring all members to comply with sanctions decisions of the Board.

Even if not binding on member states, a Board directive to curtail assistance would probably suffice as a basis for *allowing* a state to do so, in spite of any contractual commitment it might otherwise have to provide the supplies in question.

In this connection it should also be noted that the "assistance" referred to in the Statute presumably is not restricted solely to materials or equipment being provided on concessional terms, but would also encompass items provided on normal commercial conditions. The concept that the supply of any nuclear item necessarily implies an element of assistance presupposes that such items are so relatively scarce that they are not readily available for mere lucre—a situation that generally prevailed in the mid-1950s, when the Statute was being negotiated, but is increasingly inapplicable today. For the same reason it is becoming increasingly difficult to impose meaningful nuclear supply-related sanctions on errant states.

The decisive question therefore is whether the member states of the Agency, acting collectively at the behest and under the direction of the Board, can: (*a*) effectively prevent a state that violates Agency safeguards from carrying out any military nuclear programme at all, or at least any significant one; or (*b*) induce an errant state, by depriving it of supplies for its peaceful nuclear energy programme, to comply with the Board's demands for effective safeguards, lest its power production and its economy be painfully constricted.

In considering the first question, account must be taken of the fact that any government seriously contemplating a diversion under circumstances in which the Agency may learn of a safeguards violation (though probably not of its precise object) is also likely to take into account the consequences of such a detection and, in anticipation of sanctions, accumulate sufficient inventories of materials and equipment to be able to carry out its objective in spite of possible sanctions.[17] Collective nuclear-related sanctions, even if consistently maintained, will therefore usually only curtail but not preclude a military nuclear programme. In particular, the offending state may calculate that the self-interest of exporters will in any event keep any sanctions imposed short-lived and incomplete.

With respect to the possibility of striking at an actual or presumed military programme indirectly through pressures exerted on the country's nuclear power production, it should be noted that so far few countries have become so dependent on nuclear power that even a complete shut-down of such facilities would induce them to terminate activities considered vital for the national defence. Again, it is likely that a government that is planning measures that might lead to the imposition of Agency-ordered sanctions would attempt to accumulate larger than usual inventories for its peaceful programme which, when added to those maintained on a normal basis, would permit it to withstand such pressures for an extended period of time.

An additional factor to be considered in respect of both questions is the general expansion in the number of suppliers: official state agencies, legitimate commercial firms as well as 'black-market' operators. Few if any states are so completely politically isolated and without liquid resources that, especially over a sufficient period of time, they could not locate sources of supplies not responsive to the Agency's ban. Naturally, this might be less true in a situation in which the outlaw government is considered to be a general menace to the world community, but experience shows that such perceptions are rarely shared on a sufficiently wide basis to assure a seamless web of sanctions proof against even substantial economic inducements.

Thus, the tentative conclusion must be that the exclusively nuclear-related collective sanctions that the Agency might orchestrate would be unlikely to suffice to prevent or markedly inhibit a determined violator. However, together with some of the other measures discussed above, they are likely to discourage violations consequent on less serious motives.

Withdrawal of assistance already supplied

Both Articles XII.A.7 and XII.C of the Statute explicitly foresee as a possible sanction the withdrawal or recall of any material or equipment made available to the violating state(s) by the Agency or by a member for an Agency-supported project.

In limine, it is obvious that this sanction is at best an imperfect one, suffering from one inevitable and one potential defect:

1. Unlike all other sanctions discussed herein, this measure requires some positive action by the state being sanctioned, rather than merely by other entities; evidently, any 'withdrawal' of supplies already provided depends either on the

voluntary co-operation of that state or the threat or exercise of sufficient force (or other effective sanctions) to coerce compliance.

2. Even if the state concerned is prepared to release and return the supplies in question, either the supplier thereof or someone else must be prepared to take them back, a step that may be expensive and physically dangerous (e.g., in case of irradiated fuel elements). So far, the Agency has not sought or secured assurances from any of the supplier states whose customers are subject to Agency safeguards that the former would be prepared to co-operate with and assume the burdens of such an exercise—which of course does not mean that, if a sufficiently serious situation should arise, these or other states would not be prepared to do so. Finally, it should be noted that, up to now, the Agency has not itself secured any storage facilities in which it could hold any supplies returned in response to a sanctions order.

Nevertheless, this particular sanction need not therefore be written off entirely. While obviously ineffective against a violator determined to carry out a military programme no matter what the expected consequences, it may be an appropriate remedy in a situation in which a government merely desires to resist some or all Agency safeguards—evidently due to a change in national policy, probably resulting from a major domestic political upset. In such a situation, the government may be willing to cancel all the incidence of a currently unacceptable policy, including the surrender of any nuclear supplies that attract unwelcome controls—presumably, provided that the economic burden of doing so need not be borne entirely by that state. It might also be noted that the language of Article XII.A.7 suggests that the materials and equipment to be withdrawn are those supplied for a specific project, so that if the difficulty relates solely to a particular facility assisted by the Agency, then this sanction would be restricted to that facility. This would then be an entirely logical and appropriate consequence of the cancellation of an arrangement whereby the Agency originally provided or brokered assistance on condition that it would be permitted to control such supplies effectively and it later develops that for some reason, whether general or project-specific, the government is not allowing it to do so.

Suspension of the privileges and rights of Agency membership

The last penalty mentioned in Article XII of the Statute is the possibility of suspending any non-complying member from the exercise of the privileges and rights of membership, as specified in Article XIX. The reference is evidently to paragraph B of the latter provision, which provides for such suspension in respect of a member that has persistently violated the Statute or agreements (presumably especially safeguards agreements) entered into pursuant thereto; such action requires a recommendation of the Board (taken by a simple majority) and a decision by the General Conference acting by a two-thirds majority.

What, then, would be affected by such a suspension?[18] Principally, of course, the right to receive assistance for so-called 'Agency projects', that is, national projects that are approved by the Board as worthy beneficiaries of Agency assistance. Also suspended would be the right to receive non-specific assistance, for example, information generated, assembled or otherwise processed by the Agency for the benefit of its members—such as participation in the International Nuclear Information System (INIS). Since, however, the provision of most such information is not restricted to members, or even to states, and since most of it is in any event otherwise available, this aspect of the suspension would at most have limited, symbolic and in practice easily avoidable consequences. Probably more annoying, though still not unduly onerous, would be the exclusion from all types of Agency meeting, including those merely designed to exchange information and especially those at which regulatory principles (such as those relating to health and safety) are developed. For the rest, suspension of the rights and privileges of membership would imply curtailment of the ability to participate in the political life of the Agency, though the precise conditions under which this might be done are somewhat problematic.

Expulsion from the Agency is not provided for. However, voluntary withdrawal is easy, and presumably would be the option chosen by a state whose rights and privileges are suspended under conditions unlikely to permit early restoration—for example, because of some fundamental disagreement about the member's safeguards obligations—since meanwhile the obligations of membership, in particular that of paying assessed contributions, would continue.

Finally, it should be noted that since the exercise of Agency safeguards is not restricted to members, but depends solely on agreements between the Agency and the state concerned (whether or not a member), suspension of the rights and privileges of membership, and even the withdrawal of a state from membership, in no way diminishes the safeguards-related rights and obligations of either the Agency or a state.

All in all, the sanction of suspension can therefore be classified as primarily a symbolic one, signifying a conclusion that the member in question is a persistent violator of its safeguards obligations. It is only to the extent that governments naturally seek to avoid being so characterized that they may consider modifying their behaviour in response to this particular threat.

Cancellation of safeguards

It is probably not surprising that the cancellation of safeguards is not itself mentioned by the Statute as a possible sanction. Indeed, this possibility appears solely in certain safeguards agreements (none concluded in the past decade) which relate to arrangements where the Agency neither has a statutory obligation to exercise its controls (i.e., in respect of Agency projects), nor has such obligation in effect thrust upon it by the General Assembly (e.g., through the Non-Proliferation Treaty), but under which the Agency in effect provides a service by controlling the use of materials or equipment supplied to a particular state on the specific condition that such controls be exercised.

If the Agency should conclude that it is not able, because of the non-co-operation of a state concerned, to exercise the controls it has contracted to perform, one option open to it—whether explicitly stated in the safeguards agreement or merely implied by the general rules relating to the consequences to be drawn by one party to an international agreement from a violation thereof by the other party[19]—must be the right to suspend or terminate the responsibilities the Agency has assumed under the agreement. Presumably it would only do so if the consequences of such a withdrawal of its control functions would not leave the world community in a worse situation, in respect of the nuclear items in question, than if the Agency were to continue to exercise controls as best it can.

The reason why such a suspension or termination of safeguards may be characterized as a sanction is that bilateral or multilateral supply arrangements frequently provide for the exercise of Agency safeguards as a condition for the transaction, and the cancellation of such safeguards would therefore lead to the termination of such assistance and probably also to an obligation to restore any assistance already provided. The consequences of such a reaction by the suppliers concerned would be similar to those discussed above in respect of the direct curtailment of assistance by states.

United Nations sanctions

As already pointed out, the principle that the United Nations should be in a position to back up any sanctions measures decided by the Agency's Board is implied by the several provisions of the Statute whereby the Security Council and the General Assembly are to be notified of any safeguards non-compliance that the Board has found to have occurred.[20] Though naturally neither the Statute nor the UN/IAEA Relationship Agreement provide whether or how the UN organs are to react to such a notification, it is evident that each may do so within the competence granted to it by the UN Charter.

The Security Council

Should the Security Council be notified that the Board of Governors of the IAEA had made a finding of non-compliance, and especially if it later learns that the state in question has failed to comply and the Board has consequently decided on some of the sanctions available to it, the Council has available to it a range of possible reactions to supplement, reinforce or perhaps even modify the IAEA's sanctions.

First of all, the Security Council can consider the matter under Chapter VI of the UN Charter as a "situation which might lead to international friction" and "recommend appropriate procedures or methods of adjustment". Such recommendation could be addressed to the state concerned, to other states or even to the Agency itself. More importantly, under Chapter VII the Council could determine that the safeguards violation in question constitutes a "threat to the peace''—an entirely plausible conclusion in respect of an act that endangers the nuclear non-proliferation regime. Consequent on such a determination, the Council can under Charter Article 41 call on UN members to apply economic sanctions such as ''complete or partial interruption of economic relations and of [all] means of communication, and the severance of diplomatic relations''. Furthermore, under Article 42, military sanctions can be ordered, including ''demonstrations, blockade, and other operations by air, sea, or land forces of Members of the United Nations''. These members, and to a considerable extent even non-members, as well as the international organizations controlled by these states, are required to co-operate and comply with such economic and military sanctions. Finally, the Security Council can also recommend to the General Assembly the suspension of the rights and privileges of UN membership, and even expulsion from the organization.

Potentially, therefore, the Security Council has the means available to reinforce Agency safeguards to whatever extent may be necessary to assure compliance from any state (except a superpower or even one of the other nuclear weapon states—which are unlikely to be engaged in nuclear safeguards violations). In practice, of course, the situation is quite different. Because of the veto power of each of the five permanent members, and to a lesser extent because of the need to secure the votes of at least some of the developing states elected to the Council, the latter has, with the notable exception of ordering general economic sanctions against Southern Rhodesia and prohibiting certain weapons exports to South Africa, never been able to agree on any forceful measures against any state,[21] no matter how offensive its international or domestic conduct might have been. And even in the above-mentioned instances in which sanctions were imposed these were always less than the maximum available to the Council and, more importantly, less than required to secure prompt compliance from the target state. More importantly, the Council has never been able to secure the whole-hearted co-operation of all the states required to have particular sanctions fully applied and consequently effective.

The practical difficulty posed by the veto in mobilizing the UN's formidable potential power was one of which the founders of the Agency were well aware. Indeed, the first attempt to accomplish on a grander scale, by means of the Baruch-proposed International Atomic Development Authority (IADA), the tasks assigned a decade later to the IAEA, came to grief on this very issue: should the control organ of IADA be veto-free, or be subject to the Security Council? Ultimately the Agency's Board was established without a veto but able to project only the relatively weak sanctions discussed in the previous sub-section; the powerful sanctions remain the sole province of the veto-ridden Security Council.

The General Assembly

The General Assembly is, of course, not subject to the veto, though the need to secure a two-thirds majority on any recommendation with respect to the maintenance of international peace and security may make it difficult to secure a decision against any of the states that constitute part of the largest voting block in the Assembly. Unlike the Security Council, the Assembly in this respect only has the power to make non-binding recommendations: to states, to other international organizations, to the Security Council and to other UN organs (though the latter may be bound by an Assembly decision). Even the suspension or termination of UN membership cannot be voted by the General Assembly, without a prior, vetoable recommendation of the Security Council.

Thus, while it might be easier to secure a recommendation from the General Assembly that extensive and effective sanctions be imposed on a state that violates Agency safeguards, neither the state concerned nor other states would be bound by such a decision. Indeed, a General Assembly recommendation probably cannot (unlike a Security Council decision under Chapter VII of the Charter) absolve states that might wish to comply therewith from the obligation to observe the ordinary rules of international intercourse: such as the duty to refrain from the threat or use of force or the obligation to comply with the bi- and multilateral agreements regulating trade, commerce and communications. Consequently, in spite of several attempts, the General Assembly has never been able to fashion an effective set of sanctions measures against a state, except by persuading the Security Council (i.e., its permanent members) to exercise its undoubted powers.

IV. Summary and conclusions

As the above analysis demonstrates, the Agency's safeguards, while not entirely without bite, are equipped with teeth that are certainly weaker than the corresponding eyes and ears of the control system. Though probably sufficient to dissuade most states from casually violating their safeguards obligations and even to compel a weak or not particularly determined country back to the path of rectitude, the collective threats and punishments that are likely to be conjured up against a safeguards violator would hardly suffice to induce or force a government determined to acquire nuclear weapons in violation of an international obligation to abandon that purpose.

In the present state of the international nuclear market any non-universal suppliers' boycott would almost certainly be ineffective, and even the Agency might have difficulty in orchestrating a sufficiently comprehensive ban against any but the most unpopular and economically weak state. If the imposition of sanctions can be anticipated, a country will generally be able to build up sufficient stocks for at least a modest military programme, and few states are yet so dependent on nuclear energy that they can be checkmated by a cut-off directed against its power reactors. While in principle the Security Council could mobilize sufficient force to compel almost any state to comply with safeguards measures, in the political constellation prevailing now or at any time since the United

Nations was founded no such decisive action can realistically be expected from that quarter.

In many circumstances the most persuasive sanction could be the unsystematic, unorchestrated reaction of neighbouring states, ranging from an acceptance of the challenge of a localized nuclear arms race to the illegal though effective threat or use of force. As few states are impervious to all such pressures, and also because of the general desire of governments to avoid the opprobrium of being labelled law-breakers, the most effective sanction actually available to the Agency may be the apparently most innocuous one: the mere publication of a finding by the Board of a safeguards violation, or even information that the Board is considering such action. Indeed, the most important instrument available to the Agency in enforcing its safeguards is the very mechanism that determines that a violation has taken place: the technical report of the inspectors accepted by the Board, a realistically composed, representative but specialized decision-making body unhampered by a veto—in other words, a body that can reach decisions and whose decisions are likely to be respected.

Thus, it must be concluded that though the sanctions in support of safeguards are not very strict, they are probably sufficient for their purpose: to permit the safeguards system to function without destructive interference from casually motivated obstructions (which are likely to be flushed out by even the weak enforcement mechanism available), thereby helping to guarantee that the peaceful programmes that the Agency is controlling genuinely do not present any immediate threats to other states.

Finally, in evaluating the potential efficacy of the sanctions available to support the IAEA's safeguards system, account must be taken of the only imperfect development of the legal structure of the world community, in which multilateral control systems of any sort are rare and enforcement mechanisms of any type are even rarer. Against that background the sanctions available to the Agency, while certainly puny, still represent a promising development that may serve as a model for other control systems that might evolve in the future.

Notes and references

1   For a general discussion of sanctions in support of nuclear safeguards, see Szasz, P., 'Sanctions and International Nuclear Controls', *Connecticut Law Review*, Vol. 11, No. 3, Spring 1979, pp. 545–581.
2   INFCIRC/153, para. 28.
3   INFCIRC/153, para. 19.
4   For a discussion of some of the legal aspects of sanctions relating to IAEA safeguards, see Szasz, P., *The Law and Practices of the International Atomic Energy Agency* (IAEA, Vienna, 1970), Sections 21.7.2.4 (pp. 601–605) and 21.12.5 (pp. 632–633).
5   As pointed out under *General publicity*, pp. 138–139, even before the statutory notifications are made, a state may in effect be sanctioned by leaks of information about its non-co-operation with safeguards. This informal device evidently helped to resolve the long drawn-out dispute with Pakistan about safeguarding the KANUPP reactor.

6 INFCIRC/153, para. 18.

7 INFCIRC/153, para. 19. This provision would appear to make the reports facultative (even indicating certain considerations the Board is to take into account in taking any action), by providing that the Agency "may" make the reports provided for in Statute Article XII.C. However, it should be noted that Article III.2 of the 1957 Relationship Agreement between the United Nations and the IAEA (UN *Treaty Series*, Vol. 281, p. 369) repeats the statutory obligation of the Agency to report to the Security Council and the General Assembly "any case of non-compliance" within the meaning of Statute Article XII.C. Naturally, this would not apply in those situations in which the Agency's inability to verify non-diversion is not due to non-compliance by the state, and consequently the apparent option given to the Board might be interpreted as permitting non-reporting solely in those situations.

8 It should be noted that not all unresolvable differences about safeguards implementation necessarily lead to accusations of non-compliance or threaten impairment of the Agency's ability to verify non-diversion. Thus differences with EURATOM about safeguarding certain facilities have persisted for the better part of a decade, but since the Director General has never suggested that these created a genuine doubt about the Communities' compliance with safeguards undertakings, they have been under no great pressure to accept the Agency's demands.

9 Individual action, in the sense used in this text, means any action other than collective action under IAEA or UN auspices. Thus, it may include concerted actions by two or more states, such as those foreseen under paragraph 14 of the so-called London Guidelines for nuclear transfers (for which, see Goldblat, J., *Agreements for Arms Control: A Critical Survey* (Taylor & Francis, London, 1982, pp. 232–233 [a SIPRI book]). Such actions would, presumably, in no case be more effective than the collective curtailment of assistance discussed under the heading *Curtailment of assistance by states*, pp. 143–144.

10 Except where specifically mentioned, the present study does not analyse the specific rights that states may have to react to a safeguards violation by another state, nor are the 'sanctions' referred to in this study necessarily acts that would be wrongful except if taken in response to such a violation. For a technical discussion of these issues, see Ago, R., 'Eighth report [to the International Law Commission] on state responsibility' (UN document A/CN.4/318 and Add. 1–4 (1979), reproduced in UN document A/CN.4/Ser. A/1979/Add. 1 (Part 1), pp. 39–47, chapter V.3, Legitimate application of a sanction), as well as the ILC's Commentary on Article 30 (Countermeasures in respect of an internationally wrongful act) of its draft articles on State Responsibility (A/CN.4/Ser. A/1979/Add. 1 (Part 2), chapter III, pp. 115–122).

11 In particular, Article X.1 of the Non-Proliferation Treaty allows any party "in exercising its national sovereignty . . . to withdraw from the Treaty if it decides that extraordinary events, related to the subject matter of this Treaty, have jeopardized the supreme interests of its country", upon giving an explanation and three months' notice to the other parties and to the Security Council.

12 For a general survey of economic sanctions in support of foreign policy goals see the study by Hufbauer, G. C., Schott, J. J. and Elliott, K. A., *Policy Analyses in International Economics*, No. 6 (Institute for International Economics, Washington, DC, 1983), as well as the works cited in the General Bibliography of that study (pp. 101–102), and by the same authors and publisher, *Economic Sanctions Reconsidered: History and Current Policy* (1983).

[13] It should be noted that the action of Israel in bombing the Iraqi reactor in June 1982 was not taken in response to a safeguards violation determined by the IAEA Board, but was indeed taken in spite of the Agency's repeated assurance that it was applying effective safeguards. As a result, the Israeli action was roundly condemned by the Agency's Board and General Conference (IAEA document GC(XXV)/RES/381) as well as by the Security Council (UN document S/RES/487(1981)) and the General Assembly (UN documents A/RES/37/18 and A/RES/38/9). However, such condemnation, and even possible punitive measures (threats to withhold Agency research contracts and discontinue purchases from Israel, and to refrain from holding meetings in Israel—see UN document GC(XXVII)/RES/409, paras 3–4) do not constitute 'sanctions' within the meaning of IAEA Statute Article XII.C or even the formal suspension of privileges pursuant to Article XIX.B.

[14] *Charter of the United Nations, Statute and Rules of Court and other Documents* (International Court of Justice, The Hague, 1978).

[15] See Szasz (note 4), chapters 16 and 17.

[16] For an analysis of the proposition that sanctions would be facilitated if parts of the nuclear fuel cycle were internationalized, see Szasz, P., 'Sanctions as an aspect of international nuclear fuel cycles', Paper 20 in SIPRI, *Internationalization to Prevent the Spread of Nuclear Weapons* (Taylor & Francis, London, 1980).

[17] If the safeguards that the state intends to violate are merely those required under the NPT, the state could instead simply withdraw from that Treaty on giving the three-months' notice required by Article X.1 (see note 11). However, while the effect of such a public withdrawal would be that the IAEA could thereafter no longer legally impose sanctions for the violation of a no-longer existent obligation, the supplying states could in effect agree to take the same actions as they would in response to a call for Agency sanctions. Moreover, any withdrawal from the NPT and NPT-related safeguards would lead to the automatic restoration of any pre-existing non-NPT safeguards applicable to that state.

[18] See Szasz (note 4), Section 13.1.13, p. 333.

[19] See *Vienna Convention of the Law of Treaties* (1969), Article 60.

[20] See IAEA Statute, Articles III.B.4, XII.C and XVI.B.1, as well as Articles III.1(b) and IX of the UN/IAEA Relationship Agreement (note 7).

[21] The actions taken in respect of the invasion of South Korea by North Korea in June 1950, and in particular the establishment of the Unified Command (UN Security Council resolutions 82–85 (1950)) constitute only an apparent exception to this statement. In the first place, these actions were taken in a situation, most unlikely to be repeated, of a permanent member of the Council voluntarily absenting itself from its meetings; more important, the Council did not actually call on states to take any military action pursuant to Charter Article 42 but merely made non-binding recommendations to that effect.

Part III

Conclusions and recommendations

Conclusions and recommendations

Despite some inherent limitations and remediable weaknesses international safeguards have come to play an indispensable part in the world's efforts to stop or slow down the spread of nuclear weapons—efforts that have been more successful than many believed possible 25 years ago. IAEA safeguards and the NPT, even if only partially effective, are in fact one of the few successes in the depressing chronicle of the attempts to limit nuclear arms. A return to bilateral safeguards or a renegotiation of the NPT so as to assign safeguards to an international body other than the IAEA is now inconceivable.

I. Safeguards institutions

The Board of Governors has a central role in the administration of IAEA safeguards. However, changes in its size and make-up have made it much more difficult for the Board to take major initiatives of the type that it launched in the 1960s and 1970s in adopting the two safeguards systems. The prospects for improving or extending either system are therefore poor and becoming poorer. Moreover, to have practical effect, any changes in either would require renegotiating the IAEA's safeguards agreements with states, a nettle that none of the parties concerned is likely to grasp. Fortunately, despite a number of defects, both systems have proved workable and robust. Improvements will therefore have to be made within the existing systems and, in most cases, within the existing agreements. The task of adapting and improving will fall more and more upon the IAEA Secretariat.

Nevertheless, attention must be given to means of making the IAEA's Board more effective in dealing with safeguards matters. This may depend upon a change in the perceptions of many Third World countries about the way in which the IAEA can best serve their interests. A Statute amendment may perhaps be required delegating the IAEA's safeguards functions to a special statutory commission, membership of which would be limited to states with significant nuclear programmes. In the meantime, the pros and cons of establishing a safeguards committee of the Board of Governors should be examined. There may also be ways of focusing the Board's attention on specific safeguards issues. Selected action-oriented proposals might be put to the Board about such problems as reporting delays, difficulties with EURATOM, notifications of exports and notifications of new plant construction.

It is of fundamental importance that governments should provide staff of high calibre, as they have usually done in the past, to serve in the safeguards operation. At the same time, the IAEA should take further steps to build up a well-trained career inspectorate, recruiting more staff directly from universities and offering good career prospects. The IAEA experiment in making use of technicians as inspection assistants has been successful; more use should be made of inspectors in this category.

At present, the IAEA has resident inspectors only in Canada and Japan. The number of inspection man-days put in each year by the resident inspectors is nearly twice that of Vienna (headquarters)-based inspectors. Resident 'inspectorates' reduce or eliminate travel costs, time spent travelling, visa formalities, and so on, and make it easier to carry out unannounced inspections. Greater use should accordingly be made of resident inspectors outposted for lengthy periods to the countries or regions where they are to work.

The IAEA must also make every effort to ensure that its inspectors comport themselves, and are seen by states, as impartial officials of an international organization and not as national officials wearing an international cap. Progress towards a career inspectorate would help in this regard. So would a policy of increasing the proportion of inspectors from smaller NPT countries universally regarded as neutral or non-aligned.

Among the operating problems of safeguards one of the most intractable lies in the political difficulties that many countries put in the way of designating inspectors who are citizens of an opposing military bloc or of certain other nations. After deteriorating for several years, the situation showed some improvement in 1984, but unless it improves further it may be necessary for the Board to deal vigorously with the more serious cases.

Better use might be made of the Standing Advisory Group on Safeguards Implementation—SAGSI, a body which includes top-level safeguards experts from all the leading nuclear industrial states. It might be asked to advise on such problems as designation of inspectors, safeguards equipment requirements or better use and functioning of equipment. SAGSI might also undertake a more detailed review of the Safeguards Implementation Reports (SIR) each year than the Board does. The conclusions drawn from such a review could be presented to the Board.

A significant change in the European Atomic Energy Community's attitude towards IAEA safeguards is desirable. In the first place, EURATOM should recognize that effective IAEA safeguards serve the interests of the European Community and its members. Attempts to restrict the IAEA's inspection effort in the Community are bound to have repercussions on the effectiveness of IAEA safeguards in other states which may seek to impose similar restrictions on the inspection of their own plants.

In practical terms, this means that: (*a*) EURATOM should agree to greater use of the joint (EURATOM–IAEA) team approach, in particular wherever large quantities of sensitive material are involved; (*b*) the IAEA should agree to reduce the size of the joint teams by arrangements to share rather than duplicate the inspectors' tasks (ideally the combined EURATOM–IAEA team should not be significantly larger than a single team from either organization); and (*c*) the IAEA's right to 'observe' EURATOM safeguarding operations must not be interpreted in a way that would diminish its ability to reach independent conclusions and to provide assurance to other states that no diversion is taking place.

II. Safeguards instruments

While most of the serious defects of the IAEA document INFCIRC/66/Rev. 2 (regarding non-NPT safeguards) have been remedied in safeguards agreements concluded since 1975, the precedents now established should be maintained in future agreements. Some new departures may be needed to secure full application of the Treaty of Tlatelolco in Argentina, Brazil and Chile, but they should not compromise the principle that nuclear material may not be used for a nuclear explosive of any kind. Procedures will have to be worked out for safeguarding uranium enrichment plants (in addition to those already existing for plutonium separation plants). While such safeguards must be effective, they must not be unduly intrusive or raise an undue risk of contributing to proliferation rather than preventing it.

Future non-NPT safeguards agreements should provide that the IAEA will inform the supplier when adequate facility attachments have been concluded for safeguarding the supplied plant or material. Where possible, plant and material should only be transferred after these detailed safeguarding arrangements have been made.

Although the difficulties of amending IAEA documents INFCIRC/66/Rev. 2 or INFCIRC/153 (especially the latter) are probably insuperable at this time, sight must not be lost of the long-term goal of adapting the documents to technological and political change. Adaptations, if and when they come, are more likely to be extensions or accretions, as the International Plutonium Storage scheme would be.

III. Action by states

Non-proliferation and safeguards must be given high priority among foreign policy objectives. Each of the NWS has special relations with one or more of the 'nuclear threshold' countries, and the latter have sometimes made use of political strains between the superpowers to advance their own nuclear programmes or to negate constraints that might have been imposed on unsafeguarded activities. However, commercial motives have even more often taken priority over non-proliferation aims, for example, in the 1960s US and Canadian supplies to India, Pakistan and Taiwan, or in the 1970s West German supplies to Brazil, French supplies to Pakistan and South Africa, French and Italian supplies to Iraq and, possibly, also Soviet supplies to Libya.

Despite their understandable negative reactions in the late 1970s, it seems probable that many of the importing countries are now learning to live with the 1977 London (Suppliers') Guidelines for nuclear transfers and perhaps also with the 1978 US Nuclear Non-Proliferation Act in the more flexible way it is being applied today. In any case, much of the substance of the complaints themselves has been drained away by the collapse of the international market for power reactors (except in the Far East) and by the fact that most countries that wanted to obtain enrichment or reprocessing capacity have succeeded in doing so in recent years. The time might be ripe to complete the work done in London in the 1970s, for the following reasons.

1. Outside India, no non-NPT NNWS will be able to build its own nuclear power plant for several years to come. The suppliers are therefore in a position to propose full-scope safeguards as a condition for future sales of nuclear power plants. If this is not yet achievable, the suppliers can at least require that, as a condition for the supply of nuclear power plants, all plants capable of making nuclear weapon material in an NNWS that has not formally foresworn nuclear weapons be placed under IAEA safeguards. This would bring pressure to bear where it is most likely to be effective, namely, on the leaders of the national nuclear energy commissions who would have to choose between taking the path towards a peaceful, safeguarded expansion of their power programmes or going alone on a path leading towards nuclear weapons or the weapon option.

2. There is no economic justification for adding to the surplus uranium enrichment capacity of today. Moreover, the receding prospects for the commercial fast breeder have removed the main justification for additional spent-fuel-reprocessing capacity. The exporters should therefore maintain and confirm the present restraint on the export of sensitive technologies. Exceptions might be made in the case of NPT states that already have either technology (e.g., Japan).

The Soviet Union's policy is to take back spent fuel from the reactors it supplies. Other suppliers might include such a requirement in new supply agreements with states that are introducing nuclear power or buying their first research reactors. In many cases, problems of waste disposal have set back nuclear energy plans (e.g., Austria, Sweden, Switzerland) and will probably do so again in other countries. A requirement to return spent fuel (or send it to a third country) might thus be welcomed by many rather than resented.

Steps must be taken to encourage those countries that are now becoming exporters of nuclear items to require, at a minimum, IAEA safeguards on their exports and generally to follow the NPT and, if possible, also the London Guidelines for nuclear transfers.

Most exporting states, whether or not parties to the NPT, inform the IAEA of exports of nuclear material and plants or plant components to NNWS that are not parties to the NPT. They also inform the IAEA of exports of nuclear material but do not inform it of exports of nuclear plants or plant components to the NNWS that *are* parties to the NPT. As a result an entire enrichment or reprocessing plant can be sent to any of the NPT NNWS without the IAEA receiving any official notification of the transfer. So too, an NPT NNWS is not required to inform the IAEA of any nuclear plant it might be building or has built. The obligation on the importing or constructing country is only to send design information to the IAEA "as early as possible" before it moves nuclear material into the plant.

NPT NNWS are required to inform the IAEA of their imports or exports of uranium concentrates, but not of the location of such uranium; nor has the IAEA the right to check the material. As a result an NPT NNWS can export or re-export uranium concentrates to a non-NPT NNWS without the IAEA knowing about the transfer. It is probable that at least one such unreported transfer from an NPT NNWS to a non-NPT NNWS has taken place (Libya to Pakistan).

Steps should be taken to fill these gaps in the IAEA's knowledge of nuclear activities that it is expressly required to safeguard (under all agreements with NPT NNWS). The easiest and in some ways the most important step would be to ensure that the IAEA is informed of all exports of nuclear plants and of significant plant components to NPT NNWS. The second step would be to ensure that the IAEA has adequate early information about the construction of new nuclear plants in NPT NNWS. The gap concerning transfers of uranium concentrates can be important in certain cases, but would be difficult to fill unless the main exporters of uranium, as well as the transshipping states, were prepared voluntarily to give the IAEA the right to inspect the concentrates whenever the IAEA deems it necessary. (The non-NPT safeguards system, unlike the NPT safeguards system, does foresee inspection of uranium concentrates if the safeguards agreement so provides, but there is only one such non-NPT safeguards agreement.)

The states concerned (chiefly the USA and the USSR) should provide the IAEA with relevant satellite information whenever this would help to ensure full coverage of safeguards. The French-proposed International Satellite Monitoring Agency (ISMA), while intended for other purposes, could also be useful as a supplementary means of verifying whether IAEA coverage was complete. To the same end, the IAEA should explore the possibility of using "special inspections" under the model NPT safeguards agreement, if it has reason to believe that an undeclared plant exists. Inspection 'by challenge', conducted at the request of a suspecting party or a party suspected of violation (as provided for in the Treaty of Tlatelolco), could perhaps also be considered as an extension of the present IAEA rules.

It is important to note that the application of full-scope safeguards in all NNWS could close the most critical loopholes in the safeguards system and would have no more than a marginal impact on the IAEA's total safeguards effort. Therefore, supplier states should insist that they will only export nuclear material and equipment to NNWS that accept full-scope safeguards.

Exporting states should as a rule take part in the IAEA's negotiations with importing states and should help the IAEA ensure that the safeguards agreements are as effective and extensive as possible. The exporting states should be parties to such agreements and should share the responsibility with the importing states of reporting to the IAEA all transfers of plant, plant components, technology and fuel.

The exporting states should also accept a measure of responsibility for notifying the IAEA of any replicated plant (that is, a plant newly constructed by the importing state and modelled on the one previously supplied) if it is not so notified by the importing state. (France accepted such a responsibility in the unimplemented safeguards agreements covering the supply of reprocessing plants to Pakistan and the Republic of Korea.)

The European Community should be encouraged to give more attention to the risks of proliferation caused in the past by the exports of some of its member states, two of which (France and FR Germany) are now among the world's major exporters of nuclear plants. West European controls have become more effective since the mid-1970s, but a great number of the world's proliferation problems are still traceable to supplies from or co-operation with Community countries.

IV. Safeguards resources and practices

Even though some economies may be possible, the IAEA will need increasing resources to give greater confidence that no diversion of nuclear material is taking place and to be able to detect more promptly any diversion that might take place. For this, the IAEA will have to acquire more and better safeguards instruments and equipment, including costly equipment now being developed and tested. It is essential that the IAEA member states be ready to provide the needed funds.

The governments and organizations concerned should continue and expand the research and development programmes they are now carrying out on safeguards instruments, equipment and procedures; and governments and plant operators should co-operate more readily with the IAEA in providing opportunities for testing and installing existing as well as new equipment.

As a general rule, safeguards equipment should be designed as an integral part of a reactor or any other nuclear facility (when it is manufactured) and its cost, like that of safety features, should be an integral part of the price of new nuclear plants. This is particularly important for CANDU and other on-load reactors and certain bulk-handling plants (reprocessing, enrichment, fuel fabrication) since they require costly and complex safeguards equipment. The IAEA should use its experience to give guidance to plant designers and manufacturers on ways of making it easier to apply effective safeguards.

All diversion scenarios so far considered in detail by the IAEA assume that safeguards are in full operation and that diversion would take the form of misleading the IAEA's accounting and inspection system. The IAEA should explore additional diversion scenarios, in particular scenarios under which the state would attempt to hide a diversion by making it difficult for the IAEA to apply safeguards effectively. The IAEA should also define as far as possible the procedures it should follow if it is unable to apply safeguards effectively (because of accident, war, deliberate frustration, etc.).

In this context the IAEA should establish more systematically the circumstances under which it might have to declare that it was unable any longer to verify the absence of diversion. The following pointers would be relevant: attempts to limit the number of inspectors below the minimum needed for effective verification; frustration or refusal of entry into the country or plant concerned; refusal to accept essential containment/surveillance equipment; and continued failure of the national system of material accountancy and control to provide accurate and reasonably prompt reports, or prior notification of inventory takings, and so on.

In certain cases, resistance by governments and operators to the installation of containment and surveillance equipment may not be easily overcome. In some circumstances, genuine questions of safety, of plant efficiency, or fears of technology proliferation may arise. Nevertheless, it is essential that the Board of Governors should continue to give full support to the Secretariat when the installation of new equipment is required for safeguards purposes.

The transmission and processing of information must be expedited through the use of real-time containment/surveillance devices giving the IAEA nearly immediate information on any breach of containment (e.g., removal of seals or opening of a store). Steps must also be taken by national authorities to facilitate and expedite transmission of samples taken by inspectors by licensing IAEA-recommended air transport containers and rationalizing regulations.

There is much that national authorities could do to improve the quality and expedite the transmission of routine reports. The IAEA Secretariat might consider means of bringing the problem more explicitly to the notice of governments and the Board of Governors. Moreover, differences between exporters' and importers' reports about the quantity and composition of the material to which they relate can point up discrepancies important for safeguards. Such differences can only be detected, however, if both the exporters' and importers' reports make a comparison possible, so national authorities must co-operate with the IAEA in standardizing their format.

The largest single 'consumer' of safeguards manpower is the EURATOM group of states, followed by Japan. If economies can be made in IAEA and EURATOM operations in Western Europe without impairing the effectiveness of safeguards, they are likely to have a visible impact on the cost of safeguards. However, it must always be remembered that the total cost of IAEA safeguards is negligible compared with the political and security risks of a further spread of nuclear weapons, and that the contribution they make to nuclear exchanges is vital.

V. Concluding remarks

The chief function of international safeguards is to build confidence between nations by showing that other states are keeping their non-proliferation commitments. States must therefore perceive safeguards as being able to detect any significant anomaly and to do so promptly.

Technical improvement of safeguards is feasible, but their main limitations and weaknesses are political, not technical. Effective safeguards depend on the political will of states at many levels, collectively expressed through the IAEA and to some extent through the United Nations, regionally through groups of states such as EURATOM and the states that established the Latin American nuclear weapon-free zone (through the Treaty of Tlatelolco), and individually when states ratify treaties, negotiate safeguards agreements, accept or reject inspectors and co-operate with or withhold their co-operation from the IAEA in applying safeguards.

Safeguards depend critically, therefore, on the international climate, on reasonably good relations among the NWS and between the major alliances (so that control is not sacrificed to the competition between them), on greater stability in strife-torn regions, on fair treatment of even 'outcast' states and on the attitudes and policies of individual states and the importance they attach to the goal of non-proliferation and nuclear arms control.

While the majority of developing countries has joined the NPT or the Treaty of Tlatelolco a large number has not, and the latter includes most of the developing countries that are leaders in the use of nuclear technology and some of the most populous and influential nations. It is therefore essential that more developing countries should come to share the perception of the dangers of proliferation. It is especially important that they should do so since the voice of the Third World in the IAEA is becoming stronger.

The chief priority is to make nuclear safeguards as universal as possible, through further accessions to the treaties in question or through acceptance of full-scope controls even without accession to these treaties. It is disturbing to note that the number of NNWS operating unsafeguarded plants that can make weapon material has now risen to five (Argentina, India, Israel, Pakistan and South Africa) and perhaps even six (Brazil).

The future of IAEA safeguards is now to a great extent linked to that of the NPT. Largely because of the lack of progress in nuclear arms control, which drives home more and more sharply the inequality of rights and obligations between the 3 NWS and over 100 NNWS parties to the NPT, confidence in the Treaty may in time erode.

An important measure which could reduce the inequality referred to above, and thereby render the NPT more attractive to the NNWS, would be the cessation of the production of plutonium and highly enriched uranium for military purposes and the placing of the relevant plants under safeguards. To ensure that such a cut-off could be implemented without undue delay, the IAEA should consider gradually extending its safeguards coverage. This would mean the NWS placing *all* their civilian nuclear plants on the "eligible lists" for IAEA safeguards. (The USA and the UK have done so in agreements with the IAEA; France has done so, in part; and the Soviet Union may do so, also in part; and there is no safeguards agreement with China.) It would also imply that the NWS inform the IAEA of all relevant transfers to other NWS.

A major political test will come in 10 years' time at the 1995 NPT Conference which must decide whether the Treaty shall continue in force indefinitely or shall be extended only "... for an additional fixed period or periods". It is essential therefore that the main foundation of safeguards, the non-proliferation regime itself, should be strengthened before 1995. In the first place this requires that the NWS take substantial steps towards nuclear arms control and disarmament and downgrade the role of nuclear weapons in international relations and their own dependence on them. It is also most important that the present nuclear threshold states continue to refrain from tests whether of nuclear weapons or of so-called 'peaceful' nuclear devices. Concerted diplomacy of the major powers can do much to foster such restraint; and even more effective would be the measure that the NPT itself implicitly promises: a treaty banning all tests in all environments "for all time".

Appendix I. Facts about the IAEA

I. Its origins and how it has evolved

In December 1953 President Eisenhower put forward to the UN General Assembly the idea of setting up an international atomic energy agency, under UN auspices, to make nuclear material and technology available for peaceful uses to all nations and to 'syphon off' some of the nuclear materials from the arsenals of the nuclear weapon states. On the initiative of the USA a group of 8 and later 12, and eventually a conference of 81 nations drew up the statute of the new body which came into being in Vienna on 29 July 1957. Its twin aims are:

> ...to seek to accelerate and enlarge the contribution of atomic energy to peace, health and prosperity throughout the world ... [and] ... to ensure so far as it is able, that assistance provided by it or at its request or under its supervision or control is not used in such a way as to further any military purpose ...

II. The IAEA today

The structure and methods of work of the IAEA are similar to those of other specialized UN organizations. However, the IAEA differs from them in its second main aim. This is essentially to contribute to *international confidence and security* by applying its safeguards. In other words, the IAEA does not only aim like most other UN agencies to promote economic and social development.

A Board of Governors of 35 and a General Conference of 112 states (1985 figures) direct the IAEA. Its annual budget in 1985 is US$98 million and it receives nearly US$50 million more in the form of voluntary contributions for technical assistance to the developing countries, for particular safeguards projects and for other special activities. Its staff is somewhat over 1 700.

Today the IAEA's two main tasks are to apply safeguards in the nations that do not have nuclear weapons (the non-nuclear weapon states) to verify that their nuclear activities are peaceful and, in particular, that they are not making nuclear weapons or other nuclear explosives and to help the developing countries to make use of nuclear techniques and technology and to do so safely. IAEA safeguards will cost nearly US$40 million (including special contributions) and technical aid for developing countries about US$34 million (chiefly in voluntary contributions) in 1985. But the IAEA also serves as a meeting place and as a means of exchanging information between the scientists and engineers of the industrial countries.

III. Help to the Third World

With the IAEA's help, developing countries are using nuclear techniques to breed new crops, to make better use of soil and water, to control insect pests, to produce more or better quality meat and milk, to preserve food, to develop underground water resources, to improve the quality of industrial products and cut costs. In a few cases the IAEA is helping developing countries to introduce or expand nuclear power programmes for the production of electricity. Nuclear medicine is now a recognized speciality and the IAEA helps developing countries in research on tropical and endemic diseases and in the diagnosis and treatment of cancer. In most cases nuclear techniques are one of several means of achieving the same end. For instance, one can use chemical agents instead of radiation to control insects or to treat cancer just as one can use coal or water power rather than nuclear energy to produce electricity. The research or field worker or technologist must weigh the pros and cons of the alternative means at his disposal.

IV. Exchanging nuclear information

The IAEA's information programme is built around INIS (the International Nuclear Information System). This was the first international project to combine decentralized information input with internationally centralized processing. Participating institutes, governments and organizations send the results of their research to the IAEA. The IAEA checks and merges the input and sends it back to the users on magnetic tape or in a monthly abstract journal. In this way, for instance, a scientist working on certain biological effects of radiation can obtain a monthly review of all new work going on anywhere in his field.

V. Making nuclear energy safer

Each government must be responsible for nuclear safety in its own country and for any radioactive pollution that might spread beyond its own frontiers. But the IAEA helps governments, especially those that have modest nuclear safety resources, to find safe sites for nuclear reactors, to make sure that their nuclear plants are safely built and run and to deal with nuclear wastes.

Also, by working together at the IAEA, experts from many parts of the world can draw up nuclear guides and standards that distil the experience of those countries that have large nuclear programmes. Uniform international guides and codes plainly help trade in nuclear plant and material. For several years the IAEA has also helped research on the effects of nuclear radiation on man.

VI. Other programmes

The IAEA runs an international energy data bank (covering all sources of energy and not only nuclear) and gives general advice to governments on their electrical energy programmes. It helps them to find and develop uranium resources. It also operates a service laboratory near Vienna to support its various programmes including safeguards, and an international laboratory at Monaco to study the effect of radioactivity in the seas and oceans. Together with Unesco, the IAEA operates the International Centre for Theoretical Physics at Trieste in Italy which has gained world-wide scientific recognition and support.

VII. IAEA safeguards

The main clauses of the IAEA's Statute, which lay down how and when it should apply its safeguards and what they should be, are Article III.A.5 and Article XII. The first (Article III.A.5) reads as follows:

> Article III. *Functions*
>   A. The agency is authorized:
>   . . .
>   5. To establish and administer safeguards designed to ensure that special fissionable and other materials, services, equipment, facilities, and information made available by the Agency or at its request or under its supervision or control are not used in such a way as to further any military purpose; and to apply safeguards, at the request of the parties, to any bilateral or multilateral arrangement, or at the request of a State, to any of that State's activities in the field of atomic energy.

Article XII is much more detailed:

> Article XII. *Agency safeguards*
>   A. With respect to any Agency project, or other arrangement where the Agency is requested by the parties concerned to apply safeguards, the Agency shall have the following rights and responsibilities to the extent relevant to the project or arrangement:

1. To examine the design of specialized equipment and facilities, including nuclear reactors, and to approve it only from the view-point of assuring that it will not further any military purpose, that it complies with applicable health and safety standards, and that it will permit effective application of the safeguards provided for in this article;

2. To require the observance of any health and safety measures prescribed by the Agency;

3. To require the maintenance and production of operating records to assist in ensuring accountability for source and special fissionable materials used or produced in the project or arrangement;

4. To call for and receive progress reports;

5. To approve the means to be used for the chemical processing of irradiated materials solely to ensure that this chemical processing will not lend itself to diversion of materials for military purposes and will comply with applicable health and safety standards; to require that special fissionable materials recovered or produced as a by-product be used for peaceful purposes under continuing Agency safeguards for research or in reactors, existing or under construction, specified by the member or members concerned; and to require deposit with the Agency of any excess of any special fissionable materials recovered or produced as a by-product over what is needed for the above-stated uses in order to prevent stock-piling of these materials, provided that thereafter at the request of the member or members concerned special fissionable materials so deposited with the Agency shall be returned promptly to the member or members concerned for use under the same provisions as stated above;

6. To send into the territory of the recipient State or States inspectors, designated by the Agency after consultation with the State or States concerned, who shall have access at all times to all places and data and to any person who by reason of his occupation deals with materials, equipment, or facilities which are required by this Statute to be safeguarded, as necessary to account for source and special fissionable materials supplied and fissionable products and to determine whether there is compliance with the undertaking against use in furtherance of any military purpose referred to in sub-paragraph F-4 of article XI, with the health and safety measures referred to in sub-paragraph A-2 of this article, and with any other conditions prescribed in the agreement between the Agency and the State or States concerned. Inspectors designated by the Agency shall be accompanied by representatives of the authorities of the State concerned, if that State so requests, provided that the inspectors shall not thereby be delayed or otherwise impeded in the exercise of their functions;

7. In the event of non-compliance and failure by the recipient State or States to take requested corrective steps within a reasonable time, to suspend or terminate assistance and withdraw any materials and equipment made available by the Agency or a member in furtherance of the project.

B. The Agency shall, as necessary, establish a staff of inspectors. The staff of inspectors shall have the responsibility of examining all operations conducted by the Agency itself to determine whether the Agency is complying with the health and safety measures prescribed by it for application to projects subject to its approval, supervision or control, and whether the Agency is taking adequate measures to prevent the source and special fissionable materials in its custody or used or produced in its own operations from being used in furtherance of any military purpose. The Agency shall take remedial action forthwith to correct any non-compliance or failure to take adequate measures.

C. ... The inspectors shall report any non-compliance to the Director General who shall thereupon transmit the report to the Board of Governors. The Board shall call upon the recipient State or States to remedy forthwith any non-compliance which it finds to have occurred. The Board shall report the non-compliance to all members and to the Security Council and General Assembly of the United Nations. In the event of failure of the recipient State or States to take fully corrective action within a reasonable time, the Board may take one or both of the following measures: direct curtailment or suspension of assistance being provided by the Agency or by a member, and call for the return of materials and equipment made available to the recipient member or group of members. The Agency may also, in accordance with article XIX, suspend any non-complying member from the exercise of the privileges and rights of membership.

When the diplomats and scientists met in Washington in 1954 and 1955 to draw up the Statute of the IAEA they expected that its main work would be to arrange for supplies of nuclear material from the nuclear weapon states and of uranium from the countries producing that still scarce element, and that the IAEA would apply its safeguards chiefly as a result of such "assistance". It would do so at the request of the exporting and importing governments or in connection with an IAEA project—for instance, a research reactor that the country had requested from the IAEA.

In fact the IAEA's role as a broker for nuclear material or as a launcher of nuclear projects never amounted to much. Instead IAEA safeguards came into action when the IAEA took over responsibility to verify existing bilateral supply arrangements where no element of IAEA assistance was involved. However, the real take-off came in a way that the IAEA's statute could not foresee. This was when the Nuclear Non-Proliferation Treaty (NPT) and the Treaty for the Prohibition of Nuclear Weapons in Latin America came into force, and because the parties to each treaty undertake to place their nuclear activities under IAEA safeguards.

Safeguards equipment and technology are playing a growing role in the IAEA's work. They make safeguards more certain and effective and less intrusive. They also enable the IAEA to detect any suspicious event at a nuclear plant much more quickly than it could by the essential but slow process of accounting periodically for all material at the plant. The next Appendix describes some of the main equipment and techniques that the IAEA is using and that certain of its member states are helping it to obtain in the future.

List of IAEA member states, as of 1 January 1985

Afghanistan
Albania
Algeria
Argentina
Australia
Austria
Bangladesh
Belgium
Bolivia
Brazil
Bulgaria
Burma
Byelorussia
Cameroon
Canada
Chile
China
Colombia
Costa Rica
Cuba
Cyprus
Czechoslovakia
Denmark
Dominican Republic
Ecuador
Egypt
El Salvador
Ethiopia
Finland
France
Gabon
German Democratic Republic
Germany, Federal Republic of
Ghana
Greece
Guatemala
Haiti
Holy See
Hungary
Iceland
India
Indonesia
Iran
Iraq
Ireland
Israel

Italy
Ivory Coast
Jamaica
Japan
Jordan
Kampuchea, Democratic
Kenya
Korea, North
Korea, South
Kuwait
Lebanon
Liberia
Libya
Liechtenstein
Luxembourg
Madagascar
Malaysia
Mali
Mauritius
Mexico
Monaco
Mongolia
Morocco
Namibia
Netherlands
New Zealand
Nicaragua
Niger
Nigeria
Norway
Pakistan
Panama
Paraguay
Peru
Philippines
Poland
Portugal
Qatar
Romania
Saudi Arabia
Senegal
Sierra Leone
Singapore
South Africa
Spain
Sri Lanka

Sudan
Sweden
Switzerland
Syrian Arab Republic
Tanzania, United Republic of
Thailand
Tunisia
Turkey
Uganda
Ukraine

Union of Soviet Socialist Republics
United Arab Emirates
United Kingdom
United States of America
Uruguay
Venezuela
Viet Nam
Yugoslavia
Zaire
Zambia

Appendix II. Safeguards techniques and equipment

Nuclear safeguards are a comprehensive system of nuclear material accountancy and containment/surveillance (C/S) measures. Their main method—*nuclear material accountancy*—is designed to keep track of the nuclear material within the various areas of a plant. To do so requires measurements of, for instance 'amount', 'enrichment' and 'number of specific items'. IAEA inspectors also use *containment* and/or *surveillance* instruments and techniques (see Glossary) in support of nuclear material accountancy.

This appendix describes some of the instruments and techniques that IAEA inspectors use in the field.

I. Nuclear material accountancy

Under safeguards agreements the operator of a nuclear facility must keep accurate accounts of the movement of nuclear material into and out of his plant, as well as through the various plant processes. This is esential for safe and economical operation. Much of the IAEA's verification consists of checking and auditing these accounts. For instance, countries are required to report periodically to the IAEA headquarters in Vienna on every change in the quantities of nuclear material in each of their nuclear plants. The IAEA checks, analyses and compares these reports both at headquarters and during inspections. IAEA inspectors make regular visits to check the correctness of the plant records and compare them with the reports sent to the IAEA. They also verify by measurements and other means whether the amounts of nuclear material actually in the plants, and the increases or decreases since the last inspection, agree with the amounts shown or calculated from records and reports.

Measuring, counting and analysing safeguarded material

IAEA inspectors measure the content of nuclear material, either by taking a representative sample, and sending it to an analytical laboratory (e.g., the IAEA's safeguards laboratory near Vienna) or by non-destructive (ND) analysis 'on the spot'. Both procedures have their problems and require sophisticated instruments and expertise.

Chemical analysis at the IAEA or other laboratories

Chemical analyses usually lead to very accurate and precise results, but they are expensive, the samples have to be transported, and the results are only available after 3–5 weeks. ND analyses (which do not involve any taking of samples) are often less accurate but in many cases are available immediately.

The IAEA's analytical laboratory is designed and equipped for chemical analysis of materials containing plutonium. The laboratory uses a fully automated instrument—a mass spectrometer—to analyse uranium and plutonium in samples collected during inspections.

Chemical analysis provides a great deal of the quantitative information that the IAEA needs about safeguarded nuclear material. It is either used directly to obtain the results or indirectly to calibrate the standards required for ND testing techniques. More than 1 100 samples of uranium, plutonium and spent fuel were analysed by the IAEA in 1983.

Inspector's aids

Non-destructive analysis at the plant

A fuel assembly worth some $100 000 cannot be destroyed in order to find out whether the declared nuclear material is actually present. In many situations, therefore, sampling and chemical analysis are not possible: for instance, if the nuclear material is contained in cans, rods, pins, fuel assemblies, gas (UF_6) cylinders or other containers and a sample cannot readily be taken without destroying the integrity of the container. In such cases ND testing techniques are used to check the type and quality of the contained nuclear material.

Since uranium and plutonium are in continuous radioactive decay they emit characteristic radiation. This is an inherent physical property that cannot be altered or readily imitated, and it enables the type and quantity of the radioactive material to be determined.

Because of the great variety of types of information that the IAEA needs and of the forms and situations in which the nuclear material has to be measured, the IAEA needs a broad range of specialized instruments to carry out particular ND analyses.

Most of the nuclear materials of concern to safeguards emit gamma rays. Gamma rays have well-defined energies which are characteristic 'fingerprints' of the isotopes emitting them. The most common ND safeguards techniques are based on the measurement of gamma radiation as it interacts with the material of a detector. Instruments which perform this task are called multi-channel analysers.

The main kind of gamma-ray detectors used are scintillation (light-pulse emitting) detectors and semiconductor detectors. The ability of scintillation detectors to distinguish between gamma rays of different energies is low, but they can detect extremely small amounts of nuclear material. The semiconductor detectors can resolve complex gamma spectra and give much more information about the materials being examined. For instance, they can measure accurately the ratios between various isotopes of plutonium in plutonium samples and in spent fuel, thus giving information about the burn-up of the fuel. However, most semiconductor detectors must be operated at a very low temperature; and the more convenient scintillation detectors can be used in many more situations.

Examples of scintillation detectors (low-resolution gamma spectrometers)

The simplest gamma-ray detecting instrument used by inspectors is a battery-operated gamma monitor. It can detect gamma rays in different energy ranges, and can thereby distinguish between uranium and plutonium. One instrument of this type is a hand-held gamma assay monitor, used mainly for measurements on unirradiated uranium materials.

At present the most widely used instrument of this type is the stabilized assay meter (SAM-2). This is a compact, lightweight, two-channel gamma spectro-meter. (The two channels can separate the gamma-ray energies into 'high' or 'low' energy channels.) The SAM-2 unit is able to display directly the results of the measurements being made, for instance the uranium enrichment (as a percentage of uranium-235). This instrument has been in use since 1976, giving good results in *the measurement of uranium enrichment* and useful qualitative results on other materials.

Examples of semiconductor detectors (high-resolution gamma spectrometers)

In recent years, portable high-resolution spectrometers have become available. Two types of this instrument, the portable mini-multichannel analyser (PMCA), are shown in figure 1.

The PMCA can be used to measure accurately the *uranium enrichment* as well as *uranium-235 content* in various physical and chemical forms of nuclear material. It can also provide an effective means of rapid, positive identification for various uranium and plutonium samples, coupons, foils, pellets, and so on. Because of its versatility and ease of use, the PMCA is expected to become the future main 'work-horse' for on-site verification of both the uranium and plutonium content in many different types of material.

Another high-resolution gamma spectrometer allows an inspector working in the field to measure *plutonium isotopic composition*. The system is easy to use and guides the inspector through the entire measurement procedure.

Neutron-counting methods

Unlike gamma rays, neutrons readily penetrate high-density materials such as uranium and plutonium. This makes neutron techniques very useful for assaying large, dense, heterogeneous samples of uranium and/or plutonium in various types of nuclear material and configuration (e.g., pins, rods). Neutron-counting methods are generally simpler and easier to use than high-resolution gamma-ray equipment.

The high-level neutron-coincidence counter (HLNCC) shown in figure 2 is widely used for the *assay of bulk plutonium* in amounts ranging from a few grams to about 3 kg. By fitting specialized detector heads this instrument can be used to analyse *plutonium in different shapes and structures*, for instance: in plutonium 'birdcage' containers (plutonium is normally stored or transported in structures that look like birdcages and that keep plutonium in less-than-critical amounts clearly separated); in fast critical-assembly fuel assemblies; in fuel pins for fast breeder reactors; and in small samples such as those taken during inventory verification.

Another neutron-counting instrument, called the active well coincidence counter (AWCC), is used to ascertain the *uranium-235 content in enriched uranium materials*; for instance in bulk uranium dioxide samples, high-enrichment uranium metals, and light water reactor (LWR) fuel pellets. The AWCC can also be used in safeguarding some types of fuel assembly used in research reactors such as material-testing reactors.

A very important instrument in this group is the uranium neutron-coincidence collar (UNCL), designed for safeguarding LWR fuel assemblies. (The LWR is by far the most common type of power and of research reactor.) In different modes it can be operated either to *measure the uranium-235 or -238 content of fuel assemblies*. Its sensitive response to uranium-235 allows an inspector to detect the removal or substitution of as few as 3–4 rods in a pressurized water reactor fuel assembly (of 225 rods) and one rod in a boiling water reactor assembly (of 49 rods). Because it is reliable, relatively easy to operate and non-intrusive, the UNCL is expected to come into increasingly widespread use in the future.

Cherenkov glow observation

Irradiated reactor fuel emits Cherenkov radiation—a glow caused by the interaction of the intense radiation from spent fuel with the water of the storage pool. The glow varies in intensity, and for highly active fuel can be seen in darkness by the naked eye. An inspector at a LWR site can verify the presence of irradiated fuel in a pool by seeing whether the Cherenkov glow is being emitted. Since the glow is not normally visible under ordinary lighting conditions, a check of irradiated fuel requires a night-viewing device with light-amplifying capabilities. A hand-held Cherenkov viewing device routinely used by IAEA inspectors thus intensifies the image of the Cherenkov glow. When using the observation device in semi-darkness, an inspector standing on the pool bridge can scan and verify the characteristic patterns formed by the arrangements of rods and holes in fuel assemblies.

Measurement of radiation from spent fuel

Measurement of radiation from spent fuel is important because from such measurements an estimate of burn-up can be obtained which in turn enables assessment of plutonium build up and uranium-235 depletion in the fuel. (Direct measurement of these is precluded by the intense radioactivity of the fuel.) Gamma spectrometers can give good estimates of burn-up, but require that the fuel be moved to a special measurement location. To simplify the verification of spent fuel, a new technique has been developed at the Los Alamos National Laboratories, USA, which requires only minimal movement of spent fuel assemblies during measurement at the storage location.

Calorimetry

When the isotopes of plutonium decay most of the energy of the decay process is normally dissipated in the material as heat. By measuring the heat produced the mass of an amount of plutonium can be determined if its isotopic composition is known. Calorimeters are extremely precise instruments, but they take a long time to reach thermal equilibrium during the measurement. Calorimetry is thus being developed mainly as a reference method for the calibration of standards for use in other ND analysis techniques.

Weighing

One of the most important quantities to be verified by inspectors is the weight of items containing nuclear materials. In many cases this can be done by using standard weights to check the calibration of a plant operator's weighing machine, but in the case of very large items such as cylinders containing uranium hexafluoride (UF_6), this is not possible.

A transportable system for weighing 30-inch (about 75 cm) UF_6 cylinders was therefore developed by the US National Bureau of Standards and has now been approved for routine inspection use (see figure 3). The device is equipped with gauges that accurately sense the weight of the suspended cylinder and display the results directly on an electronic indicator unit.

Permanently installed instruments

Instruments which are permanently installed enable the IAEA to obtain higher quality measurements. They are particularly suitable for and useful in large bulk-handling plants such as large reprocessing, enrichment and fuel fabrication plants. The use of resident (essentially full-time) IAEA inspectors is also foreseen for some of the larger bulk-handling facilities.

The IAEA has used several installed instruments but three deserve special mention; two of them are already in regular use at reprocessing plants while the third may be used in centrifuge enrichment plants: (*a*) the 'K-edge densitometer' which measures the concentration of plutonium in separated product solutions: (*b*) the electromanometer, which is essentially an automated volume measuring system; and (*c*) the gas-phase enrichment monitor (for use in gas centrifuges).

II. C/S instruments and techniques

The IAEA is increasingly using instruments to survey and record any movement of nuclear materials in the plant between inspections, and seals to seal off stores of nuclear material between inspections or to seal the cores of the reactors themselves (i.e., the fuel in the reactor). Much work is being done to make these devices more tamper-resistant.

Sealing systems

A sealing system consists of the containment enclosing the nuclear material to be safeguarded, the means of applying the seal (i.e., a metal wire) and the seal itself. All seals are numbered and have unique identification marks placed inside the cap, which are photographed and documented before the seals are issued for use. On the return of a used seal to IAEA headquarters, the identity is verified by re-photographing and comparing with the original record. Currently some 10 000 of these seals are applied and checked by inspectors every year.

For short-term applications the seal used is an adhesive label, a deliberately fragile vinyl sheet with a pattern of small cuts, which cannot be removed without destroying it. An improved adhesive seal using reflective tamper-indicating material is being developed.

Most of the R&D in this area is aimed at producing seals which are uniquely identifiable and verifiable *in the field*. These fall into two main categories:

1. *Fibre-optic seals*, in which the seal wire (widely used today) is replaced by a multi-strand plastic fibre-optic loop, the ends of which are enclosed in a seal in such a way that a unique random pattern is formed. This can be verified by shining a light into the ends of the loop and observing the magnified pattern of the fibre ends.

2. *Ultrasonic seals* contain a unique random pattern of, say, metal pieces in a lighter substrate, or a randomly oriented coil of wire. The seal is checked by transmitting ultrasonic pulses through the seal with a suitable transducer and observing the pattern of reflections obtained, using a specifically developed pattern-reading device.

Photographic surveillance

The basic photo-surveillance unit used by the IAEA is a twin-camera (Minolta) system, mounted in a sealed case. It takes one picture at a time at intervals of 10–30 minutes. About 200 of these units are now in service. Inspectors use a variety of projection equipment to review the film taken. They include a film scanner which is capable of storing questionable images for later review.

Television surveillance

Television is preferred to photographic systems if light levels are low, if radiation is present which could fog film, if a high picture capacity is required, or if there is a need for immediate play-back of the video tape to provide quick detection of any anomalies. Since the mid-1970s the IAEA has been routinely using the 'Psychotronic' television surveillance system. Films are automatically annotated with date and time. The units have been greatly improved since their introduction and have recently been equipped with new cassette video-recorders.

An advanced television surveillance system is now being brought into field use. This is a microprocessor-controlled system (STAR) developed by Sandia Laboratories, USA; it uses solid-state cameras and has provision for back-up and slave cassette video recorders. A 'motion detector' (which picks up any movement in the field of vision of the camera) can be used to start the machine or it can operate automatically at timed intervals. Canada is developing a television surveillance system for use with CANDU reactors (see Glossary).

Bundle counter

CANDU reactors, unlike LWRs, are refuelled without reactor shut-down. Safeguards measures for CANDU reactors concentrate on the verification of irradiated fuel discharged from the core into the spent-fuel bay (and subsequent shipment off-site). Under the Canadian Support Programme, a counter for bundles of spent fuel (CSFC) has been developed specifically for safeguarding CANDU reactors. The counter consists of four Geiger-Müller radiation counters mounted along the path that the irradiated CANDU fuel bundles follow from the reactor to the spent-fuel bay. Signals are processed by a unit which determines the number and direction of travel of the bundles.

Underwater surveillance instruments

Two instruments are under evaluation for reading identification numbers on irradiated fuel in storage pools. One is a periscope which can be mounted at the pool side or on the pool bridge. The basic periscope can be used in clear water with good illumination. The extended periscope is needed when the pool water is not clear, lighting is poor, or viewing of the identification numbers is difficult.

The second instrument is a closed-circuit television system with an underwater camera. The camera has built-in lighting and is remotely controlled, enabling it to be operated from the ppol bridge.

Radiation dosimeters

Radiation dosimeters can be used as 'yes/no' monitors to confirm that radio-active materials have or have not passed through a containment barrier (e.g., reactor containment vessel, transport cask). Currently available for use are radio-photoluminescent glass dosimeters, which can be obtained with ranges from about 10 mR to several thousand roentgen. After exposure to radiation, exposure to ultra-violet light causes a luminescent glow; the luminescent intensity is proportional to the radiation dose. Heating to about 400°C destroys the lumines-cence, allowing the dosimeters to be re-used.

Inspectors also use less sophisticated thermoluminescent dosimeters, for which commercially available heat source and light measuring equipment are used.

III. R&D support programme

The IAEA does not have the resources needed for R&D to improve safeguards equipment and techniques. It is, however, co-ordinating and monitoring the extensive safeguards support programmes that some of its members and EURATOM are carrying out. Their expenditures amount to tens of millions of dollars.

Sources

Keepin, G. R., 'State of the art technology for measurement and verification of nuclear materials', in Hafemeister, D. and Tsipis, K. (eds), *Technical Means of Verification of Arms Control Treaties* (MIT Press, Cambridge, MA, 1984).

Rundquist, D. E. and Watkins, L. M., 'Improving safeguard techniques: instru-mentation', *IAEA Bulletin*, Vol. 26, No. 3, September 1984, pp. 13–19.

IAEA Safeguards Glossary (IAEA/SG/INF/1) (1980).

IAEA Safeguards: Guidelines for States' Systems of Accounting for and Control of Nuclear Materials (IAEA/SG/INF/2) (1980).

IAEA Safeguards: An Introduction (IAEA/SG/INF/3) (1981).

IAEA Safeguards: Aims, Limitations, Achievements (IAEA/SG/INF/4) (1983).

IAEA Safeguards: Techniques and Equipment (IAEA/SG/INF/5) (1984).

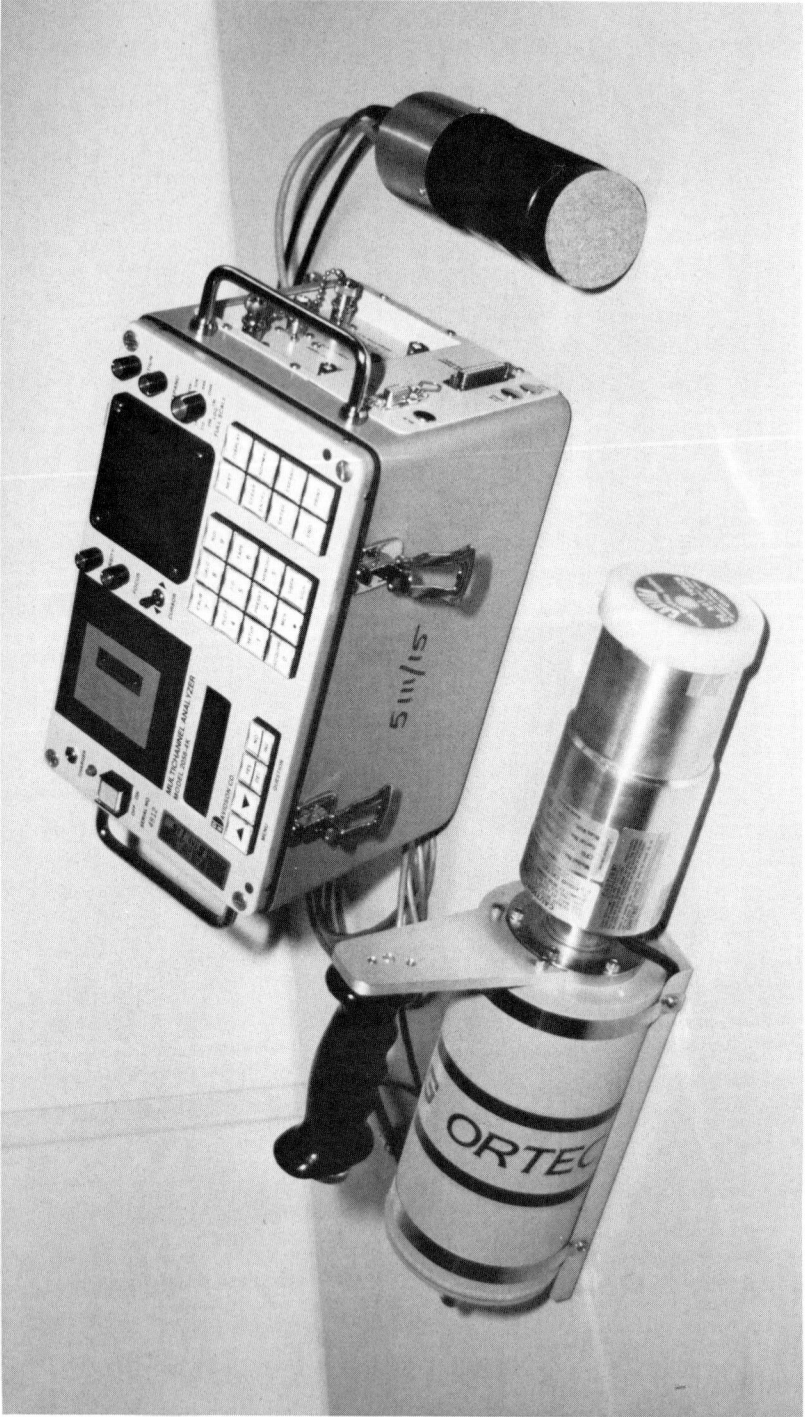

Figure 1. Two types of portable mini-multichannel analyser used to measure the uranium enrichment and ^{235}U content in nuclear materials

Photograph courtesy of Katholitzky.

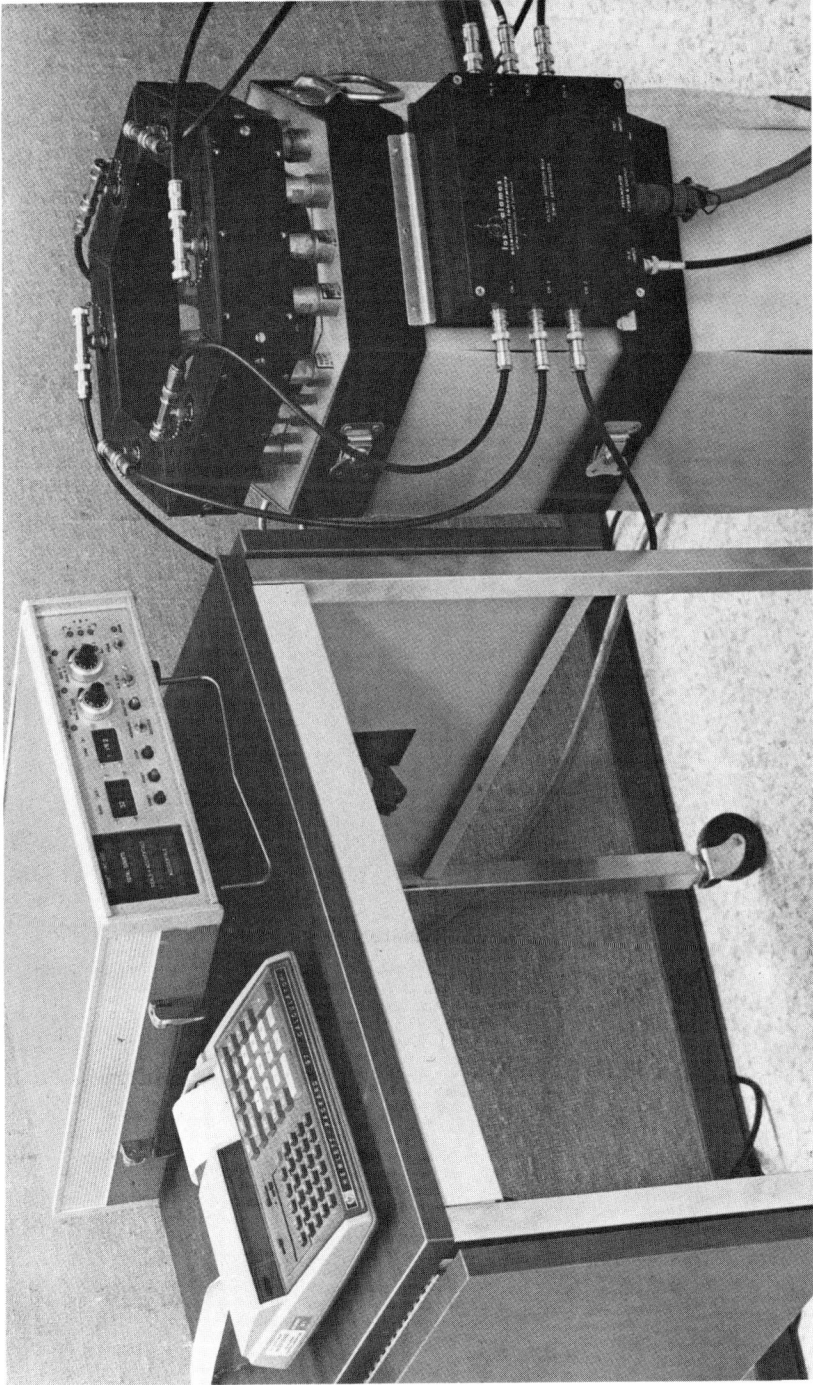

Figure 2. The high-level neutron coincidence counter (HLNCC), used for the assay of bulk plutonium in amounts ranging from a few grams to about 3 kg

Figure 3. Load-cell-based weighing system—a transportable system for weighing 30-inch UF$_6$ cylinders. The results are directly displayed on an electronic indicator unit

Appendix III. Nuclear plants[1] under construction or operating in the developing countries outside Europe (power and research reactors and significant fuel facilities)

Unsafeguarded plants are underlined.

Argentina
   3 HWR power reactors
   6 small research reactors[2]
   3 fuel fabrication plants
   2 heavy water production plants (1 unsafeguarded)
   1 pilot reprocessing plant (under safeguards when, as today, reprocessing safeguarded fuel)
   1 pilot enrichment plant[3]
   1 uranium oxide conversion plant (possibly a second unsafeguarded plant)
   1 UF$_6$ plant

Brazil
   3 LWR power reactors
   3 small research reactors
   1 pilot reprocessing plant (construction status not clear)
   1 pilot enrichment plant
   1 fuel fabrication plant
   1 uranium oxide conversion plant
   1 UF$_6$ plant

Cuba
   2 LWR power reactors[4]
   1 small LWR research reactor[4]

India
  10 power reactors (8 HWRs and 2 LWRs, 6 HWRs unsafeguarded)
   6 research reactors (including 1 large HWR)[5]
   3 reprocessing plants[5] (1 under safeguards while reprocessing safeguarded fuel)
   2 fuel fabrication plants (1 unsafeguarded)
   7 heavy water production plants
   3 uranium oxide conversion plants (2 unsafeguarded)
   1 thorium oxide fuel fabrication plant
   1 fast breeder fuel fabrication plant

Israel	2 research reactors (<u>including 1 large HWR[5]</u>)
	<u>1 reprocessing plant[5]</u>
	<u>1 heavy water production plant</u>
	<u>1 fuel fabrication plant</u>
Korea, South	9 power reactors (8 LWRs and 1 HWR)
	3 small research reactors
	2 fuel fabrication plants (1 pilot)
	1 uranium oxide conversion plant
Mexico	1 LWR power reactor (construction of second power reactor reportedly suspended)
	2 small research reactors
Pakistan	1 HWR power reactor
	1 small research reactor
	<u>2 reprocessing plants (possibly 3 including 2 pilot reprocessing plants)</u>
	<u>1 pilot enrichment plant[6]</u>
	<u>1 fuel fabrication plant</u>
	<u>2 heavy water production plants (1 upgrader)</u>
	<u>1 UF$_6$ plant</u>
Philippines	1 LWR power reactor
	1 small research reactor
South Africa[7]	2 LWR power reactors
	1 large LWR research reactor
	2 enrichment plants (<u>1 pilot plant in operation,</u>[3]
	1 commercial plant under construction)
	<u>1 fuel fabrication plant</u>
	<u>2 uranium oxide conversion plants</u>
	<u>1 UF$_6$ plant</u>
	(also extensive uranium mining, milling and processing)
Taiwan	6 LWR power reactors
	6 research reactors (including 1 large HWR)
	1 fuel fabrication plant
	1 uranium oxide conversion plant

The nuclear plant in each of the following developing countries is confined essentially to a single small research reactor, usually an LWR using enriched US or Soviet fuel:

Colombia	Iran
Peru (building a second)	Iraq[8]
Uruguay	Libya[9]
Venezuela	Thailand
Zaire	Viet Nam
Egypt	Malaysia

A further four developing countries each have two research reactors[10]:

Chile
Turkey
Indonesia
Korea, North

Notes

[1] Other than uranium mills producing U_3O_8.
[2] 'Small' means less than 5 MW(th). The fuel content of such reactors is normally well below a 'significant quantity', i.e., the amount needed to make a single nuclear explosive. LWRs use enriched uranium fuel chiefly of US, Soviet or West German origin (French, in the case of South Africa and India).
[3] Producing unsafeguarded enriched uranium.
[4] All supplied by the USSR and using Soviet low-enriched fuel.
[5] Producing unsafeguarded plutonium.
[6] Believed to be nearing completion.
[7] Although not usually classified as a developing country, South Africa is included in this list as one of the 5 NNWS that produce unsafeguarded nuclear weapon material.
[8] Since the Tamuz 1 reactor was destroyed.
[9] There are unconfirmed reports that Libya is also obtaining a power reactor (LWR) from the USSR.
[10] Among the industrial countries, Greece, Portugal and Norway each operate a single small research reactor while Denmark has two (none has or is building a power reactor). Albania has recently shown interest in acquiring a research reactor.

Appendix IV. The IAEA safeguards system of 1965–68, INFCIRC/66/Rev. 2

The Agency's safeguards system (1965, as provisionally extended in 1966 and 1968)

I. GENERAL CONSIDERATIONS

A. The purpose of this document

1. Pursuant to Article II of its Statute the Agency has the task of seeking "to accelerate and enlarge the contribution of atomic energy to peace, health and prosperity throughout the world". Inasmuch as the technology of nuclear energy for peaceful purposes is closely coupled with that for the production of materials for nuclear weapons, the same Article of the Statute provides that the Agency "shall ensure, so far as it is able, that assistance provided by it or at its request or under its supervision or control is not used in such a way as to further any military purpose".

2. The principal purpose of the present document is to establish a system of controls to enable the Agency to comply with this statutory obligation with respect to the activities of Member States in the field of the peaceful uses of nuclear energy, as provided in the Statute. The authority to establish such a system is provided by Article III.A.5. of the Statute, which authorizes the Agency to "establish and administer safeguards designed to ensure that special fissionable and other materials, services, equipment, facilities, and information made available by the Agency or at its request or under its supervision or control are not used in such a way as to further any military purpose". This Article further authorizes the Agency to "apply safeguards, at the request of the parties, to any bilateral or multilateral arrangement, or at the request of a State, to any of that State's activities in the field of atomic energy". Article XII.A sets forth the rights and responsibilities that the Agency is to have, to the extent relevant, with respect to any project or arrangement which it is to safeguard.

3. The principles set forth in this document and the procedures for which it provides are established for the information of Member States, to enable them to determine in advance the circumstances and manner in which the Agency would administer safeguards, and for the guidance of the organs of the Agency itself, to enable the Board and the Director General to determine readily what provisions should be included in agreements relating to safeguards and how to interpret such provisions.

4. Provisions of this document that are relevant to a particular project, arrangement or activity in the field of nuclear energy will only become legally binding upon the entry into force of a *safeguards agreement*[1] and to the extent that they are incorporated therein. Such incorporation may be made by reference.

5. Appropriate provisions of this document may also be incorporated in bilateral or multilateral arrangements between Member States, including all those that provide for the transfer to the Agency of responsibility for administering safeguards. The Agency will not assume such responsibility unless the principles of the safeguards and the procedures to be used are essentially consistent with those set forth in this document.

6. Agreements incorporating provisions from the earlier version of the Agency's safeguards system[2] will continue to be administered in accordance with such provisions, unless all States parties thereto request the Agency to substitute the provisions of the present document.

7. Provisions relating to types of *principal nuclear facilities*, other than *reactors*, which may produce, process or use safeguarded *nuclear material* will be developed as necessary.

8. The principles and procedures set forth in this document shall be subject to periodic review in the light of the further experience gained by the Agency as well as of technological developments.

B. General principles of the Agency's safeguards

The Agency's obligations

9. Bearing in mind Article II of the Statute, the Agency shall implement safeguards in a manner designed to avoid hampering a State's economic or technological development.

10. The safeguards procedures set forth in this document shall be implemented in a manner designed to be consistent with prudent management practices required for the economic and safe conduct of nuclear activities.

11. In no case shall the Agency request a State to stop the construction or operation of any *principal nuclear facility* to which the Agency's safeguards procedures extend, except by explicit decision of the Board.

12. The State or States concerned and the Director General shall hold consultations regarding the application of the provisions of the present document.

13. In implementing safeguards, the Agency shall take every precaution to protect commercial and industrial secrets. No member of the Agency's staff shall disclose, except to the Director General and to such other members of the staff as the Director General may authorize to have such information by reason of their official duties in connection with safeguards, any commercial or industrial secret or any other confidential information coming to his knowledge by reason of the implementation of safeguards by the Agency.

14. The Agency shall not publish or communicate to any State, organization or person any information obtained by it in connection with the implementation of safeguards, except that:

(*a*) Specific information relating to such implementation in a State may be given to the Board and to such Agency staff members as require such knowledge by reason of their official duties in connection with safeguards, but only to the extent necessary for the Agency to fulfil its safeguards responsibilities;

(*b*) Summarized lists of items being safeguarded by the Agency may be published upon decision of the Board; and

(*c*) Additional information may be published upon decision of the Board and if all States directly concerned agree.

Principles of implementation

15. The Agency shall implement safeguards in a State if:

(*a*) The Agency has concluded with the State a *project agreement* under which materials, services, equipment, facilities or information are supplied, and such agreement provides for the application of safeguards; or

(*b*) The State is a party to a bilateral or multilateral arrangement under which materials, services, equipment, facilities or information are supplied or otherwise transferred, and:

(i) All the parties to the arrangement have requested the Agency to administer safeguards; and

(ii) The Agency has concluded the necessary *safeguards agreement* with the State; or

(*c*) The Agency has been requested by the State to safeguard certain nuclear activities under the latter's jurisdiction, and the Agency has concluded the necessary *safeguards agreement* with the State.

16. In the light of Article XII.A.5 of the Statute, it is desirable that *safeguards agreements* should provide for the continuation of safeguards, subject to the provisions of this document, with respect to produced special fissionable material and to any materials substituted therefor.

17. The principal factors to be considered by the Board in determining the relevance of particular provisions of this document to various types of materials and facilities shall be the form, scope and amount of the assistance supplied, the character of each individual project and the degree to which such assistance could further any military purpose. The related *safeguards agreement* shall take account of all pertinent circumstances at the time of its conclusion.

18. In the event of any non-compliance by a State with a *safeguards agreement*, the Agency may take the measures set forth in Articles XII.A.7 and XII.C of the Statute.

II. CIRCUMSTANCES REQUIRING SAFEGUARDS

A. Nuclear materials subject to safeguards

19. Except as provided in paragraphs 21–28, *nuclear material* shall be subject to the Agency's safeguards if it is being or has been:

(*a*) Supplied under a *project agreement*; or

(*b*) Submitted to safeguards under a *safeguards agreement* by the parties to a bilateral or multilateral arrangement; or

(*c*) *Unilaterally submitted* to safeguards under a *safeguards agreement*; or

(*d*) Produced, processed or used in a *principal nuclear facility* which has been:

(i) Supplied wholly or substantially under a *project agreement*; or

(ii) Submitted to safeguards under a *safeguards agreement* by the parties to a bilateral or multilateral arrangement; or

(iii) *Unilaterally submitted* to safeguards under a *safeguards agreement*; or

(*e*) Produced in or by the use of safeguarded *nuclear material*; or

(*f*) Substituted, pursuant to paragraph 26(*d*), for safeguarded *nuclear material*.

20. A *principal nuclear facility* shall be con-

sidered as substantially supplied under a *project agreement* if the Board has so determined.

B. Exemptions from safeguards

General exemptions

21. *Nuclear material* that would otherwise be subject to safeguards shall be exempted from safeguards at the request of the State concerned, provided that the material so exempted in that State may not at any time exceed:

(*a*) 1 kilogram in total of special fissionable material, which may consist of one or more of the following:

  (i)   Plutonium;
  (ii) Uranium with an *enrichment* of 0.2 (20%) and above, taken account of by multiplying its weight by its *enrichment*;
  (iii) Uranium with an *enrichment* below 0.2 (20%) and above that of natural uranium, taken account of by multiplying its weight by five times the square of its *enrichment*;

(*b*) 10 metric tons in total of natural uranium and depleted uranium with an *enrichment* above 0.005 (0.5%);

(*c*) 20 metric tons of depleted uranium with an *enrichment* of 0.005 (0.5%) or below; and

(*d*) 20 metric tons of thorium.

Exemptions related to reactors

22. Produced or used *nuclear material* that would otherwise be subject to safeguards pursuant to paragraph 19(*d*) or (*e*) shall be exempted from safeguards if:

(*a*) It is plutonium produced in the fuel of a *reactor* whose rate of production does not exceed 100 grams of plutonium per year; or

(*b*) It is produced in a *reactor* determined by the Agency to have a maximum calculated power for continuous operation of less than 3 thermal megawatts, or is used in such a *reactor* and would not be subject to safeguards except for such use, provided that the total power of the *reactors* with respect to which these exemptions apply in any State may not exceed 6 thermal megawatts.

23. Produced special fissionable material that would otherwise be subject to safeguards pursuant only to paragraph 19(*e*) shall in part be exempted from safeguards if it is produced in a *reactor* in which the ratio of fissionable isotopes within safeguarded *nuclear material* to all fissionable isotopes is less than 0.3 (calculated each time any change is made in the loading of the *reactor* and assumed to be maintained until the next such change). Such fraction of the produced material as corresponds to the calculated ratio shall be subject to safeguards.

C. Suspension of safeguards

24. Safeguards with respect to *nuclear material* may be suspended while the material is transferred, under an arrangement or agreement approved by the Agency, for the purpose of processing, reprocessing, testing, research or development within the State concerned or to any other Member State or to an international organization, provided that the quantities of *nuclear material* with respect to which safeguards are thus suspended in a State may not at any time exceed:

(*a*) 1 *effective kilogram* of special fissionable material;

(*b*) 10 metric tons in total of natural uranium and depleted uranium with an *enrichment* above 0.005 (0.5%);

(*c*) 20 metric tons of depleted uranium with an *enrichment* of 0.005 (0.5%) or below; and

(*d*) 20 metric tons of thorium.

25. Safeguards with respect to *nuclear material* in irradiated fuel which is transferred for the purpose of reprocessing may also be suspended if the State or States concerned have, with the agreement of the Agency, placed under safeguards substitute *nuclear material* in accordance with paragraph 26(*d*) for the period of suspension. In addition, safeguards with respect to plutonium contained in irradiated fuel which is transferred for the purpose of reprocessing may be suspended for a period not to exceed six months if the State or States concerned have, with the agreement of the Agency, placed under safeguards a quantity of uranium whose *enrichment* in the isotope uranium-235 is not less than 0.9 (90%) and the uranium-235 content of which is equal in weight to such plutonium. Upon expiration of the said six months or the completion of reprocessing, whichever is earlier, safeguards shall, with the agreement of the Agency, be applied to such plutonium and shall cease to apply to the uranium substituted therefor.

D. Termination of safeguards

26. *Nuclear material* shall no longer be subject to safeguards after:

(*a*) It has been returned to the State that originally supplied it (whether directly or through the Agency), if it was subject to safeguards only by reason of such supply and if:

  (i) It was not *improved* while under safeguards; or

  (ii) Any special fissionable material that was produced in it under safeguards has been separated out, or safeguards with respect to such produced material have been terminated; or

(*b*) The Agency has determined that:

  (i)   It was subject to safeguards only by reason of its use in a *principal nuclear facility* specified in paragraph 19(*d*);

  (ii) It has been removed from such facility; and

  (iii) Any special fissionable material that was produced in it under safeguards has been separated out, or safeguards with respect to such produced material have been terminated; or

(*c*) The Agency has determined that it has

been consumed, or has been diluted in such a way that it is no longer usable for any nuclear activity relevant from the point of view of safeguards, or has become practicably irrecoverable; or

(*d*) The State or States concerned have, with the agreement of the Agency, placed under safeguards, as a substitute, such amount of the same element, not otherwise subject to safeguards, as the Agency has determined contains fissionable isotopes:

(i) Whose weight (with due allowance for processing losses) is equal to or greater than the weight of the fissionable isotopes of the material with respect to which safeguards are to terminate; and

(ii) Whose ratio by weight to the total substituted element is similar to or greater than the ratio by weight of the fissionable isotopes of the material with respect to which safeguards are to terminate to the total weight of such material;

provided that the Agency may agree to the substitution of plutonium for uranium-235 contained in uranium whose *enrichment* is not greater than 0.05 (5.0%); or

(*e*) It has been transferred out of the State under paragraph 28(*d*), provided that such material shall again be subject to safeguards it if is returned to the State in which the Agency had safeguarded it; or

(*f*) The conditions specified in the *safeguards agreement* pursuant to which it was subject to Agency safeguards, no longer apply, by expiration of the agreement or otherwise.

27. If a State wishes to use safeguarded source material for non-nuclear purposes, such as the production of alloys or ceramics, it shall agree with the Agency on the circumstances under which the safeguards on such material may be terminated.

E. Transfer of safeguarded nuclear material out of the State

28. No safeguarded *nuclear material* shall be transferred outside the jurisdiction of the State in which it is being safeguarded until the Agency has satisfied itself that one or more of the following conditions apply:

(*a*) The material is being returned, under the conditions specified in paragraph 26(*a*), to the State that originally supplied it; or

(*b*) The material is being transferred subject to the provisions of paragraph 24 or 25; or

(*c*) Arrangements have been made by the Agency to safeguard the material in accordance with this document in the State to which it is being transferred; or

(*d*) The material was not subject to safeguards pursuant to a *project agreement* and will be subject, in the State to which it is being transferred, to safeguards other than those of the Agency but generally consistent with such safeguards and accepted by the Agency.

III. SAFEGUARDS PROCEDURES

A. General procedures

Introduction

29. The safeguards procedures set forth below shall be followed, as far as relevant, with respect to safeguarded *nuclear materials*, whether they are being produced, processed or used in any *principal nuclear facility* or are outside any such facility. These procedures also extend to facilities containing or to contain such materials, including *principal nuclear facilities* to which the criteria in paragraph 19(*d*) apply.

Design review

30. The Agency shall review the design of *principal nuclear facilities*, for the sole purpose of satisfying itself that a facility will permit the effective application of safeguards.

31. The design review of a *principal nuclear facility* shall take place at as early a stage as possible. In particular, such review shall be carried out in the case of:

(*a*) An Agency project, before the project is approved;

(*b*) A bilateral or multilateral arrangement under which the responsibility for administering safeguards is to be transferred to the Agency, or an activity *unilaterally submitted* by a State, before the Agency assumes safeguards responsibilities with respect to the facility;

(*c*) A transfer of safeguarded *nuclear material* to a *principal nuclear facility* whose design has not previously been reviewed, before such transfer takes place; and

(*d*) A significant modification of a *principal nuclear facility* whose design has previously been reviewed, before such modification is undertaken.

32. To enable the Agency to perform the required design review, the State shall submit to it relevant design information sufficient for the purpose, including information on such basic characteristics of the *principal nuclear facility* as may bear on the Agency's safeguards procedures. The Agency shall require only the minimum amount of information and data consistent with carrying out its responsibility under this section. It shall complete the review promptly after the submission of this information by the State and shall notify the latter of its conclusions without delay.

Records

33. The State shall arrange for the keeping of records with respect to *principal nuclear facilities* and also with respect to all safeguarded *nuclear material* outside such facilities. For this purpose the State and the Agency shall agree on a system of records with respect to each facility and also with respect to such material, on the basis of proposals to be

submitted by the State in sufficient time to allow the Agency to review them before the records need to be kept.

34. If the records are not kept in one of the working languages of the Board, the State shall make arrangements to facilitate their examination by inspectors.

35. The records shall consist, as appropriate, of:

(a) Accounting records of all safeguarded *nuclear material*; and

(b) Operating records for *principal nuclear facilities*.

36. All records shall be retained for at least two years.

Reports

General requirements

37. The State shall submit to the Agency reports with respect to the production, processing and use of safeguarded *nuclear material* in or outside *principal nuclear facilities*. For this purpose the State and the Agency shall agree on a system of reports with respect to each facility and also with respect to safeguarded *nuclear material* outside such facilities, on the basis of proposals to be submitted by the State in sufficient time to allow the Agency to review them before the reports need to be submitted. The reports need include only such information as is relevant for the purpose of safeguards.

38. Unless otherwise provided in the applicable *safeguards agreement*, reports shall be submitted in one of the working languages of the Board.

Routine reports

39. Routine reports shall be based on the records compiled in accordance with paragraphs 33–36 and shall consist, as appropriate, of:

(a) Accounting reports showing the receipt, transfer out, inventory and use of all safeguarded *nuclear material*. The inventory shall indicate the nuclear and chemical composition and physical form of all material and its location on the date of the report; and

(b) Operating reports showing the use that has been made of each *principal nuclear facility* since the last report and, as far as possible, the programme of future work in the period until the next routine report is expected to reach the Agency.

40. The first routine report shall be submitted as soon as:

(a) There is any safeguarded *nuclear material* to be accounted for; or

(b) The *principal nuclear facility* to which it relates is in a condition to operate.

Progress in construction

41. The Agency may, if so provided in a *safeguards agreement*, request information as to when particular stages in the construction of

a *principal nuclear facility* have been or are to be reached.

Special reports

42. The State shall report to the Agency without delay:

(a) If any unusual incident occurs involving actual or potential loss or destruction of, or damage to, any safeguarded *nuclear material* or *principal nuclear facility*; or

(b) If there is good reason to believe that safeguarded *nuclear material* is lost or unaccounted for in quantities that exceed the normal operating and handling losses that have been accepted by the Agency as characteristic of the facility.

43. The State shall report to the Agency, as soon as possible, and in any case within two weeks, any transfer not requiring advance notification that will result in a significant change (to be defined by the Agency in agreement with the State) in the quantity of safeguarded *nuclear material* in a facility, or in a complex of facilities considered as a unit for this purpose by agreement with the Agency. Such report shall indicate the amount and nature of the material and its intended use.

Amplification of reports

44. At the Agency's request the State shall submit amplifications or clarifications of any report, in so far as relevant for the purpose of safeguards.

Inspections

General procedures

45. The Agency may inspect safeguarded *nuclear materials* and *principal nuclear facilities*.

46. The purpose of safeguards inspections shall be to verify compliance with *safeguards agreements* and to assist States in complying with such agreements and in resolving any questions arising out of the implementation of safeguards.

47. The number, duration and intensity of inspections actually carried out shall be kept to the minimum consistent with the effective implementation of safeguards, and if the Agency considers that the authorized inspections are not all required, fewer shall be carried out.

48. Inspectors shall neither operate any facility themselves nor direct the staff of a facility to carry out any particular operation.

Routine inspections

49. Routine inspections may include, as appropriate:

(a) Audit of records and reports;

(b) Verification of the amount of safeguarded *nuclear material* by physical inspection, measurement and sampling;

(c) Examination of *principal nuclear facilities*, including a check of their measuring instruments and operating characteristics; and

(*d*) Check of the operations carried out at *principal nuclear facilities* and at *research and development facilities* containing safeguarded *nuclear material*.

50. Whenever the Agency has the right of access to a *principal nuclear facility* at all times[3], it may perform inspections of which notice as required by paragraph 4 of the *Inspectors Document* need not be given, in so far as this is necessary for the effective application of safeguards. The actual procedures to implement these provisions shall be agreed upon between the parties concerned in the *safeguards agreement*.

Initial inspections of principal nuclear facilities

51. To verify that the construction of a *principal nuclear facility* is in accordance with the design reviewed by the Agency, an initial inspection or inspections of the facility may be carried out, if so provided in a *safeguards agreement*:

(*a*) As soon as possible after the facility has come under Agency safeguards, in the case of a facility already in operation; or

(*b*) Before the facility starts to operate, in other cases.

52. The measuring instruments and operating characteristics of the facility shall be reviewed to the extent necessary for the purpose of implementing safeguards. Instruments that will be used to obtain data on the *nuclear materials* in the facility may be tested to determine their satisfactory functioning. Such testing may include the observation by inspectors of commissioning or routine tests by the staff of the facility, but shall not hamper or delay the construction, commissioning or normal operation of the facility.

Special inspections

53. The Agency may carry out special inspections if:

(*a*) The study of a report indicates that such inspection is desirable; or

(*b*) Any unforeseen circumstance requires immediate action.

The Board shall subsequently be informed of the reasons for and the results of each such inspection.

54. The Agency may also carry out special inspections of substantial amounts of safeguarded *nuclear material* that are to be transferred outside the jurisdiction of the State in which it is being safeguarded, for which purpose the State shall give the Agency sufficient advance notice of any such proposed transfer.

B. Special procedures for reactors

Reports

55. The frequency of submission of routine reports shall be agreed between the Agency and the State, taking into account the frequency established for routine inspections. However, at least two such reports shall be submitted each year and in no case shall more than 12 such reports be required in any year.

Inspections

56. One of the initial inspections of a *reactor* shall if possible be made just before the reactor first reaches criticality.

57. The maximum frequency of routine inspections of a *reactor* and of the safeguarded *nuclear material* in it shall be determined from the following table:

Whichever is the largest of: (*a*) Facility inventory (including loading); (*b*) Annual *throughput*; (*c*) Maximum potential annual production of special fissionable material (*Effective kilograms of nuclear material*)	Maximum number of routine inspections annually
Up to 1	0
More than 1 and up to 5	1
More than 5 and up to 10	2
More than 10 and up to 15	3
More than 15 and up to 20	4
More than 20 and up to 25	5
More than 25 and up to 30	6
More than 30 and up to 35	7
More than 35 and up to 40	8
More than 40 and up to 45	9
More than 45 and up to 50	10
More than 50 and up to 55	11
More than 55 and up to 60	12
More than 60	Right of access at all times

58. The actual frequency of inspection of a *reactor* shall take account of:

(*a*) Whether the State possesses irradiated-fuel reprocessing facilities;

(*b*) The nature of the *reactor*; and

(*c*) The nature and amount of the *nuclear material* produced or used in the *reactor*.

C. Special procedures relating to safeguarded nuclear material outside principal nuclear facilities

Nuclear material in research and development facilities

Routine reports

59. Only accounting reports need be submitted in respect of *nuclear material* in *research and development facilities*. The frequency of submission of such routine reports shall be agreed between the Agency and the State, taking into account the frequency

established for routine inspections; however, at least one such report shall be submitted each year and in no case shall more than 12 such reports be required in any year.

Routine inspections

60. The maximum frequency of routine inspections of safeguarded *nuclear material* in a *research and development facility* shall be that specified in the table in paragraph 57 for the total amount of material in the facility.

Source material in sealed storage

61. The following simplified procedures for safeguarding stockpiled source material shall be applied if a State undertakes to store such material in a sealed storage facility and not to remove it therefrom without previously informing the Agency.

Design of storage facilities

62. The State shall submit to the Agency information on the design of each sealed storage facility and agree with the Agency on the method and procedure for sealing it.

Routine reports

63. Two routine accounting reports in respect of source material in sealed storage shall be submitted each year.

Routine inspections

64. The Agency may perform one routine inspection of each sealed storage facility annually.

Removal of material

65. The State may remove safeguarded source material from a sealed storage facility after informing the Agency of the amount, type and intended use of the material to be removed, and providing sufficient other data in time to enable the Agency to continue safeguarding the material after it has been removed.

Nuclear material in other locations

66. Except to the extent that safeguarded *nuclear material* outside of *principal nuclear facilities* is covered by any of the provisions set forth in paragraphs 59–65, the following procedures shall be applied with respect to such material (for example, source material stored elsewhere than in a sealed storage facility, or special fissionable material used in a sealed neutron source in the field).

Routine reports

67. Routine accounting reports in respect of all safeguarded *nuclear material* in this category shall be submitted periodically. The frequency of submission of such reports shall be agreed between the Agency and the State, taking into account the frequency established for routine inspections; however, at least one such report shall be submitted each year and in

no case shall more than 12 such reports be required in any year.

Routine inspections

68. The maximum frequency of routine inspections of safeguarded *nuclear material* in this category shall be one inspection annually if the total amount of such material does not exceed five *effective kilograms*, and shall be determined from the table in paragraph 57 if the amount is greater.

IV. DEFINITIONS

69. "Agency" means the International Atomic Energy Agency.

70. "Board" means the Board of Governors of the Agency.

71. "Director General" means the Director General of the Agency.

72. "Effective kilograms" means:

(*a*) In the case of plutonium, its weight in kilograms;

(*b*) In the case of uranium with an *enrichment* of 0.01 (1%) and above, its weight in kilograms multiplied by the square of its *enrichment*;

(*c*) In the case of uranium with an *enrichment* below 0.01 (1%) and above 0.005 (0.5%), its weight in kilograms multiplied by 0.0001; and

(*d*) In the case of depleted uranium with an *enrichment* of 0.005 (0.5%) or below, and in the case of thorium, its weight in kilograms multiplied by 0.00005.

73. "Enrichment" means the ratio of the combined weight of the isotopes uranium-233 and uranium-235 to that of the total uranium in question.

74. "Improved" means, with respect to *nuclear material*, that either:

(*a*) The concentration of fissionable isotopes in it has been increased; or

(*b*) The amount of chemically separable fissionable isotopes in it has been increased; or

(*c*) Its chemical or physical form has been changed so as to facilitate further use or processing.

75. "Inspector" means an Agency official designated in accordance with the *Inspectors Document*.

76. "Inspectors Document" means the Annex to the Agency's document GC(V)/INF/39.

77. "Nuclear material" means any source or special fissionable material as defined in Article XX of the Statute.

78. "Principal nuclear facility" means a *reactor*, a plant for processing *nuclear material* irradiated in a *reactor*, a plant for separating the isotopes of a *nuclear material*, a plant for processing or fabricating *nuclear material* (excepting a mine or ore-processing plant) or a facility or plant of such other type as may be

designated by the Board from time to time, including associated storage facilities.

79. "Project agreement" means a *safeguards agreement* relating to an Agency project and containing provisions as foreseen in Article XI.F.4(b) of the Statute.

80. "Reactor" means any device in which a controlled, self-sustaining fission chain-reaction can be maintained.

81. "Research and development facility" means a facility, other than a *principal nuclear facility*, used for research or development in the field of nuclear energy.

82. "Safeguards agreement" means an agreement between the Agency and one or more Member States which contains an undertaking by one or more of those States not to use certain items in such a way as to further any military purpose and which gives the Agency the right to observe compliance with such undertaking. Such an agreement may concern:

(*a*) An Agency project;

(*b*) A bilateral or multilateral arrangement in the field of nuclear energy under which the Agency may be asked to administer safeguards; or

(*c*) Any of a State's nuclear activities *unilaterally submitted* to Agency safeguards.

83. "Statute" means the Statute of the Agency.

84. "Throughput" means the rate at which *nuclear material* is introduced into a facility operating at full capacity.

85. "Unilaterally submitted" means submitted by a State to Agency safeguards, pursuant to a *safeguards agreement*.

Notes:

1. The use of italics indicates that a term has a specialized meaning in this document and is defined in Part IV.
2. Set forth in documents INFCIRC/26 and Add.1.
3. See para. 57.

ANNEX I. PROVISIONS FOR REPROCESSING PLANTS

Introduction

1. The Agency's Safeguards System (1965) is so formulated as to permit application to *principal nuclear facilities* other than *reactors* as foreseen in paragraph 7. This Annex lays down the additional procedures which are applicable to the safeguarding of *reprocessing plants*. However, because of the possible need to revise these procedures in the light of experience, they shall be subject to review at any time and shall in any case be reviewed after two years' experience of their application has been gained.

Special procedures

Reports

2. The frequency of submission of routine reports shall be once each calendar month.

Inspections

3. A *reprocessing plant* having an annual *throughput* not exceeding 5 *effective kilograms* of *nuclear material*, and the safeguarded *nuclear material* in it, may be routinely inspected twice a year. A *reprocessing plant* having an annual *throughput* exceeding 5 *effective kilograms* of *nuclear material*, and the safeguarded *nuclear material* in it, may be inspected at all times. The arrangements for inspections set forth in paragraph 50 shall apply to all inspections to be made under this paragraph.[1]

4. When a *reprocessing plant* is under Agency safeguards only because it contains safeguarded *nuclear material*, the inspection frequency shall be based on the rate of delivery of safeguarded *nuclear material*.

5. The State and the Agency shall co-operate in making all the necessary arrangements to facilitate the taking, shipping or analysis of samples, due account being taken of the limitations imposed by the characteristics of a plant already in operation when placed under Agency safeguards.

Mixtures of safeguarded and unsafeguarded nuclear material

6. By agreement between the State and the Agency, the following special arrangements may be made in the case of a *reprocessing plant* to which the criteria in paragraph 19(*d*) do not apply, and in which safeguarded and unsafeguarded *nuclear materials* are present:

(*a*) Subject to the provisions of sub-paragraph (*b*) below, the Agency shall restrict its safeguards procedures to the area in which irradiated fuel is stored, until such time as all or any part of such fuel is transferred out of the storage area into other parts of the plant. Safeguards procedures shall cease to apply to the storage area or plant when either contains no safeguarded *nuclear material*; and

(*b*) Where possible, safeguarded *nuclear material* shall be measured and sampled separately from unsafeguarded material, and at as early a stage as possible. Where separate measurement, sampling or processing are not possible, the whole of the material being processed in that *campaign* shall be subject to the safeguards procedures set out in this Annex. At the conclusion of the processing the *nuclear material* that is thereafter to be safeguarded shall be selected by agreement between the State and the Agency from the whole output of the plant resulting from that *campaign*, due account being taken of any processing losses accepted by the Agency.

Definitions

7. "Reprocessing plant"[2] means a facility to separate irradiated *nuclear materials* and fission products, and includes the facility's head-end treatment section and its associated storage and analytical sections.

8. "Campaign" means the period during which the chemical processing equipment in a *reprocessing plant* is operated between two successive wash-outs of the *nuclear material* present in the equipment.

Notes:
1. It is understood that for plants having an annual *throughput* of more than 60 *effective kilograms*, the right of access at all times would normally be implemented by means of continuous inspection.
2. This term is synonymous with the term "a plant for processing nuclear material irradiated in a reactor" which is used in paragraph 78.

ANNEX II. PROVISIONS FOR SAFEGUARDED NUCLEAR MATERIAL IN CONVERSION PLANTS AND FABRICATION PLANTS

Introduction

1. The Agency's Safeguards System (1965, as Provisionally Extended in 1966) is so formulated as to permit application to *principal nuclear facilities* other than *reactors* as foreseen in paragraph 7. This Annex lays down the additional procedures which are applicable to safeguarded *nuclear material* in *conversion plants* and *fabrication plants*[1]. However, because of the possible need to revise these procedures in the light of experience, they shall be subject to review at any time and shall in any case be reviewed after two years' experience of their application has been gained.

Special procedures

Reports

2. The frequency of submission of routine reports shall be once each calendar month.

Inspections

3. A *conversion plant* or *fabrication plant* to which the criteria in paragraph 19(*d*) apply and the *nuclear material* in it, may be inspected at all times if the plant inventory at any time, or the annual input, of *nuclear material* exceeds five *effective kilograms*. Where neither the inventory at any time, nor the annual input, exceeds five *effective kilograms* of *nuclear material*, the routine inspections shall not

exceed two a year. The arrangements for inspection set forth in paragraph 50 shall apply to all inspections to be made under this paragraph[2].

4. When a *conversion plant* or *fabrication plant* to which the criteria in paragraph 19(*d*) do not apply contains safeguarded *nuclear material* the frequency of routine inspections shall be based on the inventory at any time and the annual input of safeguarded *nuclear material*. Where the inventory at any time, or the annual input, of safeguarded *nuclear material* exceeds five *effective kilograms* the plant may be inspected at all times. Where neither the inventory at any time, nor the annual input, exceeds five *effective kilograms* of safeguarded *nuclear material* the routine inspections shall not exceed two a year. The arrangements for inspection set forth in paragraph 50 shall apply to all inspections to be made under this paragraph[2].

5. The intensity of inspection of safeguarded *nuclear material* at various steps in a *conversion plant* or *fabrication plant* shall take account of the nature, isotopic composition and amount of safeguarded *nuclear material* in the plant. Safeguards shall be applied in accordance with the general principles set forth in paragraphs 9–14. Emphasis shall be placed on inspection to control uranium of high enrichments and plutonium.

6. Where a plant may handle safeguarded and unsafeguarded *nuclear material*, the State shall notify the Agency in advance of the programme for handling safeguarded batches to enable the Agency to make inspections during these periods, due account being also taken of the arrangements under paragraph 10 below.

7. The State and the Agency shall co-operate in making all the necessary arrangements to facilitate the preparation of inventories of safeguarded *nuclear material* and the taking, shipping and/or analysis of samples, due account being taken of the limitations imposed by the characteristics of a plant already in operation when placed under Agency safeguards.

Residues, scrap and waste

8. The State shall ensure that safeguarded *nuclear material* contained in residues, scrap or waste created during conversion or fabrication is recovered, as far as is practicable, in its facilities and within a reasonable period of time. If such recovery is not considered practicable by the State, the State and the Agency shall co-operate in making arrangements to account for and dispose of the material.

Safeguarded and unsafeguarded nuclear material

9. By agreement between the State and the Agency, the following special arrangements

may be made in the case of a *conversion plant* or a *fabrication plant* to which the criteria in paragraph 19(*d*) do not apply, and in which safeguarded and unsafeguarded *nuclear material* are both present:

(*a*) Subject to the provisions of sub-paragraph (*b*) below, the Agency shall restrict its safeguards procedures to the area in which safeguarded *nuclear material* is stored, until such time as all or any part of such *nuclear material* is transferred out of the storage area into other parts of the plant. Safeguards procedures shall cease to be applied to the storage area or plant when it contains no safeguarded *nuclear material*; and

(*b*) Where possible, safeguarded *nuclear material* shall be measured and sampled separately from unsafeguarded *nuclear material*, and at as early a stage as possible. Where separate measurement, sampling or processing is not possible, any *nuclear material* containing safeguarded *nuclear material* shall be subject to the safeguards procedures set out in this Annex. At the conclusion of processing, the *nuclear material* that is thereafter to be safeguarded shall be selected, in accordance with paragraph 11 below when applicable, by agreement between the State and the Agency, due account being taken of any processing losses accepted by the Agency.

Blending of nuclear material

10. When safeguarded *nuclear material* is to be blended with either safeguarded or unsafeguarded *nuclear material*, the State shall notify the Agency sufficiently in advance of the programme of blending to enable the Agency to exercise its right to obtain evidence, through inspection of the blending operation or otherwise, that the blending is performed according to the programme.

11. When safeguarded and unsafeguarded *nuclear material* are blended, if the ratio of fissionable isotopes in the safeguarded component going into the blend to all the fissionable isotopes in the blend is 0.3 or greater, and if the concentration of fissionable isotopes in the unsafeguarded *nuclear material* is increased by such blending, then the whole blend shall remain subject to safeguards. In other cases the following procedures shall apply:

(*a*) Plutonium/plutonium blending. The quantity of the blend that shall continue to be safeguarded shall be such that its weight, when multiplied by the square of the weight fraction of contained fissionable isotopes, is not less then the weight of originally safeguarded plutonium multiplied by the square of the weight fraction of fissionable isotopes therein, provided however that:

(i) In cases where the weight of the whole blend, when multiplied by the square of the weight fraction of contained fissionable isotopes, is less than the weight of originally

safeguarded plutonium multiplied by the square of the weight fraction of fissionable isotopes therein, the whole of the blend shall be safeguarded; and

(ii) The number of fissionable atoms in the portion of the blend that shall continue to be under safeguards shall in no case be less than the number of fissionable atoms in the originally safeguarded plutonium;

(*b*) Uranium/uranium blending. The quantity of the blend that shall continue to be safeguarded shall be such that the number of *effective kilograms* is not less than the number of *effective kilograms* in the originally safeguarded uranium, provided however that:

(i) In cases where the number of *effective kilograms* in the whole blend is less than in the safeguarded uranium, the whole of the blend shall be safeguarded; and

(ii) The number of fissionable atoms in the portion of the blend that shall continue to be under safeguards shall in no case be less than the number of fissionable atoms in the originally safeguarded uranium;

(*c*) Uranium/plutonium blending. The whole of the resultant blend shall be safeguarded until the uranium and the plutonium constituents are separated. After separation of the uranium and plutonium, safeguards shall apply to the originally safeguarded component; and

(*d*) Due account shall be taken of any processing losses agreed upon between the State and the Agency.

Definitions

12. "Conversion plant" means a facility (excepting a mine or ore-processing plant) to *improve* unirradiated *nuclear material*, or irradiated *nuclear material* that has been separated from fission products, by changing its chemical or physical form so as to facilitate further use or processing. The term *conversion plant* includes the facility's storage and analytical sections. The term does not include a plant intended for separating the isotopes of a *nuclear material*.

13. "Fabrication plant" means a plant to manufacture fuel elements or other components containing *nuclear material* and includes the plant's storage and analytical sections.

Notes:

1. This terminology is intended to be synonymous with the term "a plant for processing or fabricating *nuclear material* (excepting a mine or ore-processing plant") which is used in paragraph 78.

2. It is understood that for plants having an inventory at any time, or an annual input, of more than 60 *effective kilograms* the right of access at all times would normally be implemented by means of continuous inspection.

Where neither the inventory at any time nor the annual input exceeds one *effective kilogram* of *nuclear material* the plant would not normally be subject to routine inspection.

Source: IAEA document INFCIRC/66/Rev. 2 (IAEA, Vienna, 1968).

Appendix V. The IAEA model NPT safeguards agreement of 1971, INFCIRC/153

THE STRUCTURE AND CONTENT OF AGREEMENTS BETWEEN THE AGENCY AND STATES REQUIRED IN CONNECTION WITH THE TREATY ON THE NON-PROLIFERATION OF NUCLEAR WEAPONS

Agreed at Vienna on 10 March 1971
On 20 April 1971, the IAEA Board of Governors authorized the Director General to use the material reproduced below as the basis for negotiating safeguards agreements between the IAEA and non-nuclear weapon states parties to the NPT

PART I

Basic undertaking

1. The Agreement should contain, in accordance with Article III.1 of the Treaty on the Non-Proliferation of Nuclear Weapons, an undertaking by the State to accept safeguards, in accordance with the terms of the Agreement, on all source or special fissionable material in all peaceful nuclear activities within its territory, under its jurisdiction or carried out under its control anywhere, for the exclusive purpose of verifying that such material is not diverted to nuclear weapons or other nuclear explosive devices.

Application of safeguards

2. The Agreement should provide for the Agency's right and obligation to ensure that safeguards will be applied, in accordance with the terms of the Agreement, on all source or special fissionable material in all peaceful nuclear activities within the territory of the State, under its jurisdiction or carried out under its control anywhere, for the exclusive purpose of verifying that such material is not diverted to nuclear weapons or other nuclear explosive devices.

Co-operation between the Agency and the State

3. The Agreement should provide that the Agency and the State shall co-operate to facilitate the implementation of the safeguards provided for therein.

Implementation of safeguards

4. The Agreement should provide that safeguards shall be implemented in a manner designed:
(a) To avoid hampering the economic and technological development of the State or international co-operation in the field of peaceful nuclear activities, including international exchange of *nuclear material*;
(b) To avoid undue interference in the State's peaceful nuclear activities, and in particular in the operation of *facilities*; and
(c) To be consistent with prudent management practices required for the economic and safe conduct of nuclear activities.

5. The Agreement should provide that the Agency shall take every precaution to protect commercial and industrial secrets and other confidential information coming to its knowledge in the implementation of the Agreement. The Agency shall not publish or communicate to any State, organization or person any information obtained by it in connection with the implementation of the Agreement, except that specific information relating to such implementation in the State may be given to the Board of Governors and to such Agency staff members as require such knowledge by reason of their official duties in connection with safeguards, but only to the extent necessary for the Agency to fulfil its responsibilities in implementing the Agreement. Summarized information on *nuclear material* being safeguarded by the Agency under the Agreement may be published upon decision of the Board if the States directly concerned agree.

6. The Agreement should provide that in implementing safeguards pursuant thereto the Agency shall take full account of technological developments in the field of safeguards, and shall make every effort to ensure optimum cost-effectiveness and the application of the principle of safeguarding effectively the flow of *nuclear material* subject to safeguards under the Agreement by use of instruments and other techniques at certain *strategic points* to the extent that present or future technology permits. In order to ensure optimum cost-effectiveness, use should be made, for example, of such means as:
(a) Containment as a means of defining *material balance areas* for accounting purposes;

(*b*) Statistical techniques and random sampling in evaluating the flow of *nuclear material*; and

(*c*) Concentration of verification procedures on those stages in the nuclear fuel cycle involving the production, processing, use or storage of *nuclear material* from which nuclear weapons or other nuclear explosive devices could readily be made, and minimization of verification procedures in respect of other *nuclear material*, on condition that this does not hamper the Agency in applying safeguards under the Agreement.

National system of accounting for and control of nuclear material

7. The Agreement should provide that the State shall establish and maintain a system of accounting for and control of all *nuclear material* subject to safeguards under the Agreement, and that such safeguards shall be applied in such a manner as to enable the Agency to verify, in ascertaining that there has been no diversion of *nuclear material* from peaceful uses to nuclear weapons or other nuclear explosive devices, findings of the State's system. The Agency's verification shall include, inter alia, independent measurements and observations conducted by the Agency in accordance with the procedures specified in Part II below. The Agency, in its verification, shall take due account of the technical effectiveness of the State's system.

Provisions of information to the Agency

8. The Agreement should provide that to ensure the effective implementation of safeguards thereunder the Agency shall be provided, in accordance with the provisions set out in Part II below, with information concerning *nuclear material* subject to safeguards under the Agreement and the features of *facilities* relevant to safeguarding such material. The Agency shall require only the minimum amount of information and data consistent with carrying out its responsibilities under the Agreement. Information pertaining to *facilities* shall be the minimum necessary for safeguarding *nuclear material* subject to safeguards under the Agreement. In examining design information, the Agency shall, at the request of the State, be prepared to examine on premises of the State design information which the State regards as being of particular sensitivity. Such information would not have to be physically transmitted to the Agency provided that it remained available for ready further examination by the Agency on premises of the State.

Agency inspectors

9. The Agreement should provide that the State shall take the necessary steps to ensure that Agency inspectors can effectively discharge their functions under the Agreement. The Agency shall secure the consent of the State to the designation of Agency inspectors to that State. If the State, either upon proposal of a designation or at any other time after a designation has been made, objects to the designation, the Agency shall propose to the State an alternative designation or designations. The repeated refusal of a State to accept the designation of Agency inspectors which would impede the inspections conducted under the Agreement would be considered by the Board upon referral by the Director General with a view to appropriate action. The visits and activities of Agency inspectors shall be so arranged as to reduce to a minimum the possible inconvenience and disturbance to the State and to the peaceful nuclear activities inspected, as well as to ensure protection of industrial secrets or any other confidential information coming to the inspectors' knowledge.

Privileges and immunities

10. The Agreement should specify the privileges and immunities which shall be granted to the Agency and its staff in respect of their functions under the Agreement. In the case of a State party to the Agreement on the Privileges and Immunities of the Agency, the provisions thereof, as in force for such State, shall apply. In the case of other States, the privileges and immunities granted should be such as to ensure that:

(*a*) The Agency and its staff will be in a position to discharge their functions under the Agreement effectively; and

(*b*) No such State will be placed thereby in a more favourable position than States party to the Agreement on the Privileges and Immunities of the Agency.

Termination of safeguards

Consumption or dilution of nuclear material

11. The Agreement should provide that safeguards shall terminate on *nuclear material* subject to safeguards thereunder upon determination by the Agency that it has been consumed, or has been diluted in such a way that it is no longer usable for any nuclear activity relevant from the point of view of safeguards, or has become practically irrecoverable.

Transfer of nuclear material out of the State

12. The Agreement should provide, with respect to *nuclear material* subject to safeguards thereunder, for notification of transfers of such material out of the State, in accordance with the provisions set out in paragraphs 92–94 below. The Agency shall terminate safeguards under the Agreement on *nuclear material* when the recipient State has assumed responsibility therefor, as provided

for in paragraph 91. The Agency shall maintain records indicating each transfer and, where applicable, the re-application of safeguards to the transferred *nuclear material*.

Provisions relating to nuclear material to be used in non-nuclear activities

13. The Agreement should provide that if the State wishes to use *nuclear material* subject to safeguards thereunder in non-nuclear activities, such as the production of alloys or ceramics, it shall agree with the Agency on the circumstances under which the safeguards on such *nuclear material* may be terminated.

Non-application of safeguards to nuclear material to be used in non-peaceful activities

14. The Agreement should provide that if the State intends to exercise its discretion to use *nuclear material* which is required to be safeguarded thereunder in a nuclear activity which does not require the application of safeguards under the Agreement, the following procedures will apply:

(*a*) The State shall inform the Agency of the activity, making it clear:

(i) That the use of the *nuclear material* in a non-proscribed military activity will not be in conflict with an undertaking the State may have given and in respect of which Agency safeguards apply, that the *nuclear material* will be used only in a peaceful nuclear activity; and

(ii) That during the period of non-application of safeguards the *nuclear material* will not be used for the production of nuclear weapons or other nuclear explosive devices;

(*b*) The Agency and the State shall make an arrangement so that, only while the *nuclear material* is in such an activity, the safeguards provided for in the Agreement will not be applied. The arrangement shall identify, to the extent possible, the period or circumstances during which safeguards will not be applied. In any event, the safeguards provided for in the Agreement shall again apply as soon as the *nuclear material* is re-introduced into a peaceful nuclear activity. The Agency shall be kept informed of the total quantity and composition of such unsafeguarded *nuclear material* in the State and of any exports of such material; and

(*c*) Each arrangement shall be made in agreement with the Agency. The Agency's agreement shall be given as promptly as possible; it shall only relate to the temporal and procedural provisions, reporting arrangements, etc., but shall not involve any approval or classified knowledge of the military activity or relate to the use of the *nuclear material* therein.

Finance

15. The Agreement should contain one of the following sets of provisions:

(*a*) An agreement with a Member of the Agency should provide that each party thereto shall bear the expenses it incurs in implementing its responsibilities thereunder. However, if the State or persons under its jurisdiction incur extraordinary expenses as a result of a specific request by the Agency, the Agency shall reimburse such expenses provided that it has agreed in advance to do so. In any case the Agency shall bear the cost of any additional measuring or sampling which inspectors may request; or

(*b*) An agreement with a party not a Member of the Agency should in application of the provisions of Article XIV.C of the Statute, provide that the party shall reimburse fully to the Agency the safeguards expenses the Agency incurs thereunder. However, if the party or persons under its jurisdiction incur extraordinary expenses as a result of a specific request by the Agency, the Agency shall reimburse such expenses provided that it has agreed in advance to do so.

Third party liability for nuclear damage

16. The Agreement should provide that the State shall ensure that any protection against third party liability in respect of nuclear damage, including any insurance or other financial security, which may be available under its laws or regulations shall apply to the Agency and its officials for the purpose of the implementation of the Agreement, in the same way as that protection applies to nationals of the State.

International responsibility

17. The Agreement should provide that any claim by one party thereto against the other in respect of any damage, other than damage arising out of a nuclear incident, resulting from the implementation of safeguards under the Agreement, shall be settled in accordance with international law.

Measures in relation to verification of non-diversion

18. The Agreement should provide that if the Board, upon report of the Director General, decides that an action by the State is essential and urgent in order to ensure verification that *nuclear material* subject to safeguards under the Agreement is not diverted to nuclear weapons or other nuclear explosive devices the Board shall be able to call upon the State to take the required action without delay, irrespective of whether procedures for the settlement of a dispute have been invoked.

19. The Agreement should provide that if the Board upon examination of relevant information reported to it by the Director General finds that the Agency is not able to

verify that there has been no diversion of *nuclear material* required to be safeguarded under the Agreements to nuclear weapons or other nuclear explosive devices, it may make the reports provided for in paragraph C of Article XII of the Statute and may also take, where applicable, the other measures provided for in that paragraph. In taking such action the Board shall take account of the degree of assurance provided by the safeguards measures that have been applied and shall afford the State every reasonable opportunity to furnish the Board with any necessary reassurance.

Interpretation and application of the Agreement and settlement of disputes

20. The Agreement should provide that the parties thereto shall, at the request of either, consult about any question arising out of the interpretation or application thereof.

21. The Agreement should provide that the State shall have the right to request that any question arising out of the interpretation or application thereof be considered by the Board; and that the State shall be invited by the Board to participate in the discussion of any such question by the Board.

22. The Agreement should provide that any dispute arising out of the interpretation or application thereof except a dispute with regard to a finding by the Board under paragraph 19 above or an action taken by the Board pursuant to such a finding which is not settled by negotiation or another procedure agreed to by the parties should, on the request of either party, be submitted to an arbitral tribunal composed as follows: each party would designate one arbitrator, and the two arbitrators so designated would elect a third, who would be the Chairman. If, within 30 days of the request for arbitration, either party has not designated an arbitrator, either party to the dispute may request the President of the International Court of Justice to appoint an arbitrator. The same procedure would apply if, within 30 days of the designation or appointment of the second arbitrator, the third arbitrator had not been elected. A majority of the members of the arbitral tribunal would constitute a quorum, and all decisions would require the concurrence of two arbitrators. The arbitral procedure would be fixed by the tribunal. The decisions of the tribunal would be binding on both parties.

Final clauses

Amendment of the Agreement

23. The Agreement should provide that the parties thereto shall, at the request of either of them, consult each other on amendment of the Agreement. All amendments shall require the agreement of both parties. It might additionally be provided, if convenient

to the State, that the agreement of the parties on amendments to Part II of the Agreement could be achieved by recourse to a simplified procedure. The Director General shall promptly inform all Member States of any amendment to the Agreement.

Suspension of application of Agency safeguards under other agreements

24. Where applicable and where the State desires such a provision to appear, the Agreement should provide that the application of Agency safeguards in the State under other safeguards agreements with the Agency shall be suspended while the Agreement is in force. If the State has received assistance from the Agency for a project, the State's undertaking in the Project Agreement not to use items subject thereto in such a way as to further any military purpose shall continue to apply.

Entry into force and duration

25. The Agreement should provide that it shall enter into force on the date on which the Agency receives from the State written notification that the statutory and constitutional requirements for entry into force have been met. The Director General shall promptly inform all Member States of the entry into force.

26. The Agreement should provide for it to remain in force as long as the State is party to the Treaty on the Non-Proliferation of Nuclear Weapons.

PART II

Introduction

27. The Agreement should provide that the purpose of Part II thereof is to specify the procedures to be applied for the implementation of the safeguards provisions of Part I.

Objective of safeguards

28. The Agreement should provide that the objective of safeguards is the timely detection of diversion of significant quantities of *nuclear material* from peaceful nuclear activities to the manufacture of nuclear weapons or of other nuclear explosive devices or for purposes unknown, and deterrence of such diversion by the risk of early detection.

29. To this end the Agreement should provide for the use of material accountancy as a safeguards measure of fundamental importance, with containment and surveillance as important complementary measures.

30. The Agreement should provide that the technical conclusion of the Agency's verification activities shall be a statement, in respect of each *material balance area*, of the amount of *material unaccounted for* over a

specific period, giving the limits of accuracy of the amounts stated.

National system of accounting for and control of nuclear material

31. The Agreement should provide that pursuant to paragraph 7 above the Agency, in carrying out its verification activities, shall make full use of the State's system of accounting for and control of all *nuclear material* subject to safeguards under the Agreement, and shall avoid unnecessary duplication of the State's accounting and control activities.

32. The Agreement should provide that the State's system of accounting for and control of all *nuclear material* subject to safeguards under the Agreement shall be based on a structure of material balance areas, and shall make provision as appropriate and specified in the Subsidiary Arrangements for the establishment of such measures as:

(a) A measurement system for the determination of the quantities of *nuclear material* received, produced, shipped, lost or otherwise removed from inventory, and the quantities on inventory;

(b) The evaluation of precision and accuracy of measurements and the estimation of measurement uncertainty;

(c) Procedures for identifying, reviewing and evaluating differences in shipper/receiver measurements;

(d) Procedures for taking a *physical inventory*;

(e) Procedures for the evaluation of accumulations of unmeasured inventory and unmeasured losses;

(f) A system of records and reports showing, for each *material balance area*, the inventory of *nuclear material* and the changes in that inventory including receipts into and transfers out of the *material balance area*;

(g) Provisions to ensure that the accounting procedures and arrangements are being operated correctly; and

(h) Procedures for the provisions of reports to the Agency in accordance with paragraphs 59-69 below.

Starting point of safeguards

33. The Agreement should provide that safeguards shall not apply thereunder to material in mining or ore processing activities.

34. The Agreement should provide that:

(a) When any material containing uranium or thorium which has not reached the stage of the nuclear fuel cycle described in subparagraph (c) below is directly or indirectly exported to a non-nuclear-weapon State, the State shall inform the Agency of its quantity, composition and destination, unless the material is exported for specifically nonnuclear purposes;

(b) When any material containing uranium or thorium which has not reached the stage of the nuclear fuel cycle described in sub-paragraph (c) below is imported, the State shall inform the Agency of its quantity and composition, unless the material is imported for specifically non-nuclear purposes; and

(c) When any *nuclear material* of a composition and purity suitable for fuel fabrication or for being isotopically enriched leaves the plant or the process stage in which it has been produced, or when such *nuclear material*, or any other *nuclear material* produced at a later stage in the nuclear fuel cycle, is imported into the State, the *nuclear material* shall become subject to the other safeguards procedures specified in the Agreement.

Termination of safeguards

35. The Agreement should provide that safeguards shall terminate on *nuclear material* subject to safeguards thereunder under the conditions set forth in paragraph 11 above. Where the conditions of that paragraph are not met, but the State considers that the recovery of safeguarded *nuclear material* from residues is not for the time being practicable or desirable, the Agency and the State shall consult on the appropriate safeguards measures to be applied. It should further be provided that safeguards shall terminate on *nuclear material* subject to safeguards under the Agreement under the conditions set forth in paragraph 13 above, provided that the State and the Agency agree that such *nuclear material* is practicably irrecoverable.

Exemptions from safeguards

36. The Agreement should provide that the Agency shall, at the request of the State, exempt *nuclear material* from safeguards, as follows:

(a) Special fissionable material, when it is used in gram quantities or less as a sensing component in instruments;

(b) *Nuclear material*, when it is used in non-nuclear activities in accordance with paragraph 13 above, if such *nuclear material* is recoverable; and

(c) Plutonium with an isotopic concentration of plutonium-238 exceeding 80%.

37. The Agreement should provide that *nuclear material* that would otherwise be subject to safeguards shall be exempted from safeguards at the request of the State, provided that *nuclear material* so exempted in the State may not at any time exceed:

(a) One kilogram in total of special fissionable material, which may consist of one or more of the following:

(i) Plutonium;

(ii) Uranium with an *enrichment* of 0.2 (20%) and above, taken account of by multiplying its weight by its *enrichment*; and

(iii) Uranium with an *enrichment* below 0.2 (20%) and above that of natural uranium, taken account of by multiplying its weight by five times the square of its *enrichment*;

(*b*) Ten metric tons in total of natural uranium and depleted uranium with an *enrichment* above 0.005 (0.5%);

(*c*) Twenty metric tons of depleted uranium with an *enrichment* of 0.005 (0.5%) or below; and

(*d*) Twenty metric tons of thorium; or such greater amounts as may be specified by the Board of Governors for uniform application.

38. The Agreement should provide that if exempted *nuclear material* is to be processed or stored together with safeguarded *nuclear material*, provision should be made for the reapplication of safeguards thereto.

Subsidiary arrangements

39. The Agreement should provide that the Agency and the State shall make Subsidiary Arrangements which shall specify in detail, to the extent necessary to permit the Agency to fulfil its responsibilities under the Agreement in an effective and efficient manner, how the procedures laid down in the Agreement are to be applied. Provision should be made for the possibility of an extension or change of the Subsidiary Arrangements by agreement between the Agency and the State without amendment of the Agreement.

40. It should be provided that the Subsidiary Arrangements shall enter into force at the same time as, or as soon as possible after, the entry into force of the Agreement. The State and the Agency shall make every effort to achieve their entry into force within 90 days of the entry into force of the Agreement, a later date being acceptable only with the agreement of both parties. The State shall provide the Agency promptly with the information required for completing the Subsidiary Arrangements. The Agreement should also provide that, upon its entry into force, the Agency shall be entitled to apply the procedures laid down therein in respect of the *nuclear material* listed in the inventory provided for in paragraph 41 below.

Inventory

41. The Agreement should provide that, on the basis of the initial report referred to in paragraph 62 below, the Agency shall establish a unified inventory of all *nuclear material* in the State subject to safeguards under the Agreement, irrespective of its origin, and maintain this inventory on the basis of subsequent reports and of the results of its verification activities. Copies of the inventory shall be made available to the State at agreed intervals.

Design information

General

42. Pursuant to paragraph 8 above, the Agreement should stipulate that design information in respect of existing *facilities* shall be provided to the Agency during the discussion of the Subsidiary Arrangements, and that the time limits for the provision of such information in respect of new *facilities* shall be specified in the Subsidiary Arrangements. It should further be stipulated that such information shall be provided as early as possible before *nuclear material* is introduced into a new *facility*.

43. The Agreement should specify that the design information in respect of each *facility* to be made available to the Agency shall include, when applicable:

(*a*) The identification of the *facility*, stating its general character, purpose, nominal capacity and geographic location, and the name and address to be used for routine business purposes;

(*b*) A description of the general arrangement of the *facility* with reference, to the extent feasible, to the form, location and flow of *nuclear material* and to the general layout of important items of equipment which use, produce or process *nuclear material*;

(*c*) A description of features of the *facility* relating to material accountancy, containment and surveillance; and

d) A description of the existing and proposed procedures at the *facility* for *nuclear material* accountancy and control, with special reference to *material balance areas* established by the operator, measurements of flow and procedures for *physical inventory* taking.

44. The Agreement should further provide that other information relevant to the application of safeguards shall be made available to the Agency in respect of each *facility*, in particular on organizational responsibility for material accountancy and control. It should also be provided that the State shall make available to the Agency supplementary information on the health and safety procedures which the Agency shall observe and with which the inspectors shall comply at the *facility*.

45. The Agreement should stipulate that design information in respect of a modification relevant for safeguards purposes shall be provided for examination sufficiently in advance for the safeguards procedures to be adjusted when necessary.

Purposes of examination of design information

46. The Agreement should provide that

the design information made available to the Agency shall be used for the following purposes:

(*a*) To identify the features of *facilities* and *nuclear material* relevant to the application of safeguards to *nuclear material* in sufficient detail to facilitate verification;

(*b*) To determine *material balance areas* to be used for Agency accounting purposes and to select those *strategic points* which are *key measurement points* and which will be used to determine the *nuclear material* flows and inventories; in determining such *material balance areas* the Agency shall, inter alia, use the following criteria:

(i) The size of the *material balance area* should be related to the accuracy with which the material balance can be established;

(ii) In determining the *material balance area* advantage should be taken of any opportunity to use containment and surveillance to help ensure the completeness of flow measurements and thereby simplify the application of safeguards and concentrate measurement efforts at *key measurement points*;

(iii) A number of *material balance areas* in use at a *facility* or at distinct sites may be combined in one *material balance area* to be used for Agency accounting purposes when the Agency determines that this is consistent with its verification requirements; and

(iv) If the State so requests, a special *material balance area* around a process step involving commercially sensitive information may be established;

(*c*) To establish the nominal timing and procedures for taking of *physical inventory* for Agency accounting purposes;

(*d*) To establish the records and reports requirements and records evaluation procedures;

(*e*) To establish requirements and procedures for verification of the quantity and location of *nuclear material*; and

(*f*) To select appropriate combinations of containment and surveillance methods and techniques and the *strategic points* at which they are to be applied.

It should further be provided that the results of the examination of the design information shall be included in the Subsidiary Arrangements.

Re-examination of design information

47. The Agreement should provide that design information shall be re-examined in the light of changes in operating conditions, of developments in safeguards technology or of experience in the application of verification procedures, with a view to modifying the action the Agency has taken pursuant to paragraph 46 above.

Verification of design information

48. The Agreement should provide that the Agency, in co-operation with the State, may send inspectors to *facilities* to verify the design information provided to the Agency pursuant to paragraphs 42–45 above for the purposes stated in paragraph 46.

Information in respect of nuclear material outside facilities

49. The Agreement should provide that the following information concerning *nuclear material* customarily used outside *facilities* shall be provided as applicable to the Agency:

(*a*) A general description of the use of the *nuclear material*, its geographic location, and the user's name and address for routine business purposes; and

(*b*) A general description of the existing and proposed procedures for *nuclear material* accountancy and control, including organizational responsibility for material accountancy and control.

The Agreement should further provide that the Agency shall be informed on a timely basis of any change in the information provided to it under this paragraph.

50. The Agreement should provide that the information made available to the Agency in respect of *nuclear material* customarily used outside *facilities* may be used, to the extent relevant, for the purposes set out in sub-paragraphs 46(*b*)–(*f*) above.

Records system

General

51. The Agreement should provide that in establishing a national system of accounting for and control of *nuclear material* as referred to in paragraph 7 above, the State shall arrange that records are kept in respect of each *material balance area*. Provision should also be made that the Subsidiary Arrangements shall describe the records to be kept in respect of each *material balance area*.

52. The Agreement should provide that the State shall make arrangements to facilitate the examination of records by inspectors, particularly if the records are not kept in English, French, Russian or Spanish.

53. The Agreement should provide that the records shall be retained for at least five years.

54. The Agreement should provide that the records shall consist, as appropriate, of:

(*a*) Accounting records of all *nuclear material* subject to safeguards under the Agreement; and

(*b*) Operating records for *facilities* containing such *nuclear material*.

55. The Agreement should provide that the system of measurements on which the records used for the preparation of reports are based shall either conform to the latest

international standards or be equivalent in quality to such standards.

Accounting records

56. The Agreement should provide that the accounting records shall set forth the following in respect of each *material balance area*:

(*a*) All *inventory changes*, so as to permit a determination of the *book inventory* at any time;

(*b*) All measurement results that are used for determination of the *physical inventory*; and

(*c*) All *adjustments* and *corrections* that have been made in respect of *inventory changes, book inventories* and *physical inventories*.

57. The Agreement should provide that for all *inventory changes* and *physical inventories* the records shall show, in respect of each *batch* of *nuclear material*: material identification, *batch data* and *source data*. Provision should further be included that records shall account for uranium, thorium and plutonium separately in each *batch* of *nuclear material*. Furthermore, the date of the *inventory change* and, when appropriate, the originating *material balance area* and the receiving *material balance area* or the recipient, shall be indicated for each *inventory change*.

Operating records

58. The Agreement should provide that the operating records shall set forth as appropriate in respect of each *material balance area*:

(*a*) Those operating data which are used to establish changes in the quantities and composition of *nuclear material*:

(*b*) The data obtained from the calibration of tanks and instruments and from sampling and analyses, the procedures to control the quality of measurements and the derived estimates of random and systematic error;

(*c*) A description of the sequence of the actions taken in preparing for, and in taking, a *physical inventory*, in order to ensure that it is correct and complete; and

(*d*) A description of the actions taken in order to ascertain the cause and magnitude of any accidental or unmeasured loss that might occur.

Reports system

General

59. The Agreement should specify that the State shall provide the Agency with reports as detailed in paragraphs 60–69 below in respect of *nuclear material* subject to safeguards thereunder.

60. The Agreement should provide that reports shall be made in English, French,

Russian or Spanish, except as otherwise specified in the Subsidiary Arrangements.

61. The Agreement should provide that reports shall be based on the records kept in accordance with paragraphs 51–58 above and shall consist, as appropriate, of accounting reports and special reports.

Accounting reports

62. The Agreement should stipulate that the Agency shall be provided with an initial report on all *nuclear material* which is to be subject to safeguards thereunder. It should also be provided that the initial report shall be dispatched by the State to the Agency within 30 days of the last day of the calendar month in which the Agreement enters into force, and shall reflect the situation as of the last day of that month.

63. The Agreement should stipulate that for each *material balance area* the State shall provide the Agency with the following accounting reports:

(*a*) *Inventory change* reports showing changes in the inventory of *nuclear material*. The reports shall be dispatched as soon as possible and in any event within 30 days after the end of the month in which the *inventory changes* occurred or were established; and

(*b*) Material balance reports showing the material balance based on a *physical inventory* of *nuclear material* actually present in the *material balance area*. The reports shall be dispatched as soon as possible and in any event within 30 days after the *physical inventory* has been taken.

The reports shall be based on data available as of the date of reporting and may be corrected at a later date as required.

64. The Agreement should provide that *inventory change* reports shall specify identification and *batch data* for each *batch* of *nuclear material*, the date of the *inventory change* and, as appropriate, the originating *material balance area* and the receiving *material balance area* or the recipient. These reports shall be accompanied by concise notes:

(*a*) Explaining the *inventory changes*, on the basis of the operating data contained in the operating records provided for under subparagraph 58(*a*) above; and

(*b*) Describing, as specified in the Subsidiary Arrangements, the anticipated operational programme, particularly the taking of a *physical inventory*.

65. The Agreement should provide that the State shall report each *inventory change, adjustment* and *correction* either periodically in a consolidated list or individually. The *inventory changes* shall be reported in terms of *batches*; small amounts, such as analytical samples, as specified in the Subsidiary Arrangements, may be combined and reported as one *inventory change*.

66. The Agreement should stipulate that the Agency shall provide the State with semi-annual statements of *book inventory* of *nuclear material* subject to safeguards, for each *material balance area*, as based on the *inventory change* reports for the period covered by each such statement.

67. The Agreement should specify that the material balance reports shall include the following entries, unless otherwise agreed by the Agency and the State:

(a) Beginning *physical inventory*;

(b) *Inventory changes* (first increases, then decreases);

(c) Ending *book inventory*;

(d) *Shipper/receiver differences*;

(e) Adjusted ending *book inventory*;

(f) Ending *physical inventory*; and

(g) *Material unaccounted for*.

A statement of the *physical inventory*, listing all *batches* separately and specifying material identification and *batch data* for each *batch*, shall be attached to each material balance report.

Special reports

68. The Agreement should provide that the State shall make special reports without delay:

(a) If any unusual incident or circumstances lead the State to believe that there is or may have been loss of *nuclear material* that exceeds the limits to be specified for this purpose in the Subsidiary Arrangements; or

(b) If the containment has unexpectedly changed from that specified in the Subsidiary Arrangements to the extent that unauthorized removal of *nuclear material* has become possible.

Amplification and clarification of reports

69. The Agreement should provide that at the Agency's request the State shall supply amplifications or clarifications of any report, in so far as relevant for the purpose of safeguards.

Inspections

General

70. The Agreement should stipulate that the Agency shall have the right to make inspections as provided for in paragraphs 71–82 below.

Purposes of inspections

71. The Agreement should provide that the Agency may make ad hoc inspections in order to:

(a) Verify the information contained in the initial report on the *nuclear material* subject to safeguards under the Agreement;

(b) Identify and verify changes in the situation which have occurred since the date of the initial report; and

(c) Identify, and if possible verify the quantity and composition of, *nuclear material* in accordance with paragraphs 93 and 96 below, before its transfer out of or upon its transfer into the State.

72. The Agreement should provide that the Agency may make routine inspections in order to:

(a) Verify that reports are consistent with records;

(b) Verify the location, identity, quantity and composition of all *nuclear material* subject to safeguards under the Agreement; and

(c) Verify information on the possible causes of *material unaccounted for*, *shipper/receiver differences* and uncertainties in the *book inventory*.

73. The Agreement should provide that the Agency may make special inspections subject to the procedures laid down in paragraph 77 below;

(a) In order to verify the information contained in special reports; or

(b) If the Agency considers that information made available by the State, including explanations from the State and information obtained from routine inspections, is not adequate for the Agency to fulfil its responsibilities under the Agreement.

An inspection shall be deemed to be special when it is either additional to the routine inspection effort provided for in paragraphs 78–82 below, or involves access to information or locations in addition to the access specified in paragraph 76 for ad hoc and routine inspections, or both.

Scope of inspections

74. The Agreement should provide that for the purposes stated in paragraphs 71–73 above the Agency may:

(a) Examine the records kept pursuant to paragraphs 51–58;

(b) Make independent measurements of all *nuclear material* subject to safeguards under the Agreement;

(c) Verify the functioning and calibration of instruments and other measuring and control equipment;

(d) Apply and make use of surveillance and containment measures; and

(e) Use other objective methods which have been demonstrated to be technically feasible.

75. It should further be provided that within the scope of paragraph 74 above the Agency shall be enabled:

(a) To observe that samples at *key measurement points* for material balance accounting are taken in accordance with procedures which produce representative samples, to observe the treatment and analysis of the samples and to obtain duplicates of such samples;

(b) To observe that the measurements of

nuclear material at *key measurement points* for material balance accounting are representative, and to observe the calibration of the instruments and equipment involved;

(*c*) To make arrangements with the State that, if necessary:

(i) Additional measurements are made and additional samples taken for the Agency's use;

(ii) The Agency's standard analytical samples are analysed;

(iii) Appropriate absolute standards are used in calibrating instruments and other equipment; and

(iv) Other calibrations are carried out;

(*d*) To arrange to use its own equipment for independent measurement and surveillance, and if so agreed and specified in the Subsidiary Arrangements, to arrange to install such equipment;

(*e*) To apply its seals and other identifying and tamper-indicating devices to containments, if so agreed and specified in the Subsidiary Arrangements; and

(*f*) To make arrangements with the State for the shipping of samples taken for the Agency's use.

Access for inspections

76. The Agreement should provide that:

(*a*) For the purposes specified in sub-paragraphs 71(*a*) and (*b*) above and until such time as the *strategic points* have been specified in the Subsidiary Arrangements, the Agency's inspectors shall have access to any location where the initial report or any inspections carried out in connection with it indicate that *nuclear material* is present;

(*b*) For the purposes specified in sub-paragraph 71(*c*) above the inspectors shall have access to any location of which the Agency has been notified in accordance with sub-paragraphs 92(*c*) or 95(*c*) below;

(*c*) For the purposes specified in paragraph 72 above the Agency's inspectors shall have access only to the *strategic points* specified in the Subsidiary Arrangements and to the records maintained pursuant to paragraphs 51–58; and

(*d*) In the event of the State concluding that any unusual circumstances require extended limitations on access by the Agency, the State and the Agency shall promptly make arrangements with a view to enabling the Agency to discharge its safeguards responsibilities in the light of these limitations. The Director General shall report each such arrangement to the Board.

77. The Agreement should provide that in circumstances which may lead to special inspections for the purposes specified in paragraph 73 above the State and the Agency shall consult forthwith. As a result of such consultations the Agency may make inspections in addition to the routine inspection effort provided for in paragraphs 78–82 below, and may obtain access in agreement with the State to information or locations in addition to the access specified in paragraph 76 above for ad hoc and routine inspections. Any disagreement concerning the need for additional access shall be resolved in accordance with paragraphs 21 and 22; in case action by the State is essential and urgent, paragraph 18 above shall apply.

Frequency and intensity of routine inspections

78. The Agreement should provide that the number, intensity, duration and timing of routine inspections shall be kept to the minimum consistent with the effective implementation of the safeguards procedures set forth therein, and that the Agency shall make the optimum and most economical use of available inspection resources.

79. The Agreement should provide that in the case of *facilities* and *material balance areas* outside *facilities* with a content or *annual throughput*, whichever is greater, of *nuclear material* not exceeding five *effective kilograms*, routine inspections shall not exceed one per year. For other *facilities* the number, intensity, duration, timing and mode of inspections shall be determined on the basis that in the maximum or limiting case the inspection régime shall be no more intensive than is necessary and sufficient to maintain continuity of knowledge of the flow and inventory of *nuclear material*.

80. The Agreement should provide that the maximum routine inspection effort in respect of *facilities* with a content or *annual throughput* of *nuclear material* exceeding five *effective kilograms* shall be determined as follows:

(*a*) For reactors and sealed stores, the maximum total of routine inspection per year shall be determined by allowing one sixth of a *man-year of inspection* for each such *facility* in the State;

(*b*) For other *facilities* involving plutonium or uranium enriched to more than 5%, the maximum total of routine inspection per year shall be determined by allowing for each such *facility* $30 \times \sqrt{E}$ man-days of inspection per year, where E is the inventory or *annual throughput* of *nuclear material*, whichever is greater, expressed in *effective kilograms*. The maximum established for any such *facility* shall not, however, be less than 1.5 *man-years of inspection*; and

(*c*) For all other *facilities*, the maximum total of routine inspection per year shall be determined by allowing for each such *facility* one third of a *man-year of inspection* plus $0.4 \times E$ man-days of inspection per year, where E is the inventory or *annual throughput* of *nuclear material*, whichever is greater, expressed in *effective kilograms*.

The Agreement should further provide that the Agency and the State may agree to amend the maximum figures specified in this paragraph upon determination by the Board that such amendment is reasonable.

81. Subject to paragraphs 78–80 above the criteria to be used for determining the actual number, intensity, duration, timing and mode of routine inspections of any *facility* shall include:

(*a*) The form of *nuclear material*, in particular, whether the material is in bulk form or contained in a number of separate items; its chemical composition and, in the case of uranium, whether it is of low or high *enrichment*; and its accessibility;

(*b*) The effectiveness of the State's accounting and control system, including the extent to which the operators of *facilities* are functionally independent of the State's accounting and control system; the extent to which the measures specified in paragraph 32 above have been implemented by the State; the promptness of reports submitted to the Agency; their consistency with the Agency's independent verification; and the amount and accuracy of the *material unaccounted for*, as verified by the Agency;

(*c*) Characteristics of the State's nuclear fuel cycle, in particular, the number and types of *facilities* containing *nuclear material* subject to safeguards, the characteristics of such *facilities* relevant to safeguards, notably the degree of containment; the extent to which the design of such *facilities* facilitates verification of the flow and inventory of *nuclear material*; and the extent to which information from different *material balance areas* can be correlated;

(*d*) International interdependence, in particular, the extent to which *nuclear material* is received from or sent to other States for use or processing; any verification activity by the Agency in connection therewith; and the extent to which the State's nuclear activities are interrelated with those of other States; and

(*e*) Technical developments in the field of safeguards, including the use of statistical techniques and random sampling in evaluating the flow of *nuclear material*.

82. The Agreement should provide for consultation between the Agency and the State if the latter considers that the inspection effort is being deployed with undue concentration on particular *facilities*.

Notice of inspections

83. The Agreement should provide that the Agency shall give advance notice to the State before arrival of inspectors at *facilities* or *material balance areas* outside *facilities*, as follows:

(*a*) For ad hoc inspections pursuant to sub-paragraph 71(*c*) above, at least 24 hours; for those pursuant to sub-paragraphs 71(*a*) and (*b*), as well as the activities provided for in paragraph 48, at least one week;

(*b*) For special inspections pursuant to paragraph 73 above, as promptly as possible after the Agency and the State have consulted as provided for in paragraph 77, it being understood that notification of arrival normally will constitute part of the consultations; and

(*c*) For routine inspections pursuant to paragraph 72 above, at least 24 hours in respect of the *facilities* referred to in sub-paragraph 80(*b*) and sealed stores containing plutonium or uranium enriched to more than 5%, and one week in all other cases.

Such notice of inspections shall include the names of the inspectors and shall indicate the *facilities* and the *material balance areas* outside *facilities* to be visited and the periods during which they will be visited. If the inspectors are to arrive from outside the State the Agency shall also give advance notice of the place and time of their arrival in the State.

84. However, the Agreement should also provide that, as a supplementary measure, the Agency may carry out without advance notification a portion of the routine inspections pursuant to paragraph 80 above in accordance with the principle of random sampling. In performing any unannounced inspections, the Agency shall fully take into account any operational programme provided by the State pursuant to paragraph 64(*b*). Moreover, whenever practicable, and on the basis of the operational programme, it shall advise the State periodically of its general programme of announced and unannounced inspections, specifying the general periods when inspections are foreseen. In carrying out any unannounced inspections, the Agency shall make every effort to minimize any practical difficulties for *facility* operators and the State, bearing in mind the relevant provisions of paragraphs 44 above and 89 below. Similarly the State shall make every effort to facilitate the task of the inspectors.

Designation of inspectors

85. The Agreement should provide that:

(*a*) The Director General shall inform the State in writing of the name, qualifications, nationality, grade and such other particulars as may be relevant, of each Agency official he proposes for designation as an inspector for the State;

(*b*) The State shall inform the Director General within 30 days of the receipt of such a proposal whether it accepts the proposal;

(*c*) The Director General may designate each official who has been accepted by the State as one of the inspectors for the State, and shall inform the State of such designations; and (*d*) The Director General, acting in response to a request by the State or on his own initiative, shall immediately inform the State of the withdrawal of the designation of any official as an inspector for the State.

The Agreement should also provide, however, that in respect of inspectors needed for the purposes stated in paragraph 48 above and to carry out ad hoc inspections pursuant to sub-paragraphs 71(*a*) and (*b*) the designation procedures shall be completed if possible within 30 days after the entry into force of the Agreement. If such designation appears impossible within this time limit, inspectors for such purposes shall be designated on a temporary basis.

86. The Agreement should provide that the State shall grant or renew as quickly as possible appropriate visas, where required, for each inspector designated for the State.

Conduct and visits of inspectors

87. The Agreement should provide that inspectors, in exercising their functions under paragraphs 48 and 71–75 above, shall carry out their activities in a manner designed to avoid hampering or delaying the construction, commissioning or operation of *facilities*, or affecting their safety. In particular inspectors shall not operate any *facility* themselves or direct the staff of a *facility* to carry out any operation. If inspectors consider that in pursuance of paragraphs 74 and 75, particular operations in a *facility* should be carried out by the operator, they shall make a request therefor.

88. When inspectors require services available in the State, including the use of equipment, in connection with the performance of inspections, the State shall facilitate the procurement of such services and the use of such equipment by inspectors.

89. The Agreement should provide that the State shall have the right to have inspectors accompanied during their inspections by representatives of the State, provided that inspectors shall not thereby be delayed or otherwise impeded in the exercise of their functions.

Statements on the Agency's verification activities

90. The Agreement should provide that the Agency shall inform the State of:

(*a*) The results of inspections, at intervals to be specified in the Subsidiary Arrangements; and

(*b*) The conclusions it has drawn from its verification activities in the State, in particular by means of statements in respect of each *material balance area*, which shall be made as soon as possible after a *physical inventory* has been taken and verified by the Agency and a material balance has been struck.

International transfers

General

91. The Agreement should provide that *nuclear material* subject or required to be subject to safeguards thereunder which is transferred internationally shall, for purposes of the Agreement, be regarded as being the responsibility of the State:

(*a*) In the case of import, from the time that such responsibility ceases to lie with the exporting State, and no later than the time at which the *nuclear material* reaches its destination; and

(*b*) In the case of export, up to the time at which the recipient State assumes such responsibility, and no later than the time at which the *nuclear material* reaches its destination.

The Agreement should provide that the States concerned shall make suitable arrangements to determine the point at which the transfer of responsibility will take place. No State shall be deemed to have such responsibility for *nuclear material* merely by reason of the fact that the *nuclear material* is in transit on or over its territory or territorial waters, or that it is being transported under its flag or in its aircraft.

Transfers out of the State

92. The Agreement should provide that any intended transfer out of the State of safeguarded *nuclear material* in an amount exceeding one *effective kilogram*, or by successive shipments to the same State within a period of three months each of less than one *effective kilogram* but exceeding in total one *effective kilogram*, shall be notified to the Agency after the conclusion of the contractual arrangements leading to the transfer and normally at least two weeks before the *nuclear material* is to be prepared for shipping. The Agency and the State may agree on different procedures for advance notification. The notification shall specify:

(*a*) The identification and, if possible, the expected quantity and composition of the *nuclear material* to be transferred, and the *material balance area* from which it will come;

(*b*) The State for which the *nuclear material* is destined;

(*c*) The dates on and locations at which the *nuclear material* is to be prepared for shipping;

(*d*) The approximate dates of dispatch and arrival of the *nuclear material*; and

(*e*) At what point of the transfer the recipient State will assume responsibility for the *nuclear material*, and the probable date on which this point will be reached.

93. The Agreement should further provide that the purpose of this notification shall be to enable the Agency if necessary to identify,

and if possible verify the quantity and composition of, *nuclear material* subject to safeguards under the Agreement before it is transferred out of the State and, if the agency so wishes or the State so requests, to affix seals to the *nuclear material* when it has been prepared for shipping. However, the transfer of the *nuclear material* shall not be delayed in any way by any action taken or contemplated by the Agency pursuant to this notification.

94. The Agreement should provide that, if the *nuclear material* will not be subject to Agency safeguards in the recipient State, the exporting State shall make arrangements for the Agency to receive, within three months of the time when the recipient State accepts responsibility for the *nuclear material* from the exporting State, confirmation by the recipient State of the transfer.

Transfers into the State

95. The Agreement should provide that the expected transfer into the State of *nuclear material* required to be subject to safeguards in an amount greater than one *effective kilogram*, or by successive shipments from the same State within a period of three months each of less than one *effective kilogram* but exceeding in total one *effective kilogram*, shall be notified to the Agency as much in advance as possible of the expected arrival of the *nuclear material*, and in any case not later than the date on which the recipient State assumes responsibility therefor. The Agency and the State may agree on different procedures for advance notification. The notification shall specify:

(*a*) The identification and, if possible, the expected quantity and composition of the *nuclear material*;

(*b*) At what point of the transfer responsibility for the *nuclear material* will be assumed by the State for the purposes of the Agreement, and the probable date on which this point will be reached; and

(*c*) The expected date of arrival, the location to which the *nuclear material* is to be delivered and the date on which it is intended that the *nuclear material* should be unpacked.

96. The Agreement should provide that the purpose of this notification shall be to enable the Agency if necessary to identify, and if possible verify the quantity and composition of, *nuclear material* subject to safeguards which has been transferred into the State, by means of inspection of the consignment at the time it is unpacked. However, unpacking shall not be delayed by any action taken or contemplated by the Agency pursuant to this notification.

Special reports

97. The Agreement should provide that in the case of international transfers a special report as envisaged in paragraph 68 above shall be made if any unusual incident or circumstances lead the State to believe that there is or may have been loss of *nuclear material*, including the occurrence of significant delay during the transfer.

Definitions

98. "Adjustment" means an entry into an accounting record or a report showing a *shipper/receiver difference* or *material unaccounted for*.

99. "Annual throughput" means, for the purposes of paragraphs 79 and 80 above, the amount of *nuclear material* transferred annually out of a *facility* working at nominal capacity.

100. "Batch" means a portion of *nuclear material* handled as a unit for accounting purposes at a *key measurement point* and for which the composition and quantity are defined by a single set of specifications or measurements. The *nuclear material* may be in bulk form or contained in a number of separate items.

101. "Batch data" means the total weight of each element of *nuclear material* and, in the case of plutonium and uranium, the isotopic composition when appropriate. The units of account shall be as follows:

(*a*) Grams of contained plutonium;

(*b*) Grams of total uranium and grams of contained uranium-235 plus uranium-233 for uranium enriched in these isotopes; and

(*c*) Kilograms of contained thorium, natural uranium or depleted uranium.

For reporting purposes the weights of individual items in the *batch* shall be added together before rounding to the nearest unit.

102. "Book inventory" of a *material balance area* means the algebraic sum of the most recent *physical inventory* of that *material balance area* and of all *inventory changes* that have occurred since that *physical inventory* was taken.

103. "Correction" means an entry into an accounting record or a report to rectify an identified mistake or to reflect an improved measurement of a quantity previously entered into the record or report. Each correction must identify the entry to which it pertains.

104. "Effective kilogram" means a special unit used in safeguarding *nuclear material*. The quantity in "effective kilograms" is obtained by taking:

(*a*) For plutonium, its weight in kilograms;

(*b*) For uranium with an *enrichment* of 0.01 (1%) and above, its weight in kilograms multiplied by the square of its *enrichment*;

(*c*) For uranium with an *enrichment* below 0.01 (1%) and above 0.005 (0.5%), its weight in kilograms multiplied by 0.0001; and

(*d*) For depleted uranium with an *enrichment* of 0.005 (0.5%) or below, and for thorium, its weight in kilograms multiplied by 0.00005.

105. "Enrichment" means the ratio of the combined weight of the isotopes uranium-233 and uranium-235 to that of the total uranium in question.

106. "Facility" means:

(*a*) A reactor, a critical facility, a conversion plant, a fabrication plant, a reprocessing plant, an isotope separation plant or a separate storage installation; or

(*b*) Any location where *nuclear material* in amounts greater than one *effective kilogram* is customarily used.

107. "Inventory change" means an increase or decrease, in terms of *batches*, of *nuclear material* in a *material balance area*; such a change shall involve one of the following:

(*a*) Increases:

(i) Import;

(ii) Domestic receipt: receipts from other *material balance areas*, receipts from a non-safeguarded (non-peaceful) activity or receipts at the starting point of safeguards;

(iii) Nuclear production: production of special fissionable material in a reactor; and

(iv) De-exemption: reapplication of safeguards on *nuclear material* previously exempted therefrom on account of its use or quantity.

(*b*) Decreases:

(i) Export;

(ii) Domestic shipment: shipments to other *material balance areas* or shipments for a non-safeguarded (non-peaceful) activity;

(iii) Nuclear loss: loss of *nuclear material* due to its transformation into other element(s) or isotope(s) as a result of nuclear reactions;

(iv) Measured discard: *nuclear material* which has been measured, or estimated on the basis of measurements and disposed of in such a way that it is not suitable for further nuclear use;

(v) Retained waste: *nuclear material* generated from processing or from an operational accident, which is deemed to be unrecoverable for the time being but which is stored;

(vi) Exemption: exemption of *nuclear material* from safeguards on account of its use or quantity; and

(vii) Other loss: for example, accidental loss (that is, irretrievable and inadvertent loss of *nuclear material* as the result of an operational accident) or theft.

108. "Key measurement point" means location where *nuclear material* appears in such a form that it may be measured to determine material flow or inventory. "Key measurement points" thus include, but are not limited to, the inputs and outputs (including measured discards) and storages in *material balance areas*.

109. "Man-year of inspection" means, for the purposes of paragraph 80 above, 300 man-days of inspection, a man-day being a day during which a single inspector has access to a *facility* at any time for a total of not more than eight hours.

110. "Material balance area" means an area in or outside of a *facility* such that:

(*a*) The quantity of *nuclear material* in each transfer into or out of each "material balance area" can be determined; and

(*b*) The *physical inventory* of *nuclear material* in each "material balance area" can be determined when necessary, in accordance with specified procedures, in order that the material balance for Agency safeguards purposes can be established.

111. "Material unaccounted for" means the difference between *book inventory* and *physical inventory*.

112. "Nuclear material" means any source or any special fissionable material as defined in Article XX of the Statute. The term source material shall not be interpreted as applying to ore or ore residue. Any determination by the Board under Article XX of the Statute after the entry into force of this Agreement which adds to the materials considered to be source material or special fissionable material shall have effect under this Agreement only upon acceptance by the State.

113. "Physical inventory" means the sum of all the measured or derived estimates of *batch* quantities of *nuclear material* on hand at a given time within a *material balance area*, obtained in accordance with specified procedures.

114. "Shipper/receiver difference" means the difference between the quantity of *nuclear material* in a *batch* as stated by the shipping *material balance area* and as measured at the receiving *material balance area*.

115. "Source data" means those data, recorded during measurement or calibration or used to derive empirical relationships, which identify *nuclear material* and provide *batch data*. "Source data" may include, for example, weight of compounds, conversion factors to determine weight of element, specific gravity, element concentration, isotopic ratios, relationship between volume and manometer readings and relationship between plutonium produced and power generated.

116. "Strategic point" means a location selected during examination of design information where, under normal conditions and when combined with the information from all "strategic points" taken together, the information necessary and sufficient for the implementation of safeguards measures is obtained and verified; a "strategic point" may include any location where key measurements related to material balance account-

ancy are made and where containment and
surveillance measures are executed.

Source: IAEA document INFCIRC/153 (Corrected)
(IAEA, Vienna, 1983)

Appendix VI. Duration and termination of INFCIRC/66 agreements, GOV/1621 of 1973

Item 1(b) of the provisional agenda (GOV/1620)

SAFEGUARDS

(b) THE FORMULATION OF CERTAIN PROVISIONS IN AGREEMENTS UNDER THE AGENCY'S SAFEGUARDS SYSTEM (1965, AS PREVIOUSLY EXTENDED IN 1966 AND 1968)

Memorandum by the Director General

1. A substantial number of Governors have urged that there should be a greater degree of standardization than in the past with respect to the duration and termination of such agreements as may henceforth be concluded under the Agency's Safeguards System (1965, as Provisionally Extended in 1966 and 1968)[1] for the application of safeguards in connection with nuclear material, equipment, facilities or non-nuclear material supplied to States by third parties. To achieve this, it is recommended that the following two concepts should be reflected in these agreements:

(*a*) That the duration of the agreement should be related to the period of actual use of the items in the recipient State; and

(*b*) That the provisions for terminating the agreement should be formulated in such a way that the rights and obligations of the parties continue to apply in connection with supplied nuclear material and with special fissionable material produced, processed or used in or in connection with supplied nuclear material, equipment, facilities or non-nuclear material, until such time as the Agency has terminated the application of safeguards thereto, in accordance with the provisions of paragraph 26 or 27 of the Agency's Safeguards System.

A short exposition with respect to the application of these concepts is annexed hereto.

2. The proposed standardization would appear likely to facilitate the uniform application of safeguards measures. It is furthermore to be noted that the combined operation of the two concepts would be consistent with the application of the general principle embodied in paragraph 16 of the Agency's Safeguards System.

Requested action by the Board

3. In bringing this matter to the Board's attention, the Director General seeks the views of the Board as to whether it concurs with the two concepts set out in paragraph 1 above.

ANNEX

1. In the case of receipt by a State of source or special fissionable material, equipment facilities or non-nuclear material from a supplier outside that State, the duration of the relevant agreement under the Agency's Safeguards System[1] would be related to the actual use in the recipient State of the material or items supplied. This may be accomplished by requiring, in accordance with present practice, that the material or items supplied be listed in the inventory called for by the agreement.

2. The primary effect of termination of the agreement, either by act of the parties or effluxion of time, would be that no further sup-

plied nuclear material, equipment, facilities or non-nuclear material could be added to the inventory. On the other hand, the rights and obligations of the parties, as provided for in the agreement, would continue to apply in connection with any supplied material or items and with any special fissionable material produced, processed or used in or in connection with supplied material or items which had been included in the inventory, until such material or items had been removed from the inventory.

3. With respect to nuclear material, conditions for removal are those set out in paragraph 26 or 27 of the Agency's Safeguards System; with respect to equipment, facilities and non-nuclear material, conditions for removal could be based on paragraph 26. A number of agreements already concluded have prescribed such conditions in part, by providing for deletion from the inventory of nuclear material, equipment and facilities which are returned to the supplying State or transferred (under safeguards) to a third State. The additional provisions contemplated would stipulate that items or non-nuclear material could be removed from the purview of the agreement if they had been consumed, were no longer usable for any nuclear activity relevant from the point of view of safeguards or had become practicably irrecoverable.

4. The effect of reflecting the two concepts in agreements would be that special fissionable material which had been produced, processed or used in or in connection with supplied material or items before they were removed from the scope of the agreement, would remain or be listed in the inventory, and such special fissionable material, together with any supplied nuclear material remaining in the inventory, would be subject to safeguards until the Agency had terminated safeguards on that special fissionable and nuclear material in accordance with the provisions of the Agency's Safeguards System. Thus, the actual termination of the operation of the provisions of the agreement would take place only when everything had been removed from the inventory.

Note:

1. The Agency's Safeguards System (1965, as Provisionally Extended in 1966 and 1968) set forth in document INFCIRC/66/Rev. 2.

Source: IAEA document Gov/1621 (IAEA, Vienna, 1973).

Appendix VII. The IAEA Inspectors' Document GC(V)INF/39 of 1961

THE AGENCY'S INSPECTORATE

MEMORANDUM BY THE DIRECTOR GENERAL

1. The General Conference will recall that in connection with its fourth regular session the Board transmitted to it for information a memorandum on the Agency's inspectors.[1] In that document the Board indicated that until certain issues relevant to the recruitment and sources of members of the Agency's inspectorate had been resolved, it would not consider its examination of the problems connected therewith as complete.

2. The Board reverted to the subject at meetings held in April and June 1961, and on 29 June decided that the Inspector General and all officers of Professional grade of the Division of Inspection would be appointed by the Director General as staff officials of the Agency after he had submitted applications recommended by him to the Board for approval. As a corollary to that decision the Board also decided that its consideration of the establishment of the Agency's inspectorate was concluded, and that the detailed provisions relating to the Agency's inspectors which it had annexed to its memorandum of last year were in effect.

3. As the Board pointed out last year, that Annex – which deals with matters that arise in the appliction of the Agency's safeguards and health and safety measures – is intended to serve as a guide to the parties concerned in negotiating provisions that are normally included in project agreements, and in agreements for the application of Agency safeguards and the Agency's health and safety measures to bilateral or multilateral arrangements or to a State's own activities in the field of atomic energy, to the extent that such provisions are relevant to each project or arrangement. The provisions of the Annex are not mandatory, and they and other provisions that may be agreed in negotiation will only be given legal effect by the entry into force of the particular agreement which incorporates them.

4. The Board has requested the communication of this memorandum to the General Conference, together with the text of the Annex to its memorandum of last year, for information at the fifth regular session.

Note:
1. IAEA document GC(IV)/INF/27.

ANNEX. THE AGENCY'S INSPECTORS

I. **Designation[1] of Agency inspectors**

1. When it is proposed to designate an Agency inspector for a State, the Director General shall inform the State in writing of the name, nationality and grade of the Agency inspector proposed, shall transmit a written certification of his relevant qualifications and shall enter into such other consultations as the State may request. The State shall inform the Director General, within 30 days of receipt of such a proposal, whether it accepts the designation of that inspector. If so, the inspector may be designated as one of the Agency's inspectors for that State, and the Director General shall notify the State concerned of such designation.

2. If a State, either upon proposal of a designation or at any time after a designation has been made, objects to the designation of an Agency inspector for that State, it shall inform the Director General of its objection. In this event, the Director General shall propose to the State an alternative designation or designations. The Director General may refer to the Board, for its appropriate action, the repeated refusal of a State to accept the designation of an Agency inspector if, in his opinion, this

214

refusal would impede the inspections provided for in the relevant project or safeguards agreement.

3. Each State shall as speedily as possible grant or renew appropriate visas, where required, for persons whose designation as Agency inspectors that State has accepted.

II. Visits of Agency inspectors

4. The State shall be given at least one week's notice of each inspection, including the names of the Agency's inspectors, the place and approximate time of their arrival and departure, and the facilities and materials to be inspected. Such notice need not exceed 24 hours for any inspection to investigate any incident requiring a "special inspection".[2]

5. Agency inspectors shall be accompanied by representatives of the State concerned, if the State so requests, provided that the inspectors shall not thereby be delayed or otherwise impeded in the exercise of their functions. Agency inspectors shall use such points of entry into and departure from the State, and such routes and modes of travel within it, as may be designated by the State.

6. Agency inspectors, in locations where this is necessary, shall be provided, on request and for reasonable compensation if agreed on, with appropriate equipment for carrying out inspections and with suitable accommodation and transport.

7. The visits and activities of the Agency's inspectors shall be so arranged as to ensure on the one hand the effective discharge of their functions and on the other hand the minimum possible inconvenience to the State and disturbance to the facilities inspected.

8. Consultations shall take place with the State to ensure that consistent with the effective discharge of the functions of the Agency's inspectors, their activities will be conducted in harmony with the laws and regulations existing in the State.

III. Rights of access and inspection

9. After submitting their credentials, and to the extent relevant to the project or arrangement, Agency inspectors shall have access, depending upon the type of inspection to be carried out, either:

(a) To all materials, equipment and facilities to which Agency safeguards against diversion are applied under the relevant provisions of document INFCIRC/26; or

(b) To all radiation sources, equipment and facilities which can be inspected by those Agency inspectors who are making inspections in relation to the provisions of paragraphs 31 and 32 of the Agency's health and safety measures set forth in document INFCIRC/18. They shall have access at all times to all places and data and to any person, to the extent provided for in Article XII.A.6 of the Statute. The State shall direct all such persons under its control to co-operate fully with Agency inspectors, and shall indicate the exact location of and identify all such materials, equipment and facilities.

10. With respect to all materials, equipment and facilities to which Agency safeguards against diversion are applied, the Agency's inspectors shall be permitted to carry out their inspections in accordance with the pertinent agreements which may include provisions for:

(a) Examination of the facility and/or materials to which Agency safeguards are applied;

(b) Audit of reports and records;

(c) Verification of the amounts of material to which Agency safeguards are applied, by physical inspection, measurement and sampling; and

(d) Examination and testing of the measurement instruments.

11. Agency inspectors for health and safety measures may perform inspections in accordance with each individual agreement, which may necessitate:

(a) Tests of radiation sources, of radiation detection and monitoring instruments and of other equipment or devices in connection with the use, storage, transportation or disposal as waste of radiation sources;

(b) Examination of facilities wherein radiation sources are used or stored, of waste disposal facilities and of all records on which reports to the Agency are based; and

(c) Examinations related to the evaluation of the radiation exposure of persons who have or may have been over-exposed.

The State shall perform, in a manner prescribed by the Agency, or arrange for the Agency to perform those tests and examinations deemed necessary by the Agency.

12. After an inspection has been carried out, the State concerned shall be duly informed by the Agency of its results. In case the State disagrees with the report of the Agency's inspectors, it shall be entitled to submit a report on the matter to the Board of Governors.

IV. The privileges and immunities of the Agency's inspectors

13. Agency inspectors shall be granted the privileges and immunities necessary for the performance of their functions. Suitable provision shall be included in each project or safeguards agreement for the application, in so far as relevant to the execution of that agreement, of the provisions of the Agreement on the Privileges and Immunities of the International Atomic Energy Agency[3] excepting Articles V and XII thereof, provided that all parties to the project or safeguards agreement so agree.

14. Disputes between a State and the Agency arising out of the exercise of the functions of Agency inspectors will be settled according to an appropriate disputes clause in the pertinent project or safeguards agreement.

Notes:
1. The term "designation" as used in this Annex refers to the assignment of Agency inspectors to a particular task or tasks and not to the recruitment or appointment of Agency inspectors.
2. "Special inspections" are provided for in paragraphs 58 and 59 of the Agency's safeguards system (INFCIRC/26); they are also provided for in paragraph 32 of the Agency's health and safety measures (INFCIRC/18).
3. INFCIRC/9/Rev. 1.

Source: IAEA document GC(V)INF/39 (IAEA, Vienna, 1961).

Appendix VIII. Guidelines for nuclear transfers, INFCIRC/254 of 1977

Agreed at London on 21 September 1977 by the Nuclear Supplier Group, and attached to communications addressed on 11 January 1978 to the Director General of the IAEA

1. The following fundamental principles for safeguards and export controls should apply to nuclear transfers to any non-nuclear-weapon State for peaceful purposes. In this connection, suppliers have defined an export trigger list and agreed on common criteria for technology transfers.

Prohibition on nuclear explosives

2. Suppliers should authorize transfer of items identified in the trigger list only upon formal governmental assurances from recipients explicitly excluding uses which would result in any nuclear explosive device.

Physical protection

3. (*a*) All nuclear materials and facilities identified by the agreed trigger list should be placed under effective physical protection to prevent unauthorized use and handling. The levels of physical protection to be ensured in relation to the type of materials, equipment and facilities, have been agreed by suppliers, taking account of international recommendations

(*b*) The implementation of measures of physical protection in the recipient country is the responsibility of the Government of that country. However, in order to implement the terms agreed upon amongst suppliers, the levels of physical protection on which these measures have to be based should be the subject of an agreement between supplier and recipient.

(*c*) In each case special arrangements should be made for a clear definition of responsibilities for the transport of trigger list items.

Safeguards

4. Suppliers should transfer trigger list items only when covered by IAEA safeguards, with duration and coverage provisions in conformance with the GOV/1621 guidelines.* Exceptions should be made only

after consultation with the parties to this understanding.

5. Suppliers will jointly reconsider their common safeguards requirements, whenever appropriate.

Safeguards triggered by the transfer of certain technology

6. (*a*) The requirements of paragraphs 2, 3 and 4 above should also apply to facilities for reprocessing, enrichment, or heavy-water production, utilizing technology directly transferred by the supplier or derived from transferred facilities, or major critical components thereof.

(*b*) The transfer of such facilities, or major critical components thereof, or related technology, should require an undertaking (1) that IAEA safeguards apply to any facilities of the same type (i.e. if the design, construction or operating processes are based on the same or similar physical or chemical processes, as defined in the trigger list) constructed during an agreed period in the recipient country and (2) that there should at all times be in effect a safeguards agreement permitting the IAEA to apply Agency safeguards with respect to such facilities identified by the recipient, or by the supplier in consultation with the recipient, as using transferred technology.

Special controls on sensitive exports

7. Suppliers should exercise restraint in the transfer of sensitive facilities, technology and weapons-usable materials. If enrichment or reprocessing facilities, equipment or technology are to be transferred, suppliers should encourage recipients to accept, as an alternative to national plants, supplier involvement and/or other appropriate multinational participation in resulting facilities. Suppliers should also promote international (including IAEA) activities concerned with multinational regional fuel cycle centres.

Special controls on export of enrichment facilities, equipment and technology

8. For a transfer of an enrichment facility, or technology therefor, the recipient nation should agree that neither the transferred facility, nor any facility based on such technology, will be designed or operated for the production of greater than 20% enriched uranium without the consent of the supplier nation, of which the IAEA should be advised.

Controls on supplied or derived weapons-usable material

9. Suppliers recognize the importance, in order to advance the objectives of these Guidelines and to provide opportunities further to reduce the risks of proliferation, of including in agreements on supply of nuclear materials or of facilities which produce weapons-usable material, provisions calling for mutual agreement between the supplier and the recipient on arrangements for reprocessing, storage, alteration, use, transfer or retransfer of any weapons-usable material involved. Suppliers should endeavour to include such provisions whenever appropriate and practicable.

Controls on retransfer

10. (*a*) Suppliers should transfer trigger list items, including technology defined under paragraph 6, only upon the recipient's assurance that in the case of:

(1) retransfer of such items,

or

(2) transfer of trigger list items derived from facilities originally transferred by the supplier, or with the help of equipment or technology originally transferred by the supplier;

the recipient of the retransfer or transfer will have provided the same assurances as those required by the supplier for the original transfer.

(*b*) In addition the supplier's consent should be required for: (1) any retransfer of the facilities, major critical components, or technology described in paragraph 6; (2) any transfer of facilities or major critical components derived from those items; (3) any retransfer of heavy water or weapons-usable material.

Supporting activities

Physical security

11. Suppliers should promote international co-operation on the exchange of physical security information, protection of nuclear materials in transit, and recovery of stolen nuclear materials and equipment.

Support for effective IAEA safeguards

12. Suppliers should make special efforts

in support of effective implementation of IAEA safeguards. Suppliers should also support the Agency's efforts to assist Member States in the improvement of their national systems of accounting and control of nuclear material and to increase the technical effectiveness of safeguards.

Similarly, they should make every effort to support the IAEA in increasing further the adequacy of safeguards in the light of technical developments and the rapidly growing number of nuclear facilities, and to support appropriate initiatives aimed at improving the effectiveness of IAEA safeguards.

Sensitive plant design features

13. Suppliers should encourage the designers and makers of sensitive equipment to construct it in such a way as to facilitate the application of safeguards.

Consultations

14. (*a*) Suppliers should maintain contact and consult through regular channels on matters connected with the implementation of these Guidelines.

(*b*) Suppliers should consult, as each deems appropriate, with other Governments concerned on specific sensitive cases, to ensure that any transfer does not contribute to risks of conflict or instability.

(*c*) In the event that one or more suppliers believe that there has been a violation of supplier/recipient understandings resulting from these Guidelines, particularly in the case of an explosion of a nuclear device, or illegal termination or violation of IAEA safeguards by a recipient, suppliers should consult promptly through diplomatic channels in order to determine and assess the reality and extent of the alleged violation.

Pending the early outcome of such consultations, suppliers will not act in a manner that could prejudice any measure that may be adopted by other suppliers concerning their current contacts with that recipient.

Upon the findings of such consultations, the suppliers, bearing in mind Article XII of the IAEA Statute, should agree on an appropriate response and possible action which could include the termination of nuclear transfers to that recipient.

15. In considering transfers, each supplier should exercise prudence having regard to all the circumstances of each case, including any risk that technology transfers not covered by paragraph 6, or subsequent retransfers, might result in unsafeguarded nuclear materials.

16. Unanimous consent is required for any changes in these Guidelines, including any which might result from the reconsideration mentioned in paragraph 5.

_____

* This is a reference to an IAEA document of 20 August 1973, entitled "The formulation of certain provisions in agreements under the Agency's safeguards system (1965, as provisionally extended in 1966 and 1968)", which recommends that the following two concepts should be reflected in the agreements: (*a*) that the duration of the agreement should be related to the period of actual use of the items in the recipient State; and (*b*) that the provisions for terminating the agreement should be formulated in such a way that the rights and obligations of the parties continue to apply in connection with supplied nuclear material and with special fissionable material produced, processed or used in or in connection with supplied nuclear material, equipment, facilities or non-nuclear material, until such time as the Agency has terminated the application of safeguards thereto.

ANNEX A. TRIGGER LIST REFERRED TO IN GUIDELINES

PART A. Material and equipment

1. Source or special fissionable material as defined in Article XX of the Statute of the International Atomic Energy Agency; provided that items specified in subparagraph (*a*) below, and exports of source or special fissionable material to a given recipient country, within a period of 12 months, below the limits specified in subparagraph (*b*) below, shall not be included:

(*a*) Plutonium with an isotopic concentration of plutonium-238 exceeding 80%.

Special fissionable material when used in gram quantities or less as a sensing component in instruments; and

Source material which the Government is satisfied is to be used only in non-nuclear activities, such as the production of alloys or ceramics;

(*b*) Special fissionable
material — 50 effective grams;
Natural uranium — 500 kilograms;
Depleted uranium — 1 000 kilograms; and
Thorium — 1 000 kilograms.

2.1. *Reactors and equipment therefor:*

2.1.1. Nuclear reactors capable of operation so as to maintain a controlled self-sustaining fission chain reaction, excluding zero energy reactors, the latter being defined as reactors with a designed maximum rate of production of plutonium not exceeding 100 grams per year.

2.1.2. Reactor pressure vessels:
Metal vessels, as complete units or as major shop-fabricated parts therefor, which are especially designed or prepared to contain the core of a nuclear reactor as defined in paragraph 2.1.1. above and are capable of withstanding the operating pressure of the primary coolant.

2.1.3. Reactor fuel charging and discharging machines: Manipulative equipment especially designed or prepared for inserting or removing fuel in a nuclear reactor as defined in paragraph 2.1.1. above capable of on-load operation or employing technically sophisticated positioning or alignment features to allow complex off-load fuelling operations such as those in which direct viewing of or access to the fuel is not normally available.

2.1.4. Reactor control rods:
Rods especially designed or prepared for the control of the reaction rate in a nuclear reactor as defined in paragraph 2.1.1 above.

2.1.5. Reactor pressure tubes:
Tubes which are especially designed or prepared to contain fuel elements and the primary coolant in a reactor as defined in paragraph 2.1.1 above at an operating pressure in excess of 50 atmospheres.

2.1.6. Zirconium tubes:
Zirconium metal and alloys in the form of tubes or assemblies of tubes, and in quantities exceeding 500 kg per year, especially designed or prepared for use in a reactor as defined in paragraph 2.1.1 above, and in which the relationship of hafnium to zirconium is less than 1:500 parts by weight.

2.1.7. Primary coolant pumps:
Pumps especially designed or prepared for circulating liquid metal as primary coolant for nuclear reactors as defined in paragraph 2.1.1 above.

2.2. *Non-nuclear materials for reactors:*

2.2.1. Deuterium and heavy water:
Deuterium and any deuterium compound in which the ratio of deuterium to hydrogen exceeds 1:5 000 for use in a nuclear reactor as defined in paragraph 2.1.1 above in quantities exceeding 200 kg of deuterium atoms for any one recipient country in any period of 12 months.

2.2.2. Nuclear grade graphite:
Graphite having a purity level better than 5 parts per million boron equivalent and with a density greater than 1.50 grams per cubic centimetre in quantities exceeding 30 metric tons for any one recipient country in any period of 12 months.

2.3.1. Plants for the reprocessing of irradiated fuel elements, and equipment especially designed or prepared therefor.

2.4.1. Plants for the fabrication of fuel elements.

2.5.1. Equipment, other than analytical instruments, especially designed or prepared for the separation of isotopes of uranium.

2.6.1. Plants for the production of heavy water, deuterium and deuterium compounds and equipment especially designed or prepared therefor.

Clarifications of certain of the items on the above list are annexed.

PART B. Common criteria for technology transfers under paragraph 6 of the Guidelines

1. "Technology" means technical data in physical form designated by the supplying country as important to the design, construction, operation, or maintenance of enrichment, reprocessing, or heavy water production facilities or major critical components thereof, but excluding data available to the public, for example, in published books and periodicals, or that which has been made available internationally without restrictions upon its further dissemination.

2. "Major critical components" are:

(a) in the case of an isotope separation plant of the gaseous diffusion type: *diffusion barrier;*

(b) in the case of an isotope separation plant of the gas centrifuge type: *gas centrifuge assemblies, corrosion-resistant to UF₆;*

(c) in the case of an isotope separation plant of the jet nozzle type: the *nozzle units;*

(d) in the case of an isotope plant of the vortex type: *the vortex units.*

3. For facilities covered by paragraph 6 of the Guidelines for which no major critical component is described in paragraph 2 above, if a supplier nation should transfer in the aggregate a significant fraction of the items essential to the operation of such a facility, together with the knowhow for construction and operation of that facility, that transfer should be deemed to be a transfer of "facilities or major critical components thereof".

4. The definitions in the preceding paragraphs are solely for the purposes of paragraph 6 of the Guidelines and this Part B, which differ from those applicable to Part A of this trigger list, which should not be interpreted as limited by such definition.

5. For the purposes of implementing paragraph 6 of the Guidelines, the following facilities should be deemed to be "of the same type (i.e. if their design, construction or operating processes are based on the same or similar physical or chemical processes)":

Where the technology transferred is such as to make possible the construction in the recipient State of a facility of the following type, or major critical components thereof:	The following will be deemed to be facilities of the same type:
(a) an isotope separation plant of the gaseous diffusion type	any other isotope separation plant using the gaseous diffusion process.
(b) an isotope separation plant of the gas centrifuge type	any other isotope separation plant using the gas centrifuge process.
(c) an isotope separation plant of the jet nozzle type..............	any other isotope separation plant using the jet nozzle process.
(d) an isotope separation plant of the vortex type..............	any other isotope separation plant using the vortex process.
(e) a fuel reprocessing plant using the solvent extraction process	any other fuel reprocessing plant using the solvent extraction process.
(f) a heavy water plant using the exchange process.........	any other heavy water plant using the exchange process.
(g) a heavy water plant using the electrolytic process	any other heavy water plant using the electrolytic process.
(h) a heavy water plant using the hydrogen distillation process......................	any other heavy water plant using the hydrogen distillation process.

Note: In the case of reprocessing, enrichment, and heavy water facilities whose design, construction, or operation processes are based on physical or chemical processes other than those enumerated above, a similar approach would be applied to define facilities "of the same type", and a need to define major critical components of such facilities might arise.

6. The reference in paragraph 6(b) of the Guidelines to "any facilities of the same type constructed during an agreed period in the recipient's country" is understood to refer to such facilities (or major critical components thereof), the first operation of which commences within a period of at least 20 years from the date of the first operation of (1) a facility which has been transferred or incorporates transferred major critical components or of (2) a facility of the same type built

after the transfer of technology. It is understood that during that period there would be a conclusive presumption that any facility of the same type utilized transferred technology. But the agreed period is not intended to limit the duration of the safeguards imposed or the duration of the right to identify facilities as being constructed or operated on the basis of or by the use of transferred technology in accordance with paragraph 6(*b*) (2) of the Guidelines.

ANNEX. CLARIFICATIONS OF ITEMS ON THE TRIGGER LIST
Clarifications of items on the trigger list

A. *Complete nuclear reactors*

(Item 2.1.1 of the trigger list)

1. A "nuclear reactor" basically includes the items within or attached directly to the reactor vessel, the equipment which controls the level of power in the core, and the components which normally contain or come in direct contact with or control the primary' coolant of the reactor core.

2. The export of the whole set of major items within this boundary will take place only in accordance with the procedures of the Guidelines. Those individual items within this functionally defined boundary which will be exported only in accordance with the procedures of the Guidelines are listed in paragraphs 2.1.1 to 2.1.5.

The Government reserves to itself the right to apply the procedures of the Guidelines to other items within the functionally defined boundary.

3. It is not intended to exclude reactors which could reasonably be capable of modification to produce significantly more than 100 grams of plutonium per year. Reactors designed for sustained operation at significant power levels, regardless of their capacity for plutonium production, are not considered as "zero energy reactors".

B. *Pressure vessels*

(Item 2.1.2. of the trigger list)

4. A top plate for a reactor pressure vessel is covered by item 2.1.1 as a major shop-fabricated part of a pressure vessel.

5. Reactor internals (e.g. support columns and plates for the core and other vessel internals, control rod guide tubes, thermal shields, baffles, core grid plates, diffuser plates, etc.) are normally supplied by the reactor supplier. In some cases, certain internal support components are included in the fabrication of the pressure vessel. These items are sufficiently critical to the safety and reliability of the operation of the reactor (and, therefore, to the guarantees and liability of the reactor supplier), so that their supply, outside the basic supply arrangement for the reactor itself, would not be common practice. Therefore, although the separate supply of these unique, especially designed and prepared, critical, large and expensive items would not necessarily be considered as falling outside the area of concern, such a mode of supply is considered unlikely.

C. *Reactor control rods*

(Item 2.1.4 of the trigger list)

6. This item includes, in addition to the neutron absorbing part, the support or suspension structures therefor if supplied separately.

D. *Fuel reprocessing plants*

(Item 2.3.1 of the trigger list)

7. A "plant for the reprocessing of irradiated fuel elements" includes the equipment and components which normally come in direct contact with and directly control the irradiated fuel and the major nuclear material and fission product processing streams. The export of the whole set of major items within this boundary will take place only in accordance with the procedures of the Guidelines. In the present state of technology, the following items of equipment are considered to fall within the meaning of the phrase "and equipment especially designed or prepared therefor":

(*a*) Irradiated fuel element chopping machines: remotely operated equipment especially designed or prepared for use in a reprocessing plant as identified above and intended to cut, chop or shear irradiated nuclear fuel assemblies, bundles or rods; and

(*b*) Critically safe tanks (e.g. small diameter, annular or slab tanks) especially designed or prepared for use in a reprocessing plant as identified above, intended for dissolution of irradiated nuclear fuel and which are capable of withstanding hot, highly corrosive liquid, and which can be remotely loaded and maintained;

8. The Government reserves to itself the right to apply the procedures of the Guidelines to other items within the functionally defined boundary.

E. *Fuel fabrication plants*

(Item 2.4.1 of the trigger list)

9. A "plant for the fabrication of fuel elements" includes the equipment:

(*a*) Which normally comes in direct contact with, or directly processes, or controls, the production flow of nuclear material, or

(*b*) Which seals the nuclear material within the cladding.

10. The export of the whole set of items for the foregoing operations will take place only in accordance with the procedures of the Guidelines. The Government will also give consideration to application of the pro-

cedures of the Guidelines to individual items intended for any of the foregoing operations, as well as for other fuel fabrication operations such as checking the integrity of the cladding or the seal, and the finish treatment to the sealed fuel.

F. *Isotope separation plant equipment*

(Item 2.5.1 of the trigger list)

11. "Equipment, other than analytical instruments, especially designed or prepared for the separation of isotopes of uranium" includes each of the major items of equipment especially designed or prepared for the separation process. Such items include:
- gaseous diffusion barriers,
- gaseous diffuser housings,
- gas centrifuge assemblies, corrosion-resistant to UF_6,
- jet nozzle separation units,
- vortex separation units,
- large UF_6 corrosion-resistant axial or centrifugal compressors,
- special compressor seals for such compressors.

ANNEX B. CRITERIA FOR LEVELS OF PHYSICAL PROTECTION

1. The purpose of physical protection of nuclear materials is to prevent unauthorized use and handling of these materials. Paragraph 3(a) of the Guidelines document calls for agreement among suppliers on the levels

Table: Categorization of nuclear material

Material	Form	Category I	Category II	Category III
1. Plutonium[a]	Unirradiated[b]	2 kg or more	Less than 2 kg but more than 500 g	500 g or less[c]
2. Uranium-235	Unirradiated[b]			
	– uranium enriched to 20% ^{235}U or more	5 kg or more	Less than 5 kg but more than 1 kg	1 kg or less[c]
	– uranium enriched to 10% ^{235}U but less than 20%	–	10 kg or more	Less than 10 kg[c]
	– uranium enriched above natural, but less than 10% ^{235}U[d]			10 kg or more
3. Uranium-233	Unirradiated[b]	2 kg or more	Less than 2 kg but more than 500 g	500 g or less[c]
4. Irradiated fuel			Depleted or natural uranium, thorium or low enriched fuel (less than 10% fissile content)[e,f]	

[a] As identified in the trigger list.
[b] Material not irradiated in a reactor or material irradiated in a reactor but with a radiation level equal to or less than 100 rads/hour at one metre unshielded.
[c] Less than a radiologically significant quantity should be exempted.
[d] Natural uranium, depleted uranium and thorium and quantities of uranium enriched to less than 10% not falling in Category III should be protected in accordance with prudent management practice.
[e] Although this level of protection is recommended, it would be open to States, upon evaluation of the specific circumstances, to assign a different category of physical protection.
[f] Other fuel which by virtue of its original fissile material content is classified as Category I or II before irradiation may be reduced one category level while the radiation level from the fuel exceeds 100 rads/hour at one metre unshielded.

of protection to be ensured in relation to the type of materials, and equipment and facilities containing these materials, taking account of international recommendations.

2. Paragraph 3(*b*) of the Guidelines document states that implementation of measures of physical protection in the recipient country is the responsibility of the Government of that country. However, the levels of physical protection on which these measures have to be based should be the subject of an agreement between supplier and recipient. In this context these requirements should apply to all States.

3. The document INFCIRC/225 of the International Atomic Energy Agency entitled "The Physical Protection of Nuclear Material" and similar documents which from time to time are prepared by international groups of experts and updated as appropriate to account for changes in the state of the art and state of knowledge with regard to physical protection of nuclear material are a useful basis for guiding recipient States in designing a system of physical protection measures and procedures.

4. The categorization of nuclear material presented in the attached table or as it may be updated from time to time by mutual agreement of suppliers shall serve as the agreed basis for designating specific levels of physical protection in relation to the type of materials, and equipment and facilities containing these materials, pursuant to paragraph 3(*a*) and 3(*b*) of the Guidelines document.

5. The agreed levels of physical protection to be ensured by the competent national authorities in the use, storage and transportation of the materials listed in the attached table shall as a minimum include protection characteristics as follows:

Category III

Use and Storage within an area to which access is controlled.

Transportation under special precautions including prior arrangements among sender, recipient and carrier, and prior agreement between entities subject to the jurisdiction and regulation of supplier and recipient States, respectively, in case of international transport specifying time, place and procedures for transferring transport responsibility.

Category II

Use and Storage within a protected area to which access is controlled, i.e. an area under constant surveillance by guards or electronic devices, surrounded by a physical barrier with a limited number of points of entry under appropriate control, or any area with an equivalent level of physical protection.

Transportation under special precautions including prior arrangements among sender,

recipient and carrier, and prior agreement between entities subject to the jurisdiction and regulation of supplier and recipient States, respectively, in case of international transport, specifying time, place and procedures for transferring transport responsibility.

Category I

Materials in this Category shall be protected with highly reliable systems against unauthorized use as follows:

Use and Storage within a highly protected area, i.e. a protected area as defined for Category II above, to which, in addition, access is restricted to persons whose trustworthiness has been determined, and which is under surveillance by guards who are in close communication with appropriate response forces. Specific measures taken in this context should have as their objective the detection and prevention of any assault, unauthorized access or unauthorized removal of material.

Transportation under special precautions as identified above for transportation of Category II and III materials and, in addition, under constant surveillance by escorts and under conditions which assure close communication with appropriate response forces.

6. Suppliers should request identification by recipients of those agencies or authorities having responsibility for ensuring that levels of protection are adequately met and having responsibility for internally co-ordinating response/recovery operations in the event of unauthorized use or handling of protected materials. Suppliers and recipients should also designate points of contact within their national authorities to co-operate on matters of out-of-country transportation and other matters of mutual concern.

Source: IAEA document INFCIRC/254, Appendix (IAEA, Vienna, 1978).

The Guidelines were agreed upon by the members of the Nuclear Supplier Group, the so-called London Club: Belgium, Canada, Czechoslovakia, France, German Democratic Republic, FR Germany, Italy, Japan, Netherlands, Poland, Sweden, Switzerland, UK, USA, USSR.

Appendix IX. The Treaty on the Non-Proliferation of Nuclear Weapons (NPT)

Signed at London, Moscow and Washington on 1 July 1968
Entered into force on 5 March 1970
Depositaries: UK, US and Soviet governments

The States concluding this Treaty, hereinafter referred to as the "Parties to the Treaty",

Considering the devastation that would be visited upon all mankind by a nuclear war and the consequent need to make every effort to avert the danger of such a war and to take measures to safeguard the security of peoples,

Believing that the proliferation of nuclear weapons would seriously enhance the danger of nuclear war,

In conformity with resolutions of the United Nations General Assembly calling for the conclusion of an agreement on the prevention of wider dissemination of nuclear weapons,

Undertaking to co-operate in facilitating the application of International Atomic Energy Agency safeguards on peaceful nuclear activities,

Expressing their support for research, development and other efforts to further the application, within the framework of the International Atomic Energy Agency safeguards system, of the principle of safeguarding effectively the flow of source and special fissionable materials by use of instruments and other techniques at certain strategic points,

Affirming the principle that the benefits of peaceful applications of nuclear technology, including any technological by-products which may be derived by nuclear-weapon States from the development of nuclear explosive devices, should be available for peaceful purposes to all Parties to the Treaty, whether nuclear-weapon or non-nuclear-weapon States,

Convinced that, in furtherance of this principle, all Parties to the Treaty are entitled to participate in the fullest possible exchange of scientific information for, and to contribute alone or in co-operation with other States to, the further development of the applications of atomic energy for peaceful purposes,

Declaring their intention to achieve at the earliest possible date the cessation of the nuclear arms race and to undertake effective measures in the direction of nuclear disarmament,

Urging the co-operation of all States in the attainment of this objective,

Recalling the determination expressed by the Parties to the 1963 Treaty banning nuclear weapon tests in the atmosphere, in outer space and under water in its Preamble to seek to achieve the discontinuance of all test explosions of nuclear weapons for all time and to continue negotiations to this end,

Desiring to further the easing of international tension and the strengthening of trust between States in order to facilitate the cessation of the manufacture of nuclear weapons, the liquidation of all their existing stockpiles, and the elimination from national arsenals of nuclear weapons and the means of their delivery pursuant to a Treaty on general and complete disarmament under strict and effective international control,

Recalling that, in accordance with the Charter of the United Nations, States must refrain in their international relations from the threat or use of force against the territorial integrity or political independence of any State, or in any other manner inconsistent with the Purposes of the United Nations, and that the establishment and maintenance of international peace and security are to be promoted with the least diversion for armaments of the world's human and economic resources,

Have agreed as follows:

Article I

Each nuclear-weapon State Party to the Treaty undertakes not to transfer to any recipient whatsoever nuclear weapons or other nuclear explosive devices or control over such weapons or explosive devices directly, or indirectly; and not in any way to assist, encourage, or induce any non-nuclear-weapon State to manufacture or otherwise acquire nuclear weapons or other nuclear explosive devices, or control over such weapons or explosive devices.

Article II

Each non-nuclear-weapon State Party to the Treaty undertakes not to receive the transfer from any transferor whatsoever of nuclear weapons or other nuclear explosive devices or of control over such weapons or explosive devices directly, or indirectly; not to manufacture or otherwise acquire nuclear weapons or other nuclear explosive devices; and not to seek or receive any assistance in the manufacture of nuclear weapons or other nuclear explosive devices.

Article III

1. Each non-nuclear-weapon State Party to the Treaty undertakes to accept safeguards, as set forth in an agreement to be negotiated and concluded with the International Atomic Energy Agency in accordance with the Statute of the International Atomic Energy Agency and the Agency's safeguards system, for the exclusive purpose of verification of the fulfilment of its obligations assumed under this Treaty with a view to preventing diversion of nuclear energy from peaceful uses to nuclear weapons or other nuclear explosive devices. Procedures for the safeguards required by this Article shall be followed with respect to source or special fissionable material whether it is being produced, processed or used in any principal nuclear facility or is outside any such facility. The safeguards required by this Article shall be applied on all source or special fissionable material in all peaceful nuclear activities within the territory of such State, under its jurisdiction, or carried out under its control anywhere.

2. Each State Party to the Treaty undertakes not to provide: (*a*) source or special fissionable material, or (*b*) equipment or material especially designed or prepared for the processing, use or production of special fissionable material, to any non-nuclear-weapon State for peaceful purposes, unless the source or special fissionable material shall be subject to the safeguards required by this Article.

3. The safeguards required by this Article shall be implemented in a manner designed to comply with Article IV of this Treaty, and to avoid hampering the economic or technological development of the Parties or international co-operation in the field of peaceful nuclear activities, including the international exchange of nuclear material and equipment for the processing, use or production of nuclear material for peaceful purposes in accordance with the provisions of this Article and the principle of safeguarding set forth in the Preamble of the Treaty.

4. Non-nuclear-weapon States Party to the Treaty shall conclude agreements with the International Atomic Energy Agency to meet the requirements of this Article either individually or together with other States in accordance with the Statute of the International Atomic Energy Agency. Negotiation of such agreements shall commence within 180 days from the original entry into force of this Treaty. For States depositing their instruments of ratification or accession after the 180-day period, negotiation of such agreements shall commence not later than the date of such deposit. Such agreements shall enter into force not later than eighteen months after the date of initiation of negotiations.

Article IV

1. Nothing in this Treaty shall be interpreted as affecting the inalienable right of all the Parties to the Treaty to develop research, production and use of nuclear energy for peaceful purposes without discrimination and in conformity with Articles I and II of this Treaty.

2. All the Parties to the Treaty undertake to facilitate, and have the right to participate in, the fullest possible exchange of equipment, materials and scientific and technological information for the peaceful uses of nuclear energy. Parties to the Treaty in a position to do so shall also co-operate in contributing alone or together with other States or international organizations to the further development of the applications of nuclear energy for peaceful purposes, especially in the territories of non-nuclear-weapon States Party to the Treaty, with due consideration for the needs of the developing areas of the world.

Article V

Each Party to the Treaty undertakes to take appropriate measures to ensure that, in accordance with this Treaty, under appropriate international observation and through appropriate international procedures, potential benefits from any peaceful applications of nuclear explosions will be made available to non-nuclear-weapon States Party to the Treaty on a non-discriminatory basis and that the charge to such Parties for the explosive devices used will be as low as possible and exclude any charge for research and development. Non-nuclear-weapon States Party to the Treaty shall be able to obtain such benefits, pursuant to a special international agreement or agreements, through an appropriate international body with adequate representation of non-nuclear-weapon States. Negotiations on this subject shall commence as soon as possible after the Treaty enters into force. Non-nuclear-weapon States Party to the Treaty so desiring may also obtain such benefits pursuant to bilateral agreements.

Article VI

Each of the Parties to the Treaty undertakes to pursue negotiations in good faith on effective measures relating to cessation of the nuclear arms race at an early date and to nuclear disarmament, and on a treaty on general and complete disarmament under strict and effective international control.

Article VII

Nothing in this Treaty affects the right of any group of States to conclude regional treaties in order to assure the total absence of nuclear weapons in their respective territories.

Article VIII

1. Any Party to the Treaty may propose amendments to this Treaty. The text of any proposed amendment shall be submitted to the Depositary Governments which shall circulate it to all Parties to the Treaty. Thereupon, if requested to do so by one-third or more of the Parties to the Treaty, the Depositary Governments shall convene a conference, to which they shall invite all the Parties to the Treaty, to consider such an amendment.

2. Any amendment to this Treaty must be approved by a majority of the votes of all the Parties to the Treaty, including the votes of all nuclear-weapon States Party to the Treaty and all other Parties which, on the date the amendment is circulated, are members of the Board of Governors of the International Atomic Energy Agency. The amendment shall enter into force for each Party that deposits its instrument of ratification of the amendment upon the deposit of such instruments of ratification by a majority of all the Parties, including the instruments of ratification of all nuclear-weapon States Party to the Treaty and all other Parties which, on the date the amendment is circulated, are members of the Board of Governors of the International Atomic Energy Agency. Thereafter, it shall enter into force for any other Party upon the deposit of its instrument of ratification of the amendment.

3. Five years after the entry into force of this Treaty, a conference of Parties to the Treaty shall be held in Geneva, Switzerland, in order to review the operation of this Treaty with a view to assuring that the purposes of the Preamble and the provisions of the Treaty are being realised. At intervals of five years thereafter, a majority of the Parties to the Treaty may obtain, by submitting a proposal to this effect to the Depositary Governments, the convening of further conferences with the same objective of reviewing the operation of the Treaty.

Article IX

1. This Treaty shall be open to all States for signature. Any State which does not sign the Treaty before its entry into force in accordance with paragraph 3 of this Article may accede to it at any time.

2. This Treaty shall be subject to ratification by signatory States. Instruments of ratification and instruments of accession shall be deposited with the Governments of the United Kingdom of Great Britain and Northern Ireland, the Union of Soviet Socialist Republics and the United States of America, which are hereby designated the Depositary Governments.

3. This Treaty shall enter into force after its ratification by the States, the Governments of which are designated Depositaries of the Treaty, and forty other States signatory to this Treaty and the deposit of their instruments of ratification. For the purposes of this Treaty, a nuclear-weapon State is one which has manufactured and exploded a nuclear weapon or other nuclear explosive device prior to 1 January, 1967.

4. For States whose instruments of ratification or accession are deposited subsequent to the entry into force of this Treaty, it shall enter into force on the date of the deposit of their instruments of ratification or accession.

5. The Depositary Governments shall promptly inform all signatory and acceding States of the date of each signature, the date of deposit of each instrument of ratification or of accession, the date of the entry into force of this Treaty, and the date of receipt of any requests for convening a conference or other notices.

6. This Treaty shall be registered by the Depositary Governments pursuant to Article 102 of the Charter of the United Nations.

Article X

1. Each Party shall in exercising its national sovereignty have the right to withdraw from the Treaty if it decides that extraordinary events, related to the subject matter of this Treaty, have jeopardized the supreme interests of its country. It shall give notice of such withdrawal to all other Parties to the Treaty and to the United Nations Security Council three months in advance. Such notice shall include a statement of the extraordinary events it regards as having jeopardized its supreme interests.

2. Twenty-five years after the entry into force of the Treaty, a conference shall be convened to decide whether the Treaty shall continue in force indefinitely, or shall be extended for an additional fixed period or periods. This decision shall be taken by a majority of the Parties to the Treaty.

Article XI

This Treaty, the English, Russian, French, Spanish and Chinese texts of which are equally authentic, shall be deposited in the archives of the Depositary Governments. Duly certified copies of this Treaty shall be transmitted by the Depositary Governments to the Governments of the signatory and acceding States.

Source: *Treaty Series*, Vol. 729 (United Nations, New York).

Appendix X. Status of the implementation of the Non-Proliferation Treaty and of the NPT safeguards agreements, as of 1 January 1985

Notes:
1. Abbreviations used in the table:
   - S: signature
   - R: deposit of instrument of ratification, accession or succession
   - SA: Safeguards agreement in force with the IAEA under the NPT

   - L: London
   - M: Moscow
   - W: Washington
   indicate the place of signature and/or deposit of the instrument of ratification, accession or succession for the NPT.

2. The texts of the statements contained in the footnotes have been abridged, but the wording is close to the original version.

Afghanistan	S:	1 Jul	1968	LMW
	R:	4 Feb	1970	W
		5 Feb	1970	M
		5 Mar	1970	L
	SA:	20 Feb	1978	
Australia	S:[1]	27 Feb	1970	LMW
	R:	23 Jan	1973	LMW
	SA:	10 Jul	1974	
Austria	S:	1 Jul	1968	LMW
	R:	27 Jun	1969	LMW
	SA:	23 Jul	1972	
Bahamas	R:[2]	11 Aug	1976	L
		13 Aug	1976	W
		30 Aug	1976	M
Bangladesh	R:	31 Aug	1979	LM
		27 Sep	1979	W
	SA:	11 Jun	1982	
Barbados	S:	1 Jul	1968	W
	R:	21 Feb	1980	W
Belgium	S:	20 Aug	1968	LMW
	R:	2 May	1975	LW
		4 May	1975	M
	SA:	21 Feb	1977	

Benin	S:	1 Jul	1968	W
	R:	31 Oct	1972	W
Bolivia	S:	1 Jul	1968	W
	R:	26 May	1970	W
Botswana	S:	1 Jul	1968	W
	R:	28 Apr	1969	L
Bulgaria	S:	1 Jul	1968	LMW
	R:	5 Sep	1969	W
		18 Sep	1969	M
		3 Nov	1969	L
	SA:	29 Feb	1972	
Burkina Faso (formerly Upper Volta)				
	S:	25 Nov	1968	W
		11 Aug	1969	M
	R:	3 Mar	1970	W
Burundi	R:	19 Mar	1971	M
Cameroon	S:	17 Jul	1968	W
		18 Jul	1968	M
	R:	8 Jan	1969	W
Canada	S:	23 Jul	1968	LW
		29 Jul	1968	M
	R:	8 Jan	1969	LMW
	SA:	21 Feb	1972	

227

Cape Verde	R:	24 Oct	1979	M

Central African Republic

	R:	25 Oct	1970	W

Chad	S:	1 Jul	1968	M
	R:	10 Mar	1971	W
		11 Mar	1971	M
		23 Mar	1971	L

Colombia	S:	1 Jul	1968	W

Congo	R:	23 Oct	1978	W

Costa Rica	S:	1 Jul	1968	W
	R:	3 Mar	1970	W
	SA:	22 Nov	1979	

Cyprus	S:	1 Jul	1968	LMW
	R:	10 Feb	1970	M
		16 Feb	1970	W
		5 Mar	1970	L
	SA:	26 Jan	1973	

Czechoslovakia	S:	1 Jul	1968	LMW
	R:	22 Jul	1969	LMW
	SA:	3 Mar	1972	

Denmark	S:	1 Jul	1968	LMW
	R:	3 Jan	1969	LMW
	SA:	21 Feb	1977	

Dominica[2]	R:	10 Aug	1984	L

Dominican Republic

	S:	1 Jul	1968	W
	R:	24 Jul	1971	W
	SA:	11 Oct	1973	

Ecuador	S:	9 Jul	1968	W
	R:	7 Mar	1969	W
	SA:	10 Mar	1975	

Egypt	S:	1 Jul	1968	LM
	R:[3]	26 Feb	1981	L
	SA:	30 Jun	1982	

El Salvador	S:	1 Jul	1968	W
	R:	11 Jul	1972	W
	SA:	22 Apr	1975	

Equatorial Guinea

	R:	1 Nov	1984	W

Ethiopia	S:	5 Sep	1968	LMW
	R:	5 Feb	1970	M
		5 Mar	1970	LW
	SA:	2 Dec	1977	

Fiji	R:[2]	21 Jul	1972	W
		14 Aug	1972	L
		29 Aug	1972	M
	SA:	22 Mar	1973	

Finland	S:	1 Jul	1968	LMW
	R:	5 Feb	1969	LMW
	SA:	9 Feb	1972	

France[4]

Gabon	R:	19 Feb	1974	W

Gambia	S:	4 Sep	1968	L
		20 Sep	1968	W
		24 Sep	1968	M
	R:	12 May	1975	W
	SA:	8 Aug	1978	

German Democratic Republic

	S:	1 Jul	1968	M
	R:	31 Oct	1969	M
	SA:	7 Mar	1972	

FR Germany	S:	28 Nov	1969	LMW
	R:[5]	2 May	1975	LW
	SA:	21 Feb	1977	

Ghana	S:	1 Jul	1968	MW
		24 Jul	1968	L
	R:	4 May	1970	L
		5 May	1970	W
		11 May	1970	M
	SA:	17 Feb	1975	

Greece	S:	1 Jul	1968	MW
	R:	11 Mar	1970	W
	SA:	1 Mar	1972	

Grenada	R:[2]	2 Sep	1975	L
		3 Dec	1975	W

Guatemala	S:	26 Jul	1968	W
	R:	22 Sep	1970	W
	SA:	1 Feb	1982	

Guinea-Bissau	R:	20 Aug	1976	M

Haiti	S:	1 Jul	1968	W
	R:	2 Jun	1970	W

Holy See (Vatican City)

	R:[6]	25 Feb	1971	LMW
	SA:	1 Aug	1972	

Honduras	S:	1 Jul	1968	W
	R:	16 May	1973	W
	SA:	18 Apr	1975	

Hungary	S:	1 Jul	1968	LMW
	R:	27 May	1969	LMW
	SA:	30 Mar	1972	

Iceland	S:	1 Jul	1968	LMW
	R:	18 Jul	1969	LMW
	SA:	16 Oct	1974	

Indonesia	S:[7]	2 Mar	1970	LMW
	R:[7]	12 Jul	1979	LMW
	SA:	14 Jul	1980	

Iran	S:	1 Jul	1968	LMW
	R:	2 Feb	1970	W
		10 Feb	1970	M
		5 Mar	1970	L

	SA:	15 May	1974	
Iraq	S:	1 Jul	1968	M
	R:	29 Oct	1969	M
	SA:	29 Feb	1972	
Ireland	S:	1 Jul	1968	MW
		4 Jul	1968	L
	R:	1 Jul	1968	W
		2 Jul	1968	M
		4 Jul	1968	L
	SA:	21 Feb	1977	
Italy	S:	28 Jan	1969	LMW
	R:[8]	2 May	1975	LW
		4 May	1975	M
	SA:	21 Feb	1977	
Ivory Coast	S:	1 Jul	1968	W
	R:	6 Mar	1973	W
	SA:	8 Sep	1983	
Jamaica	S:	14 Apr	1969	LMW
	R:	5 Mar	1970	LMW
	SA:	6 Nov	1978	
Japan	S:	3 Feb	1970	LMW
	R:[9]	8 Jun	1976	LMW
	SA:	2 Dec	1977	
Jordan	S:	10 Jul	1968	W
	R:	11 Feb	1970	W
	SA:	21 Feb	1978	
Kampuchea	R:	2 Jun	1972	W
Kenya	S:	1 Jul	1968	W
	R:	11 Jun	1970	M
Korea, Republic of (South)				
	S:[10]	1 Jul	1968	W
	R:[11]	23 Apr	1975	W
	SA:	14 Nov	1975	
Kuwait	S:	15 Aug	1968	MW
		22 Aug	1968	L
Lao People's Dem. Rep.				
	S:	1 Jul	1968	LMW
	R:	20 Feb	1970	M
		5 Mar	1970	LW
Lebanon	S:	1 Jul	1968	LMW
	R:	15 Jul	1970	LM
		20 Nov	1970	W
	SA:	5 Mar	1973	
Lesotho	S:	9 Jul	1968	W
	R:	20 May	1970	W
	SA:	12 Jun	1973	
Liberia	S:	1 Jul	1968	W
	R:	5 Mar	1970	W

Libya	S:	18 Jul	1968	L
		19 Jul	1968	W
		23 Jul	1968	M
	R:	26 May	1975	LMW
	SA:	8 Jul	1980	
Liechtenstein	R:[12]	20 Apr	1978	LMW
	SA:	4 Oct	1979	
Luxembourg	S:	14 Aug	1968	LMW
	R:	2 May	1975	LW
		4 May	1975	M
	SA:	21 Feb	1977	
Madagascar	S:	22 Aug	1968	W
	R:	8 Oct	1970	W
	SA:	14 Jun	1973	
Malaysia	S:	1 Jul	1968	LMW
	R:	5 Mar	1970	LMW
	SA:	29 Feb	1972	
Maldives	S:	11 Sep	1968	W
	R:	7 Apr	1970	W
	SA:	2 Oct	1977	
Mali	S:	14 Jul	1969	W
		15 Jul	1969	M
	R:	10 Feb	1970	M
		5 Mar	1970	W
Malta	S:	17 Apr	1969	W
	R:	6 Feb	1970	W
Mauritius	S:	1 Jul	1968	W
	R:	8 Apr	1969	W
		14 Apr	1969	L
		25 Apr	1969	M
	SA:	31 Jan	1973	
Mexico	S:[13]	26 Jul	1968	LMW
	R:	21 Jan	1969	LMW
	SA:	14 Sep	1973	
Mongolia	S:	1 Jul	1968	M
	R:	14 May	1969	M
	SA:	5 Sep	1972	
Morocco	S:	1 Jul	1968	LMW
	R:	27 Nov	1970	M
		30 Nov	1970	L
		16 Dec	1970	W
	SA:	18 Feb	1975	
Nauru	R:	7 Jun	1982	L
	SA:	13 Apr	1984	
Nepal	S:	1 Jul	1968	LMW
	R:	5 Jan	1970	W
		9 Jan	1970	M
		3 Feb	1970	L
	SA:	22 Jun	1972	
Netherlands	S:	20 Aug	1968	LMW
	R:	2 May	1975	LMW
	SA:	21 Feb	1977	

New Zealand	S:	1 Jul	1968	LMW
	R:	10 Sep	1969	LMW
	SA:	29 Feb	1972	
Nicaragua	S:	1 Jul	1968	LW
	R:	6 Mar	1973	W
	SA:	29 Dec	1976	
Nigeria	S:	1 Jul	1968	LMW
	R:	27 Sep	1968	L
		7 Oct	1968	W
		14 Oct	1968	M
Norway	S:	1 Jul	1968	LMW
	R:	5 Feb	1969	LMW
	SA:	1 Mar	1972	
Panama	S:	1 Jul	1968	W
	R:	13 Jan	1977	W
Papua New Guinea				
	R:	13 Jan	1982	L
		25 Jan	1982	W
		16 Feb	1982	M
	SA:	13 Oct	1983	
Paraguay	S:	1 Jul	1968	W
	R:	4 Feb	1970	W
		5 Mar	1970	L
	SA:	20 Mar	1979	
Peru	S:	1 Jul	1968	W
	R:	3 Mar	1970	W
	SA:	1 Aug	1979	
Philippines	S:	1 Jul	1968	W
		18 Jul	1968	M
	R:	5 Oct	1972	W
		16 Oct	1972	L
		20 Oct	1972	M
	SA:	16 Oct	1974	
Poland	S:	1 Jul	1968	LMW
	R:	12 Jun	1969	LMW
	SA:	11 Oct	1972	
Portugal	R:	15 Dec	1977	LMW
	SA:	14 Jun	1979	
Romania	S:	1 Jul	1968	LMW
	R:	4 Feb	1970	LMW
	SA:	27 Oct	1972	
Rwanda	R:	20 May	1975	LMW
Saint Lucia	R:[2]	28 Dec	1979	L
Saint Vincent and the Grenadines				
	R:[2]	6 Nov	1984	L
Samoa	R:	17 Mar	1975	M
		18 Mar	1975	W
		26 Mar	1975	L
	SA:	22 Jan	1979	
San Marino	S:[10]	1 Jul	1968	W
		29 Jul	1968	L

		21 Nov	1968	M
	R:	10 Aug	1970	L
		20 Aug	1970	M
		31 Aug	1970	W
Sao Tome and Principe				
	R:	20 Jul	1983	M
Senegal	S:	1 Jul	1968	MW
		26 Jul	1968	L
	R:	17 Dec	1970	M
		22 Dec	1970	W
		15 Jan	1971	L
	SA:	14 Jan	1980	
Sierra Leone	R:	26 Feb	1975	LMW
Singapore	S:	5 Feb	1970	LMW
	R:	10 Mar	1976	LMW
	SA:	18 Oct	1977	
Solomon Islands				
	R:[2]	17 Jun	1981	L
Somalia	S:	1 Jul	1968	LMW
	R:	5 Mar	1970	L
		12 Nov	1970	W
Sri Lanka	S:	1 Jul	1968	LMW
	R:	5 Mar	1979	LMW
	SA:	6 Aug	1984	
Sudan	S:	24 Dec	1968	M
	R:	31 Oct	1973	W
		22 Nov	1973	M
		10 Dec	1973	L
	SA:	7 Jan	1977	
Suriname	R:[2]	30 Jun	1976	W
	SA:	2 Feb	1979	
Swaziland	S:	24 Jun	1969	L
	R:	11 Dec	1969	L
		16 Dec	1969	W
		12 Jan	1970	M
	SA:	28 Jul	1975	
Sweden	S:	19 Aug	1968	LMW
	R:	9 Jan	1970	LMW
	SA:	14 Apr	1975	
Switzerland	S:	27 Nov	1969	LMW
	R:[12]	9 Mar	1977	LMW
	SA:	6 Sep	1978	
Syria	S:	1 Jul	1968	M
	R:[10]	24 Sep	1969	M
Taiwan	S:	1 Jul	1968	W
	R:	27 Jan	1970	W
Thailand	R:	7 Dec	1972	L
	SA:	16 May	1974	
Togo	S:	1 Jul	1968	W
	R:	26 Feb	1970	W

Tonga	R:[2]	7 Jul	1971	L
		15 Jul	1971	W
		24 Aug	1971	M

Trinidad and Tobago				
	S:	20 Aug	1968	W
		22 Aug	1968	L

| Tunisia | S: | 1 Jul | 1968 | LMW |
| | R: | 26 Feb | 1970 | LMW |

Turkey	S:	28 Jan	1969	LMW
	R:[14]	17 Apr	1980	LMW
	SA:	1 Sep	1981	

| Tuvalu | R:[2] | 19 Jan | 1979 | L |

| Uganda | R: | 20 Oct | 1982 | W |

Union of Soviet Socialist Republics[15]				
	S:	1 Jul	1968	LMW
	R:	5 Mar	1970	LMW

United Kingdom[16]				
	S:	1 Jul	1968	LMW
	R:[17]	27 Nov	1968	LW
		29 Nov	1968	M

United States of America[18]				
	S:	1 Jul	1968	LMW
	R:	5 Mar	1970	LMW

Upper Volta (see Burkina Faso)

Uruguay	S:	1 Jul	1968	W
	R:	31 Aug	1970	W
	SA:	17 Sep	1976	

Venezuela	S:	1 Jul	1968	W
	R:	25 Sep	1975	L
		26 Sep	1975	W
		3 Oct	1975	M
	SA:	11 Mar	1982	

| Viet Nam | R: | 14 Jun | 1982 | M |

| Yemen Arab Republic | | | | |
| | S: | 23 Sep | 1968 | M |

Yemen, People's Dem. Rep. of				
	S:	14 Nov	1968	M
	R:	1 Jun	1979	M

Yugoslavia	S:	10 Jul	1968	LMW
	R:[19]	4 Mar	1970	W
		5 Mar	1970	LM
	SA:	28 Dec	1973	

Zaire	S:	22 Jul	1968	W
		26 Jul	1968	M
		17 Sep	1968	L
	R:	4 Aug	1970	W
	SA:	9 Nov	1972	

Notes:

[1] On signing the Treaty, Australia stated, *inter alia*, that it regarded it as essential that the Treaty should not affect security commitments under existing treaties of mutual security.

[2] Notification of succession.

[3] On the occasion of the deposit of the instrument of ratification, Egypt stated that since it was embarking on the construction of nuclear power reactors, it expected assistance and support from industrialized nations with a developed nuclear industry. It called upon nuclear weapon states to promote research and development of peaceful applications of nuclear explosions in order to overcome all the difficulties at present involved therein. Egypt also appealed to these states to exert their efforts to conclude an agreement prohibiting the use or threat of use of nuclear weapons against any state, and expressed the view that the Middle East should remain completely free of nuclear weapons.

[4] France, not party to the Treaty, declared that it would behave like a state adhering to the Treaty and that it would follow a policy of strengthening appropriate safeguards relating to nuclear equipment, material and technology. On 12 September 1981 an agreement between France, the European Atomic Energy Community (EURATOM) and the IAEA for the application of safeguards in France entered into force. The agreement covers nuclear material and facilities notified to the IAEA by France.

[5] On depositing the instrument of ratification, the Federal Republic of Germany re-iterated the declaration made at the time of signing: it reaffirmed its expectation that the nuclear weapon states would intensify their efforts in accordance with the undertakings under Article VI of the Treaty, as well as its understanding that the security of FR Germany continued to be ensured by NATO; it stated that no provision of the Treaty may be interpreted in such a way as to hamper further development of European unification; that research, development and use of nuclear energy for peaceful purposes, as well as international and multinational co-operation in this field, must not be prejudiced by the Treaty; that the application of the Treaty, including the implementation of safeguards, must not lead to discrimination of the nuclear industry of FR Germany in international competition; and that it attached vital importance to the undertaking given by the United States and the United Kingdom concerning the application of safeguards to

their peaceful nuclear facilities, hoping that other nuclear weapon states would assume similar obligations.

In a separate note, FR Germany declared that the Treaty will also apply to Berlin (West) without affecting Allied rights and responsibilities, including those relating to demilitarization. In notes of 24 July, 19 August, and 25 November 1975, respectively, addressed to the US Department of State, Czechoslovakia, the Soviet Union and the German Democratic Republic stated that this declaration by FR Germany had no legal effect.

[6] On acceding to the Treaty, the Holy See stated, *inter alia,* that the Treaty will attain in full the objectives of security and peace and justify the limitations to which the states party to the Treaty submit, only if it is fully executed in every clause and with all its implications. This concerns not only the obligations to be applied immediately but also those which envisage a process of ulterior commitments. Among the latter, the Holy See considers it suitable to point out the following:

(*a*) The adoption of appropriate measures to ensure, on a basis of equality, that all non-nuclear weapon states party to the Treaty will have available to them the benefits deriving from peaceful applications of nuclear technology.

(*b*) The pursuit of negotiations in good faith on effective measures relating to cessation of the nuclear arms race at an early date and to nuclear disarmament, and on a treaty on general and complete disarmament under strict and effective control.

[7] On signing the Treaty, Indonesia stated, *inter alia,* that the government of Indonesia attaches great importance to the declarations of the United States, the United Kingdom and the Soviet Union affirming their intention to provide immediate assistance to any non-nuclear weapon state party to the Treaty that is a victim of an act of aggression in which nuclear weapons are used. Of utmost importance, however, is not the action *after* a nuclear attack has been committed but the guarantees to prevent such an attack. The Indonesian government trusts that the nuclear weapon states will study further this question of effective measures to ensure the security of the non-nuclear weapon states. On depositing the instrument of ratification, Indonesia expressed the hope that the nuclear countries would be prepared to co-operate with non-nuclear countries in the use of nuclear energy for peaceful purposes and implement the provisions of Article IV of the Treaty without discrimination. It also stated the view that the nuclear weapon states should observe the provisions of Article VI of the Treaty relating to the cessation of the nuclear arms race.

[8] Italy stated that in its belief nothing in the Treaty was an obstacle to the unification of the countries of western Europe; it noted full compatibility of the Treaty with the existing security agreements; it noted further that when technological progress would allow the development of peaceful explosive devices different from nuclear weapons, the prohibition relating to their manufacture and use shall no longer apply; it interpreted the provisions of Article IX, paragraph 3 of the Treaty, concerning the definition of a military nuclear state, in the sense that it referred exclusively to the five countries which had manufactured and exploded a nuclear weapon or other nuclear explosive device prior to 1 January 1967, and stressed that under no circumstance would a claim of pertaining to such category be recognized by the Italian government for any other state.

[9] On depositing the instrument of ratification, Japan expressed the hope that France and China would accede to the Treaty; it urged a reduction of nuclear armaments and a comprehensive ban on nuclear testing; appealed to all states to refrain from the threat or use of force involving either nuclear or non-nuclear weapons; expressed the view that peaceful nuclear activities in non-nuclear weapon states party to the Treaty should not be hampered and that Japan should not be discriminated against in favour of other parties in any aspect of such activities. It also urged all nuclear weapon states to accept IAEA safeguards in their peaceful nuclear activities.

[10] A statement was made containing a disclaimer regarding the recognition of states party to the Treaty.

[11] On depositing the instrument of ratification, the Republic of Korea took note of the fact that the depositary governments of the three nuclear weapon states had made declarations in June 1968 to take immediate and effective measures to safeguard any non-nuclear weapon state which is a victim of an act or an object of a threat of aggression in which nuclear weapons are used. It recalled that the UN Security Council adopted a resolution to the same effect on 19 June 1968.

[12] On depositing the instruments of accession and ratification, Liechtenstein and Switzerland stated that activities not prohibited under Articles I and II of the Treaty include, in particular, the whole field of energy production and related operations, research and technology concerning future generations of nuclear reactors based on fission or fusion, as well as production of isotopes. Liechtenstein and Switzerland define the term "source or special fissionable material" in Article III of the Treaty as being in accordance with Article XX of the IAEA Statute, and a modification of this interpretation requires their formal consent; they will accept only such interpretations and definitions of the terms

"equipment or material especially designed or prepared for the processing, use or production of special fissionable material", as mentioned in Article III of the Treaty, that they will expressly approve; and they understand that the application of the Treaty, especially of the control measures, will not lead to discrimination of their industry in international competition.

13 On signing the Treaty, Mexico stated, *inter alia,* that none of the provisions of the Treaty shall be interpreted as affecting in any way whatsoever the rights and obligations of Mexico as a state party to the Treaty of Tlatelolco.

It is the understanding of Mexico that at the present time any nuclear explosive device is capable of being used as a nuclear weapon and that there is no indication that in the near future it will be possible to manufacture nuclear explosive devices that are not potentially nuclear weapons. However, if technological advances modify this situation, it will be necessary to amend the relevant provisions of the Treaty in accordance with the procedure established therein.

14 The ratification was accompanied by a statement in which Turkey underlined the non-proliferation obligations of the nuclear weapon states, adding that measures must be taken to meet adequately the security requirements of non-nuclear weapon states. Turkey also stated that measures developed or to be developed at national and international levels to ensure the non-proliferation of nuclear weapons should in no case restrict the non-nuclear weapon states in their option for the application of nuclear energy for peaceful purposes.

On 21 February 1985 the Soviet Union and the IAEA signed an agreement for the application of safeguards in peaceful nuclear facilities to be designated by the USSR.

16 The United Kingdom recalled its view that if a regime is not recognized as the government of a state, neither signature nor the deposit of any instrument by it, nor notification of any of those acts, will bring about recognition of that regime by any other state.

17 This agreeement, signed by the United Kingdom, Euratom and the IAEA, provides for the submission of British non-military nuclear installations to safeguards under IAEA supervision.

18 This agreement provides for safeguards on fissionable material in all facilities within the USA, excluding those associated with activities of direct national security significance.

19 In connection with the ratification of the Treaty, Yugoslavia stated, *inter alia,* that it considered a ban on the development, manufacture and use of nuclear weapons and the destruction of all stockpiles of these weapons to be indispensable for the maintenance of a stable peace and international security; it held the view that the chief responsibility for progress in this direction rested with the nuclear weapon powers, and expected these powers to undertake not to use nuclear weapons against the countries which have renounced them as well as against non-nuclear weapon states in general, and to refrain from the threat to use them. It also emphasized the significance it attached to the universality of the efforts relating to the realization of the Non-Proliferation Treaty.

Appendix XI.   Non-NPT safeguards agreements, as of 1 January 1985

Agreements providing for safeguards, other than those in connection with the NPT, approved by the Board as of 1 January 1985

Party(ies)	Subject	Entry into force

(While the Agency is a party to each of the following agreements, only the State(s) party to them is (are) listed.)

(a) Project agreements

Party(ies)	Subject	Entry into force
Argentina	Siemens SUR-100	13 March 1970
	RAEP Reactor	2 December 1964
Chile	Herald Reactor	19 December 1969
Finland*a*	FiR-1 Reactor	30 December 1960
	FINN sub-critical assembly	30 July 1963
Greece*a*	GRR-1 Reactor	1 March 1972
Indonesia*a*	Additional core-load for TRIGA Reactor	19 December 1969
Iran*a*	UTRR Reactor	10 May 1967
Jamaica*a*	Fuel for research reactor	25 January 1984
Japan*a*	JRR-3	24 March 1959
Malaysia*a*/United States of America	TRIGA-II Reactor	22 September 1980
Mexico*a*	TRIGA-III Reactor	18 December 1963
	Siemens SUR-100	21 December 1971
	Laguna Verde Nuclear Power Plant	12 February 1974
Morocco*a*	Fuel for research reactor	2 December 1983
Pakistan	PRR Reactor	5 March 1962
	Booster rods for KANUPP	17 June 1968
Peru*a*	Research Reactor and fuel therefor	9 May 1978
Philippines*a*	PRR-1 Reactor	28 September 1966
Romania*a*	TRIGA Reactor	30 March 1973
	Experimental fuel elements	1 July 1983
Spain	Coral-I Reactor	23 June 1967
Turkey*a*	Sub-critical assembly	17 May 1974
Uruguay*a*	URR Reactor	24 September 1965
Venezuela*a*	RV-1 Reactor	7 November 1975
Viet Nam	Fuel for research reactor	1 July 1983
Yugoslavia*a*	TRIGA-II Reactor	4 October 1961
	Krško Nuclear Power Plant	14 June 1974
Zaire*a*	TRICO Reactor	27 June 1962

(b) Unilateral submissions

Party(ies)	Subject	Entry into force
Argentina	Atucha Power Reactor Facility	3 October 1972
	Nuclear material	23 October 1973
	Embalse Power Reactor Facility	6 December 1974
	Equipment and nuclear material	22 July 1977

Party(ies)	Subject	Entry into force
	Nuclear material, material, equipment and facilities	22 July 1977
	Atucha II Nuclear Power Plant	15 July 1981
	Heavy water plant	14 October 1981
	Heavy water	14 October 1981
	Nuclear material	8 July 1982
Chile	Nuclear material	31 December 1974
	Nuclear material	22 September 1982
Cuba	Nuclear research reactor and fuel therefor	25 September 1980
	Nuclear power plant and nuclear material	5 May 1980
	Zero-power nuclear reactor and fuel therefor	7 October 1983
India	Nuclear material, material and facilities	17 November 1977
Korea, North	Research reactor and nuclear material for this reactor	20 July 1977
Pakistan	Nuclear material	2 March 1977
Spain	Nuclear material	19 November 1974
	Nuclear material	18 June 1975
	Vandellos Nuclear Power Plant	11 May 1981
	Four nuclear facilities	11 May 1981
United Kingdom	Nuclear material	14 December 1972
Viet Nam	Research reactor and fuel therefor	12 June 1981

(c) *Tlatelolco Treaty*

Colombia	All nuclear material	22 December 1982
Mexico[b]	All nuclear material, equipment and facilities	6 September 1968
Panama	All nuclear material	23 March 1984

(d) *Agreements concluded with nuclear-weapon States on the basis of voluntary offers*

France	Nuclear material in facilities submitted to safeguards	12 September 1981
United Kingdom	Nuclear material in facilities designated by the Agency	14 August 1978
United States of America	Nuclear material in facilities designated by the Agency	9 December 1980

(e) *Other agreements*

Argentina/United States of America	25 July 1969
Australia[b]/United States of America	26 September 1966
Austria[b]/United States of America	24 January 1970
Brazil/Germany, Federal Republic of[b]	26 February 1976
Brazil/United States of America	31 October 1968
Colombia/United States of America	9 December 1970
India/Canada[b]	30 September 1971
India/United States of America	27 January 1971
Iran[b]/United States of America	20 August 1969
Israel/United States of America	4 April 1975
Japan[b]/Canada[b]	20 June 1966
Japan[b]/France	22 September 1972
Japan/United States of America	10 July 1968
Japan[b]/United Kingdom	15 October 1968
Korea, South/United States of America	5 January 1968
Korea, South[b]/France	22 September 1975
Pakistan/Canada	17 October 1969
Pakistan/France	18 March 1976
Philippines[b]/United States of America	19 July 1968
Portugal[b]/United States of America[c]	19 July 1969
South Africa/United States of America	26 July 1967
South Africa/France	5 January 1977

Party(ies)	Subject	Entry into force
Spain/Germany, Federal Republic of[b]		29 September 1982
Spain/United States of America		9 December 1966
Spain/Canada[b]		10 February 1977
Sweden[b]/United States of America		1 March 1972
Switzerland[b]/United States of America[c]		28 February 1972
Turkey/United States of America		5 June 1969
Venezuela[b]/United States of America[c]		27 March 1968

(f) The Agency also applies safeguards under two agreements (INFCIRC/133 and INFCIRC/158) to the nuclear facilities in Taiwan, China. Pursuant to the decision adopted by the Board of Governors on 9 December 1971 that the Government of the People's Republic of China is the only government which has the right to represent China in the Agency, the relations between the Agency and the authorities in Taiwan are non-governmental. The Agreements are implemented by the Agency on that basis.

Notes:
[a] Agency safeguards are being applied to the items required to be safeguarded under this (these) project agreement(s) pursuant to an agreement in connection with NPT covering the State indicated.
[b] Application of Agency safeguards under this agreement has been suspended in the State indicated as the State has concluded an agreement in connection with NPT.
[c] Application of Agency safeguards under this agreement has been suspended in the United States of America.

Source: The IAEA.

Index